Moral Reasons

FOR HUGH, JACK AND KATE

MORAL REASONS

Jonathan Dancy

BLACKWELL
Oxford UK & Cambridge USA

Copyright © Jonathan Dancy 1993

The right of Jonathan Dancy to be identified as author
of this work has been asserted in accordance with the
Copyright, Designs and Patents Act 1988.

First published 1993

Blackwell Publishers
108 Cowley Road
Oxford OX4 1JF
UK

238 Main Street, Suite 501
Cambridge, Massachusetts 02142
USA

British Library Cataloguing in Publication Data

A CIP catalogue record for this book is available from
the British Library.

Library of Congress Cataloging-in-Publication Data

Dancy, Jonathan.
Moral reasons / Jonathan Dancy.
p. cm.
Includes bibliographical references and index.
ISBN 0–631–17775–2 (hard). – ISBN 0–631–18792–8 (pbk.)
1. Ethics. I. Title.
BJ1012.D263 1993
170–dc20
92–21888
CIP

Typeset in 10 on 12 pt Sabon
by Graphicraft Typesetters Ltd, Hong Kong
Printed in Great Britain by T.J. Press Ltd., Padstow, Cornwall

This book is printed on acid-free paper

Contents

Introduction

I first became interested in the prospects for what is sometimes called moral realism when I read two articles by John McDowell in the early 1980s. But I had never found the sort of moral theory that I was taught as an undergraduate at Oxford in the 1960s at all satisfying. Despite my personal respect for R. M. Hare, who held the White's Chair at Corpus Christi College when I was there and was very generous with his time, I never found either his prescriptivism or the emotivism from which it developed at all plausible. Something seemed to be missing; could this be all that there was to be said? Among the problems, as I now think, was a lingering distaste for metaphysics and an oversharp distinction between the proper scope of theory (analysis) and the realities of practical moral problems. I now take there to be a sliding scale here, and would want to argue that the views I present, which I see as high theory, would none the less make a considerable difference to moral practice if accepted. (It is the particularism more than anything else that I have in mind here, of course.)

McDowell's work, and that of David Wiggins, seemed to me to trigger a rebirth of significant ethical theory. The story had been that intuition-ism, in the persons of W. D. Ross and H. A. Prichard, was effectively eclipsed by emotivism in the crude hands of A. J. Ayer and the far more subtle ones of C. L. Stevenson. But the arguments against intuitionism began to seem to have depended on features of Ross's position which could be excised without loss. Other things had to change too, of course, since all things are interconnected. But the prospects of a recognizable successor to the intuitionistic tradition began to seem much rosier. *Moral Reasons* is part of the attempt to write such a theory.

No book can attempt everything, and my choice of topics and of method is somewhat idiosyncratic. As far as method is concerned, I have eschewed attacks on the non-cognitivist alternative as far as I can, and restricted myself to laying out as persuasively as possible the views

I want to promote. Though of course I hold that if this view is true, the alternative is false, I do not hold that an ability to lay out the attractions of this or any other view need include an ability to dismantle the opposition. I spend far more time arguing the rival merits of views close to my own, especially those of Nagel and of McDowell. These forms of 'moral realism' are quite distinct from views given the same name which emanate from Cornell and Michigan (I am thinking of writers such as Sturgeon, Boyd, Railton and Brink). Again, I make no explicit reference to these views, though many of my remarks about Humeanism can be applied to them, *mutatis mutandis*. On topics, the book is ostensibly about moral reasons, and I have tried to ask and answer some hard questions about them. I start off by assuming that there are such things, and see how I get along.

My official starting point is the theory of motivation. I take it that Hume was right to rest his non-cognitivism on his theory of motivation, and that any effective opposition has to do the same, i.e. to find a rival theory of motivation that will re-establish the possibility that moral reasons are both cognitive and able to motivate in their own right. Accordingly, my first three chapters concern the theory of motivation in general, with only occasional references to moral motivation. Since, unlike some writers, I do not take the view that moral motivation is very special, there should be no defect in this approach. In these chapters I take it that the going theory of motivation is one which, though not exactly Hume's, has come to us as a descendant of Hume's views and is therefore commonly called Humeanism. I do not argue against Humeanism, but do attempt to show that a purely cognitive theory can cope with all the relevant phenomena without collapsing into Humeanism.

I then argue that the most defensible form of cognitivism in the theory of motivation adopts a particularistic rather than a generalistic account of reasons. Chapter 4 details some advantages of particularism; after that, since particularism has had such an extraordinarily bad press, I break my rule and try to undermine opposing views. The next two chapters, therefore, attempt to dismantle the two main forms of generalism that I know. I think that I have a fair amount of success in this, but my central purpose here is to make people see that there is a need for a defence of generalism, and that its truth cannot simply be assumed.

The particularism I am here promoting is not special to me. Particularistic strands can be found in various contemporary developments; it is common to hear that moral rules, or moral theory if we take the business of theory to be the provision of rules, cannot cope with the rich multiplicity of lived situations. Although in general terms I applaud this trend, in many cases its proponents seem to me to be operating in ignorance of the most subtle form of generalism they are rejecting, namely the theory of prima facie reasons. I attempt therefore to provide genuine arguments in favour of particularism and so to turn what is sometimes (mere) rhetoric into something more like reasoning.

In chapters 7 and 8 I consider two apparent difficulties for the sort of particularistic cognitivism that has by then emerged. In dealing with the first difficulty, I am encouraged to be more explicit about the metaphysics of moral reasons, and in so doing I make great play with the metaphor of shape. This metaphor, which is a recurrent theme thereafter, is the main cause of the second difficulty, which concerns the possibility of supererogation. Supererogation raises problems for everyone, and these I try to deal with in chapter 12; it raises special problems for me, which I try to handle in chapter 8.

I then turn to ask myself what sort of objectivity moral reasons, as so far conceived, are capable of. And with an answer to this question, I ask what sorts of moral reasons enjoy that degree of objectivity. The sharp edge of this question concerns the possibility of objective but agent-relative reasons. It has been common to suppose that even if there are agent-relative reasons, they can claim only a lesser degree of objectivity than that of agent-neutral reasons. I dispute this picture. In the process, I find myself unable to avoid the question whether the agent-relative reasons for whose possibility I am arguing are ones whose existence would be compatible with the truth of some form of sophisticated consequentialism, and after lengthy discussion I conclude that they are not.

R. M. Hare argued that the truth of utilitarianism was entailed by his combination of prescriptivism and universalizability. My conclusion is the mirror image of this: that the sort of objectivity that moral reasons enjoy validates some reasons whose existence is incompatible with the truth of utilitarianism (or any other form of consequentialism).

An early version of chapters 1–2 was read at a conference on moral theory held at St Andrews University in September 1988; I am grateful to Susan Wolf for her comments on that occasion. Subsequent versions have been read at universities too numerous to mention, and I have learnt more in discussions than I could ever manage to attribute to individuals. Chapter 9 contains some material which originally appeared in *Philosophical Books*. Parts of chapter 10 appeared in *Philosophical Papers*, and an early version of material from chapter 11 in *Value, Welfare and Morality* edited by R. Frey and C. Morris (Cambridge: Cambridge University Press, 1992). I am grateful to the competent authorities for permission to re-use this material.

Moral Reasons is the outward and visible sign of an excellent year I spent visiting at the University of Pittsburgh; it developed from a graduate class I gave there on moral theory. I was very grateful to the students who attended this class for sustained but highly charitable discussion, conducted in the best traditions of the subject, of the views I was trying to work out. I was especially grateful to David Gauthier and John McDowell, who also attended this class, for their attempts to help me do what I was trying to do, rather than to make me do what they were trying to do (again in the best traditions). Beyond those debts, various parts of the book were read in various forms and at various times by John Broome, Brad Hooker, Derek Parfit, Charles Swann and Candace Vogler; and I am very grateful to them, and to two anonymous referees, for their comments. I should also thank Eve Garrard for her quite correct insistence that I should both say what I mean and give some comprehensible reasons for it, and David Bakhurst for his inventiveness and enthusiasm. Finally, I owe thanks to Keele University for giving me a Research Award – an extra term free of teaching in which to convert my original manuscript into a book.

Beyond that, I have two major academic debts. When my interest in moral theory began to awaken, I started to teach a final year special option at Keele jointly with David McNaughton. This proved extremely fruitful for me. His knowledge of the literature has always been far greater than mine, and his sympathy to the views I was trying to develop was very encouraging. That process went on for ten years; *Moral Reasons* is the eventual result. In its gestation David has read every draft with great care, and caused very many changes. The most significant of these are marked as they occur, but there are many more where his influence is present unacknowledged. I owe David a deep debt of gratitude; his presence at Keele has banished the sense of isolation that can afflict those working on abstruse topics in small departments.

I owe a different sort of debt to John McDowell. Although I spend a fair amount of time in early chapters saying that he has made various unnecessary mistakes, the general structure of my approach to ethics, and indeed of my overall philosophical orientation, is owed in large measure to him. The views I express here are not McDowell's views, to be sure, but they are McDowellian in inspiration and (I hope) in general style. I owe much to him for both personal encouragement and intellectual example.

Finally, I am fortunate in that my family really is a bosom – in the sense of a warm place which envelopes one in a sense of security and love. Most of the credit for this is due to my wife Sarah, who has succeeded in combining her own studies with an interest in and support for mine. Our children, to whom this book is dedicated, are now old enough to want to engage with the topics that are concerning me here, which is exhaustingly rewarding. I even took my life in my hands and at their suggestion gave a talk on the demandingness of morality at my sons' school. Though this is not a risk I would take twice, none of us suffered any permanent damage, and the spice of danger certainly enlivened the humdrum existence of a moral theorist.

J. D.

1
Internalism and cognitivism

1 INTERNALISM AND EXTERNALISM

The classification of theories of moral motivation into those that are internalist and those that are externalist began with W. D. Falk,[1] but more recent discussion of the distinction revolves around Thomas Nagel's earlier work. Nagel wrote:

> Internalism is the view that the presence of a motivation for acting morally is guaranteed by the truth of ethical propositions themselves. On this view the motivation must be so tied to the meaning, or truth, of ethical statements that when in a particular case someone is (or perhaps merely believes that he is) morally required to do something, it follows that he has a motivation for doing it. Externalism holds, on the other hand, that the necessary motivation is not supplied by ethical principles and judgements themselves, and that an additional psychological sanction is required to motivate our compliance ... Internalism's appeal derives from the conviction that one cannot accept or assert sincerely any ethical proposition without accepting at least a prima facie motivation for action in accordance with it.[2]

Nagel's work here is pioneering but, like many other pioneers, he did not find the best road for others to follow. There are two ideas which he fails to keep apart in this passage. The first is that motivation is provided by the mere *truth* of some proposition; the second is that the motivation is provided by one's *belief* in that proposition, whether it be true or not. The second of these is much less outlandish than the first, and is what I take to have been Nagel's intention.[3] If so, his account of the choice between internalism and externalism is clearly informed by the general structure of Humean theory of motivation.[4] Humeanism (which I shall sometimes refer to as Hume) holds that there are two sorts of motivating states. The general name for the first sort is 'desire', and the general name for the second sort is 'belief'. Desires are states which are *guaranteed*[5] to motivate; they cannot exist without motivating. We can say that they are essentially or necessarily motivating states. Belief, on the other hand, requires the help of desire if it is to motivate.[6] Beliefs are able to motivate when keyed into a suitable desire, and they borrow their ability to motivate from that relation to a state of a distinctively different sort. So a belief can be present without motivating; beliefs are contingently motivating states.

So Humeanism is the view that there are two sorts of motivating states, the essentially motivating and the contingently motivating. The former are called internally motivating states and the latter externally motivating states. This is because the latter (the beliefs) get their ability to motivate from elsewhere – from the desires – while the desires motivate in their own right. Crucially, we need a state of each sort to get an action going. This is Hume's belief/desire thesis: every complete motivating state is a combination of belief and desire. Suppose that I tell you that a ton of bricks is about to fall through the ceiling. Unless there is something you care about, something you want, this information will make no difference to you. It won't be a reason for you to act in one way rather than another. It only becomes a reason for action if you care about something – your own future, for instance. Equally, if you want an orange but have no relevant beliefs – beliefs about the probable whereabouts of oranges, for instance – your desire is impotent; it is like a blind urge seeking a guide, an external agent to give it a direction. So each state needs the contribution of the other. A complete motivating state – a state which is sufficient for action – must be a combination of belief and desire. This is the belief/desire thesis.

What persuades us that desire is an essentially motivating state, one that cannot be present without motivating? Shouldn't we leave room for a desire that is dormant in us? For instance, don't I retain my desires while asleep (this is me dormant rather than the desire) when they are clearly not motivating me at all? I don't think that this is quite the right question to ask. We might admit that a desire only motivates when the agent is capable of being motivated, and cope with the sleeping agent in that way. The real question concerns the possibility of a dormant desire in a non-dormant person. Could there be a desire present while others are motivating, and which is not motivating itself? I don't think that Humeanism has any room for this possibility. What requires desire to motivate is not its content, no doubt, since a desire can share its content with a belief. Nor, I think, is it the phenomenology of desire, despite the felt thrustiness of some desires. For after all most other desires (Hume's 'calm passions') don't feel like that, and indeed most of them don't have any phenomenology; they are desires that feel like nothing. The fact is, I think, that there is nothing else for desires to do other than motivate. One way of putting this point would appeal to the notion of direction of fit. Beliefs are supposed to fit the world; they have the mind-to-world direction of fit. Desires try to get the world to fit them when it doesn't need to; they have the world-to-mind direction of fit. Given this picture of the difference between belief and desire, it seems that desires must be internally motivating states, since their essence is to try to get the world to fit them.[7]

The Humean theory of motivation, then, constitutes the backcloth against which Nagel is trying to construct a form of internalism. Now there are two ways of being an internalist in the theory of moral motivation: the cognitivist way and the non-cognitivist way.[8] (Nagel's is the cognitive, Hume's the non-cognitive.) A non-cognitivist in ethics sees moral judgements as expressions of desires. There is a classic Humean argument to drive us in this direction, which starts from the belief/desire thesis. No set of beliefs alone is sufficient to generate an action. But if we add to such a set a moral judgement, we have a new set which could be sufficient for action. So a moral judgement must either be, or at the least contain, a desire; there must be some desire which the moral judgement expresses, whatever else it does. But desires are internally motivating states. So non-cognitivists of this sort are internalists about moral motivation, holding that moral judgements are internally motivating states. Cognitivists have a choice, however. They can be internalists, holding that moral judgements express peculiar beliefs which, unlike normal beliefs, cannot be present without motivating. Or they can be externalists, holding that moral judgements express beliefs which rely on the presence of an independent desire if they are to motivate.

This is an important matter, because cognitivism (in its intuitionist guise) was often attacked for its apparent commitment to externalism.[9] For instance, Ross's intuitionist theory was held to be defective just because it left room for persons who share all our moral beliefs but see them as completely irrelevant to their choice of action – the amoralists. We will be seeing more of these people in a minute. And actually this was a fair complaint, though it is one which simply assumes against Ross the truth of internalism; it is fair in the sense that Ross was indeed an externalist about moral motivation.[10] It is not fair as a complaint against cognitivism itself, since there remains room for a cognitivist to be an internalist. This is possible; but I must admit that it is harder than being an externalist, since one seems to have to make sense of the suggestion that, while most beliefs are externally motivating states, some special ones are internally motivating states.

If it can be an intuitively plausible complaint against Ross that he was not an internalist as all good non-cognitivists are, there must be strong intuitive reasons in favour of internalism; and these reasons must be independent of any non-cognitivist associations, since otherwise the complaint would simply be that Ross was not a non-cognitivist, which though true hardly counts as any sort of an argument. And there is at least one such reason, namely the sense that morality is essentially practical, so that it would be odd for someone to say 'This action is wrong but I don't see that as at all relevant to my choice.' Even this sense of oddness may seem to amount in the dialectic merely to an assertion of internalism. But it can be backed up by the thought that moral considerations are ones whose practical relevance cannot be escaped by saying 'I don't care about that sort of thing.' The sense that this is so is not so much an expression of non-cognitivism as one of the reasons why non-cognitivism is attractive; the issue before us is whether it is a well-taken reason, or whether this sense cannot be equally well captured by a cognitivist theory. What we are learning is that the reason why a cognitivist should adopt internalism in ethics is the same reason as *a* reason for calling moral imperatives categorical; a categorical imperative, in this weak sense at least, is one whose grip on someone who 'accepts' it is not dependent on the presence of an independent desire, so that without the desire one can say that this would clearly be relevant to anyone who cares about that sort of thing, but is not relevant to oneself because one doesn't. We certainly don't *want* moral reasons to depend on independent desires in this way, though whether we can get what we do want here remains to be seen.[11]

Internalism is here being supported by an intuition. But I am not frightened by intuitions, and this seems to me to be a good one.

2   PROBLEMS FOR COGNITIVIST INTERNALISM

What can be said against this internalism? There are perhaps three types of person ruled out if it is true: the amoral person, the evil person and the person suffering from moral *accidie*.[12] Amoral people are those we met before. They can tell the difference between right and wrong well enough; it just doesn't concern them at all. Evil people are those who are attracted by evil for its own sake. They can tell the difference between right and wrong well enough too; but they take the wrongness of an action as a reason for doing it and the rightness of an action as a reason for leaving it undone. People who suffer from accidie are those who just don't care for a while about things which would normally seem to them to be perfectly good reasons for action; this is so whether the reasons are moral reasons or more ordinary ones. Depression can be a cause of accidie. The depressive is not deprived of the relevant beliefs by his depression; they just leave him indifferent. He knows that if he doesn't act now he will lose the opportunity he has been working for for two years, but he can't see that this matters.

Externalism can easily cope with all these three people, because it holds that to recognize a moral truth is one thing and to be motivated by it is another. In fact, externalism can be vindicated by the occurrence of such people, because if externalism is true there should be such people, and there are. Given the mutual independence of recognition of moral truth and motivating desire, there is room for people who, either permanently (the amoral) or temporarily (accidie), are uninfluenced by the truths they recognize; and there is even room for those who, with perverse desires, are influenced but not in the normal direction. That the latter are at least influenced is no defence of internalism, for though we only required for internalism that motivation of some sort be guaranteed by the presence of the moral judgement, it was clearly intended that the judgement should make the right difference, not just any difference.[13]

So the existence of these three sorts of people makes trouble for internalism. Or at least it would make trouble if we allowed that such people exist. But this is what wise internalists should question, at least in the cases of amorality and evil. It may be that too much is being made of phenomena which need to be distorted if they are to serve the externalists' purpose. In the case of amoralism, we may all admit that there is the person who sees the institution of morality from outside, as something whose claims on us he rejects. But this person does not accept the moral judgements whose relevance he denies; at best, he merely knows what judgement would be made by others.[14] This person is no problem for internalism. Is there an amoralist who is near enough to the thing he rejects both to understand and to accept it, but not to be moved by it at all? I see no reason for the internalist to admit that there is such a person. If there were any, this would be a problem for internalism. But it can hardly be presented as a matter of fact either that there are some or that there could be. That such a person is possible is surely more an assertion of the externalist position than independent support for it.

Similar moves can be made when we come to the evil person. We of course all know people who are occasionally bad (ourselves, if not others). But such people are surely those who don't care enough about the harm they are doing to others, rather than those who are actually attracted by it. They are no problem for internalism. What about the person in a foul mood, who just wants to make others feel uncomfortable? This person surely sees the discomfort of others as a (temporary) good; he is no counter-example to the maxim that to desire something is always to desire it *sub specie boni*. The interesting suggestion is that there are people who desire certain outcomes *sub specie mali*. Here it is common to quote Milton's account of Satan, and his remark 'Evil, be thou my good.' But the internalist should question whether this extreme degree of evil is genuinely possible. In the case of Milton's Satan, examination of the context reveals that Satan pursues evil not for its own sake (*sub specie mali*) but for extraneous reasons, such as the fact that it is his only remaining hope of empire.[15] This renders Satan's pursuit of evil comprehensible, but at the cost of making it useless to the externalist. And what this tells us is that for us to understand the pursuit of evil, we have to find some comprehensible relation between it and some good, but that in doing so we move back within the bounds of what internalism can allow. So I take it that the internalist should not allow the possibility of the really troubling case, that of the evil seeking evil for its own sake.

So far I have defended internalism against attack. But with accidie I run out of defence. I am not tempted to deny the possibility of depression depriving one's moral beliefs of their normal motivational force, and this means that if the choice between internalism and externalism has been fairly stated, the externalist is in the stronger position. I now turn to ask whether I did state the choice fairly. Initially I accepted Nagel's account of the distinction, and using that account, we find an apparently unanswerable argument in favour of externalism. But now I want to ask whether there might not be a different account of the distinction which would leave the internalist rather better off. By the end of the next chapter I hope to have emerged with a cognitive theory of moral motivation which has what one might call an internalist flavour, and yet escapes the argument from accidie. But in the sense of Nagel's original contrast, the theory I end up with will be neither internalist nor externalist. His distinction will have been left behind or transcended, since it rests on assumptions which I will reject.

I approach this question in a rather roundabout way, by looking in much greater detail at two different forms of cognitivist internalism in ethics. I hope that their weaknesses will be instructive, and enable me to construct a more defensible theory which is not troubled by accidie.

3 FORMS OF COGNITIVIST INTERNALISM

Cognitivists hold that moral judgements express beliefs, and internalists hold that moral judgement necessarily motivates. Remember the Humean claim that if we add a moral judgement to a set of beliefs, we get a state which is sufficient for action. Cognitivists accept this, and argue therefore that, since moral judgement is belief, where there is a moral belief present a set of beliefs alone can be sufficient for action. Being internalists, our cognitivists also hold that moral beliefs generate imperatives that are categorical in the weak sense mentioned above; they offer us (or are) reasons for action whose relevance cannot be got out of by claiming that one isn't actually concerned about that sort of thing.

The best known form of cognitivist internalism is that of Kant. Kant held that there are two styles of motivation. The first, and more ordinary, is Humean. We need to add an independent desire to the beliefs we have if we are to act. The second only occurs with moral motivation. Here motivation is purely cognitive; a complete reason for action is provided by a set of beliefs about the world and a moral judgement. The moral judgement is a judgement to the effect that my present maxim could (or could not) serve as a law for all rational beings. When I act morally, I act out of respect or reverence for the ability of my maxim to serve as a law for all rational beings. But Kant is at pains to say that the reverence he is talking about is not to be conceived as a sort of subjective feeling, but rather as a recognition of a feature objectively present for us and not caused by our recognition of it.[16] Those who recognize this feature are necessarily motivated by it, though they may not actually do the action which it requires of them. But if they don't, this will be because they are imperfectly rational. The moral judgement appeals to one's rationality, while other reasons appeal to one's humanity, and it is possible for imperfect beings like ourselves to find the moral reasons we recognize overwhelmed by desire. None the less, in recognizing the existence of those reasons we are necessarily motivated by them. So Kant's view is a form of cognitivist internalism. Internalism never undertook to show that we always actually do what we know we ought.

The second form of cognitivist internalism that I want to discuss (indeed, the only other that I know of) does not make this claim, but holds rather that immorality is not a failure of rationality so much as of character. This is the view that John McDowell has been developing, taking as his starting point Nagel's work on motivation. Nagel and McDowell both admit, as Kant does, that there is Humean motivation, where belief and desire contribute together to action in the sort of way that Hume described. But they want to say that there is a different form of motivation which is purely cognitive. This only occurs with reasons of prudence or of morals; prudential and moral motivation are, or at least can be, special.[17] In those cases it is possible for a purely cognitive state, one which consists entirely of beliefs, to constitute a complete motivating state – to be a complete reason for action. Facts about one's future or about the pain one's actions will cause one's neighbours can play this special role in motivation, sometimes.

Now one might be tempted to insist that in such a case the agent surely is doing what he wants to do, and doing it because he wants to do it. This special sort of motivation is not restricted to cases where the agent does his duty or looks out for himself reluctantly. Nagel is not talking about the state of mind we are in when we pay our insurance premiums. Surely normal cases of prudential motivation are cases where the agent is doing what he wants because he wants. And isn't this enough to persuade us that there is a desire here, functioning in much the sort of way that Hume describes? If so, how can Nagel's view be called a form of cognitivism, if it admits that beliefs alone are insufficient for motivation? Nagel's reply to this objection is as follows:

> The claim that a desire underlies every act is true only if desires are taken to include motivated as well as unmotivated desires, and it is true only in the sense that *whatever* may be the motivation for someone's intentional pursuit of a goal, it becomes in virtue of his pursuit *ipso facto* appropriate to ascribe to him a desire for that goal. But if the desire is a motivated one, the explanation of it will be the same as the explanation of his pursuit, and it is by no means obvious that a desire must enter into this further explanation ... That I have the appropriate desire simply *follows* from the fact that these considerations motivate me.[18]

However, it seems to me that Nagel offers here, without distinguishing them, two different cognitive theories. The first is one which allows there to be a desire present, as an independent existence (in Hume's sense), but insists that it is not playing a Humean role. It is motivated, not motivating; we know that it is there because though we know that the beliefs in the case are sufficient explanation of the action, we allow Hume the point that every action is caused by a complex which includes a desire. The desire which must be present, then, must be one which is explained by the beliefs and which does not explain the beliefs' ability to motivate. The second theory maintains that though we *ascribe* a desire to a person motivated entirely by his beliefs, for instance a care for his own physical well-being, all that is meant by this is just that his beliefs

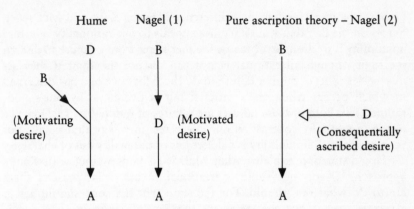

Figure 1.1. Theories of motivation. (B, belief; D, desire; A, action. The dark arrow indicates a causal relation.)

were sufficient reason for him to act. Here we do not admit the need for a desire as an independent existence; we *call* the beliefs' motivating the agent 'his doing it because he wanted'. We might dub this the 'pure ascription' theory.

Figure 1.1 is a diagram of the theories we have considered so far. The key to keeping these two interpretations apart is to see that there is an ambiguity in the notion of an 'independent desire'. In talking of independent desire, we may either mean desire as an independent existence or desire as independently intelligible. On neither interpretation is the relevant desire independently intelligible, but on the former it is an independent existence while on the latter it is not.[19]

Nagel and McDowell have often been interpreted as adherents of the pure ascription theory.[20] Among the reasons for this is the way McDowell expressed the view later,[21] claiming that a non-Humean desire is consequentially ascribed and not independently intelligible. It is true that talk of consequentially ascribed desire smacks of the pure ascription theory, and that the sense in which the desire is not independently intelligible is stronger in the pure ascription theory than in the motivated desire theory. But if asked to choose between these two theories, I suspect that they would both choose the latter.[22] So from now on I will be taking them as motivated desire theorists.

4 MOTIVATED DESIRE THEORY

Motivated desire theory is located on the philosophical map between two views. The first of these we have already seen: it is Kant's. And perhaps the most fundamental difference between Kant and McDowell hinges on the fact that Kant's picture appeals to our rationality. For him immorality is irrationality, because it either stems from a failure to discern the right (though all rational beings can discern the right if they set themselves to it) or from a failure to do the right once one has discerned it, which occurs when one's rational self is overcome by one's non-rational self. Both of these failures are failures of rationality. McDowell's picture appeals by contrast to our character (in a way that I have not yet brought out). Immorality is a defect not of rationality but of character.

This distinction explains what McDowell finds wrong with Kant's approach.[23] Kant must hold it irrational to ask what reasons there are to do what one should. For the statement that one should act in a certain way is just the statement that one's maxim in so acting is universalizable. This is the only moral reason there is, and anyone who fails to see this as a reason to act is failing in rationality, since it is to our rationality that this reason appeals rather than to our desires. So to query the status of a moral reason is to show a failure of rationality. But in fact it is not irrational to ask why this or that is a reason. The reason why one should do what one should is not expressed in the statement that one should, and being told that one should do it therefore fails to provide one with a reason if one did not have one already.

Kant's view is that one cannot really ask whether the reasons are reasons, or why they are, because he thinks that if one really understands the question one will already know the answer. This claim is supported by his view that it is the same reason at issue every time.[24] But in fact there may well be no *general* reason for doing what one should, despite Kant's assumption that there must be such a thing. The reason why you should do it will be the distress you will cause her if you don't, or the help you can give him if you do. These facts, which constitute the reason why you should act, are not ones which you are required to notice on pain of irrationality. One's conception of the circumstances, which is what overall constitutes one's reason for acting, must indeed be rational in the sense of being in accordance with reason, but will not be a conception which is required by reason. So it is not one which it is a failure of rationality not to have. Admittedly, if I do have that conception, then I can be criticized if I am not appropriately motivated. But, for internalists, to have that conception just *is* to be motivated; there would be something genuinely incoherent if these two got separated. This does not mean that all who have it will actually act on it, however, and those who do not have not failed in rationality – they have simply failed morally, revealing a defect of character.

So Kant's view that immorality is a form of irrationality should be abandoned, and with it his form of cognitivism in ethics. On the other side of McDowell's view is the suggestion of D. Z. Phillips[25] that moral reasons are purely cognitive states (beliefs), but they are beliefs which we would not have unless we already had a concern for others. On this account the moral reasons do not require the presence of independent desires in order to motivate, since the independent desires are needed at an earlier stage. The desires are not among one's reasons for action, though they are necessary for one to have the reasons one has. Phillips writes:

> Is not the form of the imperative 'You ought to heed these considerations if you care or if you are interested'? This is not so. To think otherwise is to confuse the conditions under which a man has reasons for paying attention to moral considerations with his reasons for paying attention. He will not have such reasons unless he cares, but the fact that he cares is not his reason for caring. If, hurrying to the cinema, I stop to help the victim of an epileptic fit, while it is true that, in the absence of considerations of personal advantage, I should not have stopped unless I cared, it does not follow that my reason for helping him is because I care. The reason is to be found in the suffering of the epileptic.[26]

This theory is hard to characterize. It is cognitivist, since its moral reasons are beliefs, such as the belief that the epileptic is in pain. It is internalist in the sense that the presence of a moral belief guarantees motivation, and the reasons it speaks of are categorical imperatives in our weak sense, since nobody can recognize those reasons for what they are and then attempt to escape their relevance to himself by saying that he just doesn't care about that sort of thing. It is too late for this remark, even though there can be people who don't care about that sort of thing. For to have the relevant moral belief one must already care, on Phillips' account. (This just shows how weak is our present sense of 'categorical'.) But the theory still lacks something that we held characteristic of cognitivism, namely the claim that a set of beliefs can be alone sufficient for action. It is close to this claim, but not quite there. It remains stubbornly the case that the relevant desire is a necessary part of any complete motivating state, even in the ethical case. Admittedly, the theory is not quite Humean, since the role played by the desire is not a Humean role. There is no suggestion here that the desire generates an end to which the beliefs offer probable means. But in my view the theory is not fully cognitive for all that. It has too much of the structure of Hume's theory in figure 1.1.

McDowell intends to occupy the position of Nagel's motivated desire theory. He takes it that to have a moral reason is to be in a purely

cognitive state, but one which is not in any way dependent on independent desires, either for its existence or for its motivational role. He
admits the need for desires in the story, but thinks of them as motivated
by the beliefs rather than as playing the sort of prior role that they play
in Phillips' account. The desires are present and necessary if the action
is to happen, though they do not pull their own weight in the causal
story. But won't McDowell have to admit that only those sensitive to
the needs of others can have the relevant moral beliefs? He will, but this
does not collapse the distinction between his position and that of Phillips.
The reason is that the sensitivity to the needs of others plays a different
role in McDowell's approach. For him, to be sensitive just is to see the
moral reasons in the case for what they are. It is not a prior concern
which has enough independent body to be brought to a new case, or to
be taken from case to case. The sensitivity is not an antecedent condition
for the moral belief, since having the moral beliefs is just what it is to
be sensitive. So that sensitivity should not be mistaken for a Humean
desire in drag. It is not to be thought of as affective rather than cognitive, in the way that Phillips' caring is. Perhaps the right way to think
of it is as both affective and cognitive, but if one had to choose between
the two one would go for the cognitive side.

So far, then, McDowell's adaptation of Nagel's cognitive theory of
motivation is proving the best form of cognitivism we have seen. But
does it escape the problem of accidie? Humean motivation is of course
vulnerable to accidie, but this creates no philosophical difficulty. We
simply announce that the necessary (motivating) desires can, on occasion, vanish and cease for any of a number of reasons. What about
motivated desires? It seems at the moment that motivated desire theory
faces the problem raised earlier, that if the relevant beliefs can be present
without generating any motivation whatever, they can never be the sole
source of that motivation.[27] This means that the best extant form of
cognitivist internalism is vulnerable to the problem of accidie.

In the remainder of this chapter, I lay the building blocks for a form
of cognitivism which, though internalist in general style, succeeds in
escaping the accidie problem. Effectively, what I shall suggest is that
what we need in this area is a more extreme form of cognitivism, one
which does not admit that Hume was right part of the time.

5 PURE COGNITIVISM

To build this purer form of cognitivism, I need to return to Hume's
starting point, but use it in my own way and for my own purposes.

Hume's belief/desire thesis has it that every complete motivating state is a combination of belief and desire. Neither belief nor desire alone can be sufficient for action. If this were all there was to it, the belief/desire thesis would be symmetrical; all we have so far is that belief needs desire and desire needs belief. But the relation between belief and desire in motivation is hardly symmetrical, in Hume's view. The difference between the two is that desire is active in a way that belief is not. I take this to mean that a belief is not a reason for action unless joined to a relevant desire. Add the desire and what was not a reason for action becomes one. Belief is intrinsically inert. But desires are always a reason for action. A desire without relevant belief is like a hydraulic thrust which has no means of escape. So desires are essentially 'ert', and beliefs can become 'ert' when combined with suitable desires. It is in this way that Hume tries to do justice to the common feeling that it is the desires that really do the motivating. The thrust comes really from the desire, not from the belief, despite the need for a belief in a complete motivating state.

One notable feature of this deservedly classic theory is the way it makes beliefs and desires fit each other in an asymmetrical relation. Beliefs and desires, as Hume conceives them, are made for each other. There could hardly be Humean beliefs unless there were Humean desires, and vice-versa. There is what is sometimes called a local holism here. It is not just that desires are more important than beliefs. Desires and beliefs play different roles, and the role of each is made possible by the role of the other. This must be so if Hume's argument is to work, since the asymmetry at issue constitutes Hume's explanation of why neither belief nor desire is alone sufficient for action.

Hume's argument, as I am presenting it here, comes in two stages. The first stage suggests that a complete motivating state must have two elements, labelled 'belief' and 'desire'. The second stage tells us something about the differences between those elements. It is only at the second stage that it becomes necessary for Hume to put forward his specific conceptions of belief and of desire, as explanations of what he found at the first stage. At the first stage various conceptions are still possible.

So what I want to suggest is that there is room for a theory which, while accepting and working with something like the first stage of Hume's argument, conceives of the two elements distinguished rather differently, in broadly cognitivist terms. Such a theory will start from a cognitivist version of Hume's initial question about whether belief or desire alone could generate an action. What are the formal requirements for an *intentional* and *purposive* action?[28] For there to be such an action, there need to be two distinct 'representations' in the agent. The first of these will represent the world as it now is, and the second will represent the world as it will be when and if the action is successfully completed. We can see that the first representation is necessary because without it agents would have no idea of the circumstances in which they are acting. In particular, they would have no idea whether their action is necessary or not; they would have no idea whether it would lead to a *change*. We can see that the second representation is necessary first for the same reason, and second because without it agents would have no idea what they are trying to achieve. The first representation tells them what they are working from and the second tells them what they are working to. So we can think of the first one as the 'before' and the second one as the 'after'.

This is the argument from which my cognitive theory of motivation is to grow. The general aim is to write a theory which achieves as much as possible with the very slender conceptual equipment which the argument provides. The further we get in this enterprise, the nearer we are to showing that an adequate theory of motivation need not contain any recognizable version of Hume's conception of desire. This result would serve to distinguish my purer form of cognitivism from those of Kant and of McDowell and Nagel.

So far we have, perhaps, the bare bones of the theory but not much meat. In chapter 2 I try to develop the pure theory by showing how it responds to various objections. In the final section of chapter 2 I lift the restriction to purposive action, and try to show how the theory can be expanded or adapted to deal with actions of other types.

NOTES

1 See Falk (1948) and Frankena (1958).
2 Nagel (1970), p. 7.
3 What makes this muddle unfortunate is that it tempts one to confuse two quite different questions, which are anyway easy enough to run together because they are discussed in the same vocabulary of 'internal' and 'external'. The first of these is raised by Bernard Williams (1980) as the question whether there can be both internal and external reasons; external reasons, in Williams' sense, are facts rather than beliefs. The second is what Nagel is discussing when he speaks of internalism and externalism in the theory of motivation. I discuss the relation between these two distinctions, and Williams' views on the matter, in Appendix I.
4 It is worth saying that in my view Hume was not in this sense a Humean, and when I speak of Hume in the text I do not mean to refer to the views

Hume actually held, but to the post-Humean tradition. (David Wiggins pressed me very hard to talk of Davidsonianism instead; for Humean views in Davidson, see Davidson (1980) ch. 1.) One crucial respect in which Hume differs from the Humeans is that he held that belief is a lively idea in a way that I find hard to reconcile with the insistence that belief be passive. An outstandingly non-Humean sentence in Hume is this one: '[Belief] is something *felt* by the mind, which distinguishes the ideas of the judgement from the fictions of the imagination. It gives them more force and influence; makes them appear of greater importance; infixes them in our mind; and renders them the governing principles of all our actions.' This is in the Appendix to Hume's *Treatise* (Hume, 1739/40), at p. 629. Another point of the same sort is that an insistence that desire be active while belief is passive is hard to make consistent with Hume's official account of causation. But this is not a very strong point because Hume's text is notoriously riddled with similar inconsistencies.

5 See Nagel's use of the notion of guaranteeing in the quotation above.

6 Note that this is not the strong view that beliefs don't motivate at all. They do motivate, but only when enabled to do so by the presence of a distinctively motivating state – a desire.

7 This appeal to the notion of direction of fit may be premature, since I shall have much more to say about it in chapter 2. Its appearance here is only to try to stifle a reasonable worry about the structure of the Humean position.

8 I should admit straight out that I know of no satisfactory account of the difference between cognitive and non-cognitive states. For the moment, the present paragraph could simply be taken as an arbitrary definition of cognitivism and non-cognitivism in ethics. The best I can do to define the two crucial terms is to say that belief is the paradigm case of a cognitive state and desire the paradigm case of a non-cognitive one.

9 For instance, in Warnock (1967), ch. 2.

10 See Ross (1939), pp. 226–8. In chapter 5 I suggest a motive for Ross to adopt this position. It is interesting that Prichard too can probably be counted as an externalist; see Prichard (1968), pp. 223–6. Ross was strongly influenced by Prichard.

11 There are other, stronger notions of a categorical imperative, which can be found, for example, in Wiggins (1991); I examine this matter in more detail in chapter 3, where I consider whether the theory of motivation which I prefer can give any genuine sense to the idea that moral reasons are distinctive in being or generating categorical imperatives. Wiggins' discussion conflates what I shall there be trying to keep apart, namely the claim that moral reasons are external reasons (in Williams' sense, see note 3 above), the claim that they are categorical in the weak sense given in the text, and the more authentically Kantian claim that the acts they recommend are objectively necessary without regard to any end.

12 For arguments against internalism based on people of these types, see Brink (1986) and (1989), pp. 45–50.

13 It should be no surprise that I do not include the weak-willed person in my list of problems for internalism. Weakness of will is not a problem for internalism, because the weak-willed person is motivated by every consideration he recognizes as a reason (this doesn't include the overall judgement about where the balance of reasons lies); he just doesn't act in accordance with that overall judgement. Weakness of will plays a completely different role in this debate, a role which surfaces in chapter 2.

14 There are two lines possible here. The first is to say that this amoralist does not fully understand the moral judgements which he knows that others make; the second is to say that though he does understand them, he does not accept them. Either line would be enough for the defence of internalism, and I am not here going to choose between them. Maybe there are just people of both sorts.

15 Here and generally in the discussion of amoralism and evil I follow the line taken in McNaughton (1988), ch. 9.

16 See the longer footnote on pp. 66–67 of Kant (1785), where he writes: 'Immediate determination of the will by the law and consciousness of this determination is called "*reverence*", so that reverence is regarded as the *effect* of the law on the subject and not as the *cause* of the law. Reverence is properly awareness of a value which demolishes my self-love.'

17 Nagel's discussion focuses on prudential reasons; McDowell presses the case for extending Nagel's position to ethics.

18 Nagel (1970), p. 29.

19 It is possible that an ambiguity in the notion of the 'independently intelligible' has contributed to the lack of clarity in the choice between the motivated desire theory and the pure ascription theory. In the former, the desire is 'not independently intelligible' only in the weak sense that one could not understand how it came into existence if one did not know about the beliefs; it *could*, however, have come into existence in other ways. In the latter, the desire is 'not independently intelligible' in a stronger sense, since the desire consists in the way the beliefs cause the action. In the theory I will be offering in chapter 2, we will see an account under which the desire is not independently intelligible in the strong sense, but is still an independent existence. I am grateful to Eve Garrard for discussion here.

    A further point: in the motivated desire theory, is the belief held able to motivate an action all by itself, without the help of a desire? If so, the theory is more radically anti-Humean than I have allowed. But it is not so. The desire is necessary (*causally* necessary), though it does not pull its own weight in the causal story in a way that the belief does in the motivating desire theory.

20 For example in McNaughton (1988), p. 50: 'According to the realist, to ascribe such a desire to the agent, after he has acted, is merely to acknowledge that his moral belief was here sufficient to motivate him'.

21 See McDowell (1978), p. 20.

22 For some evidence, see Nagel (1986), p. 151n. McDowell is tempted to

ask, against the pure ascription theory, 'Why say it if it isn't true?' (in conversation).

23 See McDowell (1978), p. 14.
24 David McNaughton helped me here.
25 See Phillips (1977) and Smith (1987).
26 Phillips (1977), p. 146.
27 This is so, at least, until we introduce the complications deriving from McDowell's notion of the virtuous person, in whom cognitive reasons silence any possible opposition. I introduce these complications in chapter 3; their relation to the present debate is, as we shall see, far from clear.
28 Later (in 2.6) I withdraw the restriction to purposive action, and it emerges that the need for two representations is a feature of the purposive rather than of all intentional action. The 'two representation' theory I am building up at the moment turns out to be something of a special case of a more general cognitive theory.

2
The pure theory and
its rivals

1 PURE AND HYBRID THEORIES

I need to show the difference between the theory I am trying to build up, which I have called the 'pure' cognitive theory, and the only other going alternative to Hume, the theory proposed by Nagel for the case of prudential motivation and adopted (and adapted) by McDowell for the case of moral motivation. As I argued in chapter 1, there are two ways of reading Nagel, either as 'motivated desire' theorist or as 'pure ascription' theorist. These theories agree that though in non-Humean motivation there is still desire in the story, the desire concerned is not independently intelligible. They differ on whether the desire is an independent existence in Hume's sense; the motivated desire theory sees the relevant desire as an independent existence, while the pure ascription theory does not. Of these two theories I have already suggested that Nagel and McDowell themselves in fact intend the first. I, however, prefer the second. My reason for this preference is that I don't want to start by allowing Hume the point that every action is caused by a complex which includes a desire.

However this may be, both Nagelian theories differ from my pure theory in the same two ways. First, the pure theory does not treat moral or prudential motivation as a special case in the way that the Nagel/McDowell theory does. My theory, by contrast, is especially aimed at showing that there is nothing very special about moral reasons. Even if moral (and prudential?) reasons are somehow distinct in style from others (a matter which I discuss in chapter 3), the difference between them and others is not so great that they could be alone in being non-Humean. For Nagel and McDowell there are, though, or at least can be, two distinct sorts of motivation; in that sense we can call their theory a *hybrid* theory. Second, the pure theory, as we have so far expressed it, may yet admit the need for an independent desire for each case of intentional action. It would do this, for instance, if it identified the second representation with a desire. Desires so conceived would be independent in both senses. They would be independently intelligible and independent existences.

So what role should we see desire as playing in the pure theory? There are three different ways of running the pure theory. The first and most trenchant is to say that desire does not enter into the story at all. The second is to identify one or other of the two representations with desire, presumably the 'after'. The third is to admit that there is a place for desire in the story, but to insist that neither representation is a desire. The first of these perhaps best deserves the title 'pure cognitivism', but it is hard to see that we should find no role for desire at all in our account of motivation; I reject this approach out of hand. The second amounts effectively to a cognitive theory of desire, since it identifies desire with a cognitive state. There are awkwardnesses here. Using the notion of direction of fit (of which more in a moment), we can say that if the second representation is a desire, it must be a peculiar state that has *both* directions of fit. As a belief about how things will be when my action is complete, it has the mind-to-world direction of fit. As a reason for me to make that belief true, it has the world-to-mind direction of fit. Those who understandably find this concoction unsettling might prefer the third, more subtle approach. This holds that though desire is necessary for motivation, the occurrence of a desire is never what motivates. What motivates in the case of a purposive action is always the gap between two representations, and the occurrence of the desire is *the agent's being motivated* by that gap. If we make this move we could even allow the existence of desires as independently existing non-cognitive states, and thus make room for those who are impressed by the nature of some strong desires such as lust, which have a genuine phenomenology which makes Humean analyses especially tempting in their case. We could allow the lust to be a non-cognitive state, since it is not a belief, but insist that what motivates the luster is not the lust but the combination of two representations, the 'before' and the 'after'.[1] The lust is the agent's being strongly motivated by these representations. So it is not a belief and it has phenomenal properties; and it must be an independent existence, for how otherwise could it have phenomenal properties?

Of these three possibilities, it is the third that is the most promising for pure cognitivism. But will our adoption of one or other of the three have the effect of collapsing the distinction between pure and hybrid theory? The first version of the pure theory is effectively a complex version of the pure ascription theory. We might, after all, be willing to agree that when someone acts in the light of two suitable representations he is doing what he wants and doing it because he wants to, without thinking of this as inconsistent with the purity of our cognitive approach. Here we identify neither representation with a desire, but still talk about doing what one wants. It is easy to distinguish the second version from either of the two Nagelian theories, since its desires are independently intelligible[2] which on Nagelian theories they are not. On the third version, too, our theory would be distinct from the hybrid theory (on either interpretation). It differs from the motivated desire theory in its view that the desire, though an independent existence, is not part of the causal story that takes us from beliefs to action. The desire here is to be conceived as a distinct event, that of the agent's being motivated by certain conceptions.[3] As such it is caused by those conceptions, but though necessary for the eventual action it is not a cause of that action; it does not pull its own weight in the causal story.[4] (Its occurrence does not contribute to the explanation of the action, though for logical rather than causal reasons we could not suppose the action possible in its absence.) The pure theory here is nearer to the pure ascription theory, since it agrees that the desire just is the agent's being motivated by his beliefs; on both these accounts the desire is not independently intelligible. But the pure theory differs in taking the desire still to be an independent existence, and not merely a figure of speech.

So far I have said little in favour of the pure theory. In fact, I shall never offer an explicit argument in favour of that theory, nor argue directly against its Humean rival. But I do want to argue that it is superior to the hybrid theory, and so that it emerges as the best form of cognitivism in the theory of motivation. The suggestion I want to make is that hybrid theories are for that very reason liable to objection: that the very purity of the pure theory is an advantage. To this end, I start with a question: does the hybrid theory introduce two distinct sorts of desires, Humean ones and consequentially ascribed ones? I think that the answer to this is that it does not. On the motivated desire theory, the desires come in a different place, indeed, but they are still Humean. On the pure ascription theory, one might say that consequentially ascribed desires are really not genuine desires at all – what we have here is more like desire-talk than real desires. So either way there are not two sorts of desire. But then the question becomes whether there aren't two sorts of beliefs. It is important to remember that Humean beliefs and desires are made for each other. The discovered characteristics of belief and of desire derive centrally from the way the two go together in the generation of action – the asymmetry, as I called it. This makes it hard to change one side of the pairing without changing the other, as we would expect if we are really dealing with a local holism. But this seems to be what the hybrid theory is trying to do. It holds that sometimes beliefs need the independent contribution of desire, and sometimes they don't. This seems to mean that there are two sorts of beliefs, Humean and non-Humean. But that cannot be quite right, because the very same beliefs which on one occasion need an independent non-cognitive supplement if there is to be an action, can elsewhere figure in a state which needs no such supplement at all. Beliefs are not carved up into two sorts, those that can motivate alone and those that need some help. It is the same sort of belief all the time. But in that case how is it that the extra provided by a desire can on other occasions be provided by a belief? First, if the beliefs concerned are Humean, no accumulation of them will ever be sufficient for an action; and, second, if the desires concerned are Humean, so must the beliefs be. So purely cognitive motivation cannot be conceived in terms of (or as a variation on) Humean motivation in the way that the hybrid theory tries to.

The point here is that if ever we allow ourselves to be persuaded that a set of beliefs will stand in need of the independent contribution of a desire if they are to motivate, that need will remain no matter how much we enrich the set of beliefs. So a hybrid theory will be unable to retain its insistence that purely cognitive motivation is possible if it once yields to the pressure to admit Humean motivation as a possibility. I take this to show that hybrid theories are unstable, leaving my pure cognitivism as the strongest theory in the field.

There is a way of pursuing this line of thought, which is to suggest that no *one* theory of human nature could support a hybrid theory of motivation. Humeanism is (part of) a theory of human nature, and it should not surprise us if it covers the ground in such a way that we are unable to say that it is right some of the time. So any Kantian or other theory which tries to *add* something to Humeanism must be misconceived. If the addition is well motivated, the Humean side cannot be. This is too large a story for me to follow up here. But it is the most incisive way I know of making the point against the hybrid theory that if non-Humean motivation is even possible, Humeanism is false.[5]

I still have to establish that the pure theory has an answer to the problem of accidie. But there is also another very influential standard argument against any form of cognitivism that I have not yet addressed, which I want to tackle first. I take it first because my answer to it is also an answer to the problem of accidie.

2 INTRINSICALLY MOTIVATING STATES

The argument I mean runs as follows. Take an agent's total cognitive state, and suppose that on this occasion it is sufficient for action. We must admit that the same state can be present without leading to action, because of weakness of will. But this surely contradicts our hypothesis that the state concerned was sufficient for action in the first place. We must have given an incomplete specification of that state, and since we have exhausted cognitive resources, we are left presuming that there was a non-cognitive element present as well. But to admit this is to abandon the cognitive theory altogether.

The upshot of this argument is that the phenomenon of weakness of will disproves any form of cognitivism in the theory of motivation. This is a different problem from that raised in chapter 1, which centred on the notion of accidie. As I said there, accidie focuses our attention on people who are not at all motivated by moral reasons which in some sense they recognize; it therefore generates an argument against internalism. Weakness of will focuses attention on those who share a conception with someone who is sufficiently motivated to act, but don't act. The standard argument above claims that this possibility amounts to a refutation of cognitivism. The general idea is that the obvious thing to say about weakness of will is that the relevant desires don't necessarily follow the strength of the perceived reasons (beliefs). But only a non-cognitivist can say this. The cognitivist, who either denies the need for desires or sees them as tightly tied to the beliefs, cannot make the same move. That is why this argument raises a special problem for cognitivists.

We might think of this argument as analogous to a similar argument in causal terms. Take a circumstance which we suppose to be sufficient for some outcome here. If we admit that in different conditions that circumstance would be present without the outcome occurring, we appear forced to agree that our specification of the cause here was incomplete. It is this sort of argument that leads us to accept that ordinary causal statements are 'gappy'.

I want to argue that this influential argument is in fact unsound, and that my pure cognitivism escapes it. It is unsound because it makes a basic assumption which a cognitivist does not need to share. This is that if a state is anywhere sufficient for action, it must be everywhere sufficient. This generalist assumption can and should be replaced by a different conception of a state sufficient for action, which can allow the possibility of a cognitive state being sufficient for action without supposing that wherever it occurs the action must follow.

	Essentially	Contingently
In their own right	Hume's desires	My representations
Not in their own right	?	Hume's beliefs

Figure 2.1 Grid of ways in which states can motivate.

To see the possibility of this alternative, we need to return to where we started. Hume conceives of a complete motivating state as consisting of two elements, belief and desire, asymmetrically related. The desire is an essentially or necessarily motivating state, while the belief is a state which can motivate, but which can be present without motivating. So when the belief does motivate, it does not do so in its own right, but acquires the ability to do so from its subordinate relation to a relevant desire. This distinction is often discussed in the literature by talking of the difference between internally and externally motivating states. Our concept of an internally motivating state takes as its paradigm of such a state a Humean desire: our concept of an externally motivating state is modelled on a Humean or post-Humean conception of a belief. It is clear, therefore, that cognitivists should be careful before accepting the distinction between internally and externally motivating states as it emerges straight from the opposing theory. And in fact we can see that the original distinction is a conflation of two distinctions.[6] The first is between states that are essentially and those that are contingently motivating (which can be present without motivating). The second is between those states which when they motivate do so in their own right and those which do not. Hume's theory contains the assertions, first, that there are essentially motivating states, and, second, that any state which when it motivates does so in its own right must be of that sort, – i.e. that the two distinctions coincide. But we can deny this, and so construct the notion of a sort of state which can be present without motivating, but which, when it does motivate, does so in its own right. Think of the representations with which I began as such states. A diagram of the ways in which states can motivate is given in figure 2.1.

The sort of cognitive theory I want to support maintains that there are no such things as Humean beliefs or desires. Instead of these internally and externally motivating states, there are what we might call *intrinsically* motivating states, which can be present without motivating but which when they do motivate do so in their own right. They can motivate in their own right, and so are not Humean beliefs; but they can be present without motivating, and so are not Humean desires.

This gives us a conception of a state which can in suitable circumstances be sufficient for action, but which can also be present in other cases without leading to action.[7] Of course, when this happens there will be an explanation of it, and we should expect to give this in terms of the presence of some feature in the second case which defused the ability of the original cognitive state to motivate. But that should not be taken to mean that the absence of this feature must have been among the agent's reasons for acting in the first case. Absences like this are only occasionally among one's reasons for acting, and nothing here forces us to admit that this is one of those occasions. There is an analogue of this point in the theory of causation. We might allow that the causes of my attending a conference in the US would not have been sufficient if the US had recently declared war on England, without accepting that the fact that this had not happened was among the causes of my presence there.

So I reject the thought that what was sufficient in one case must be sufficient wherever it occurs. What is a perfectly adequate reason here may be insufficient there, in a way which is to be explained by citing a *cause* that is not itself a *reason*. This possibility emerges once we accept the notion of an intrinsically motivating state. But, moving away now from the specific consideration of weakness of will, that notion also validates another possibility. This is that what are reasons *here* may not be the same reasons *there*, because of the presence of further reasons in the second case. The general line is that the ability of a consideration to motivate can be affected by background conditions which are not themselves motivators. In some circumstances a consideration will be a complete reason in favour. In others it will be an incomplete reason in favour (perhaps overwhelmed), indifferent (perhaps silenced), or even something of a reason against. If a consideration which succeeds in one place fails in another, there will be an explanation of why it fails. And this explanation will appeal to the content of some state which is present in the second case and not in the first. To give a very simple example, I might buy an ice-cream because I expect to enjoy it.[8] But if I were to accept that ice-creams damage one's teeth, I would not buy one. This should not be taken to show that among my reasons for buying the ice-cream was the fact that I did not believe that it would damage my teeth. We could harden the point by contrasting a case where it is not merely that I do not believe that they damage my teeth; instead, I positively believe that they do not damage teeth. Even in such a case we should refuse to allow that just because I would not be motivated to buy an ice-cream if I believed the opposite, my belief that ice-creams are okay for teeth must have been among my reasons for buying this one. First, my action is already sufficiently intelligible without appeal to this belief. Second, that something is okay for teeth is a peculiar reason for eating it except in special circumstances (e.g. when most things are bad for teeth and one is not very hungry anyway).

I began this book with a characterization of the distinction between internalism and externalism in the theory of motivation which I took from Nagel. Using that distinction, I argued that externalism was in a stronger position because it can make sense of the phenomenon of accidie, which internalism, as originally conceived, cannot. But now the structure of the debate seems to me to have shifted. We started in a place where it made sense to ask of any motivating state whether it was an internally motivating state or an externally motivating one. But now we see that that question embodied all sorts of Humean assumptions, in particular the identification of the distinction between essentially and contingently motivating states with that between those that motivate in their own right and those that don't. (It was the latter distinction that really embodied the asymmetry so important to Hume.) Effectively, we have rejected the distinction between internally and externally motivating states, and with it the original distinction between internalism and externalism. The theory we have ended up with is neither internalist nor externalist.

Even so, there is a lot more about it that is internalist than there is externalist; and the question for us now is whether pure cognitivism, having supposedly survived problems deriving from the phenomenon of weakness of will, can also survive those deriving from accidie. If it can, there is no remaining reason to prefer an externalist theory, and we can appeal to the original intuition in support of internalism to support pure cognitivism as well. But the flexibility introduced by the notion of an intrinsically motivating state is surely just what we need to account for accidie. What we assert is that a state which is here sufficient for action may elsewhere not be. Where it is not sufficient, there will be an explanation for this. And we have introduced no restriction on the sorts of explanation that we are prepared to countenance. Sometimes the reason will be carelessness or inattention; sometimes it will be despair; sometimes it will be an excess of alcohol; sometimes it will be a neuro-physiological disorder; and sometimes it will be clinical depression. I see no difficulty in capturing the sorts of explanation felt appropriate for accidie in this sort of net. So accidie is a problem only for internalism as we originally conceived it; it can be handled by pure cognitivism without difficulty.

Can we still appeal to our intuitions to support the pure theory? The intuition I relied on was the sense that there is something odd in saying 'This is wrong but I don't see that as relevant to my choice of action.' And we built this up by suggesting that moral considerations are not ones whose practical relevance one can escape by pleading the absence of a suitable desire. I see no difficulty in seeing the pure theory as one way of capturing this intuition, which is after all vague enough to admit of various interpretations. First, the pure theory can make good sense of moral imperatives as categorical in the weak sense of chapter 1, seeing moral judgements as cognitive states whose motivational force exists (when they have any at all) without relying on any contribution from an independent desire. Second, the pure theory is not prevented from seeing the overall moral judgement 'This is what I ought to do' as one which, though in certain unusual circumstances it may be deprived of its normal motivational force, still has a normal motivational force to be deprived of. This idea of a normal (default) force in the overall judgement is perfectly compatible with anything the pure theory has yet committed itself to. And it is surely what is gestured towards by the original intuition that there is something odd about saying 'This is wrong but I don't see that as relevant to my choice of action.' The pure theory agrees that there is something odd about this, because normally to see something as wrong is (intrinsically) to be motivated not to do it, though it admits that there may be circumstances where what normally happens does not happen.

It is worth noticing this idea that there is a normal or default tendency in the overall moral judgement, and keeping it apart from the idea that certain repeatable features of actions have a normal or default moral tendency. It is natural to think that the causation of pain has such a tendency. Whether this is so or not, and if so what it takes to annul that tendency in particular cases, will be the topic of chapter 6 and recur in chapter 11. For the moment I only want to point out that one could accept the view that overall moral judgements have such normal or default tendencies, without saying the same about the lower-level features of actions which generate the overall judgement.

So I take it therefore that the pure theory can cope with the existence of accidie and of weakness of will, and that it is a method of capturing the intuition that lay behind Nagel's formulation of the internalist position without being in that sense internalist. It is clearly superior to its hybrid rival.

3 Directions of fit

The real problem for a cognitivist is to show that one's theory is not just some form of Humeanism in disguise. There is an enormous temptation to insist that *any* theory, no matter how initially distant it may seem, must somehow respect and retain Humean asymmetries. The crucial asymmetry here is the one between two directions of fit. Humeanism claims that a belief is a cognitive state with one direction of fit, and desire is a non-cognitive state with the other direction of fit. (In claiming that desire is non-cognitive there is no intention to deny that desire is a propositional attitude. In fact, the distinction between the cognitive and the non-cognitive does not add much to the debate here, since there is no agreement about how it should be drawn or what it amounts to; the real point is the one about directions of fit and it may well be that the other distinction collapses into this.)

The notion of direction of fit is normally built up in the following way.[9] Suppose that I am going to the supermarket to do the week's shopping, and that I have in hand a list of what I am to get.[10] However, unknown to me, my wife suspects me of conducting an affair, and she has a detective on my heels writing down a list of everything I do. Once I have been through the shop, the detective's list will be the same as mine (he hopes). But the two lists have different directions of fit. The detective's list has to fit what is in my trolley, and if there is a mismatch there is something wrong with his list, not with what is in the trolley. But what is in the trolley is supposed to fit *my* list, and if it does not there is something wrong with what is in the trolley, not with my list. Here we have two lists with a common content but different directions of fit. Generalizing, we can say that a state with the first direction of fit has to fit the world, and if it does not the fault lies with the state and not with the world; a state with the second direction of fit is one which the world has to fit (or which is out to get the world to fit it), and if it doesn't the fault lies with the world and not with the state. Beliefs have the first direction of fit, and desires the second, though states such as emotions and intentions may have the second direction of fit as well.

The way I have expressed the notion of direction of fit is highly metaphorical, and a great deal of work has been recently put into taking the metaphor out.[11] The hope is that once the metaphor is removed, we will be able to see the distinction clearly for what it is, and that therefore the use of it as a weapon will be much more effective. For reasons which cannot be run through in detail here, I do not think that a sound non-metaphorical version has yet been provided. But there is no doubting the strength of the intuition which the story above is trying to capture. The best way I know of expressing the distinction without talk of whose fault the failure to fit is, or of what we should change to improve matters, is to say that a belief is a state which aims to be caused by the truth of its own content, while desire is a state which aims to cause its own content to become true. (Note that we cannot say simply that belief is caused by the world and desire is not but aims to cause the world, because any rational desire is to a great extent caused by how things are, just as belief is.)

Let us take this (probably defective) version of the distinction and see what one might try to do with it. The point for me is that it can be used to depress the pretensions of the pure cognitive theory of motivation. For here is an immediate objection to the pure theory: without the presence of two distinct states, one with each direction of fit, action is inconceivable. If this were true, then either the first or the second representation must have the direction of fit of a desire (which really amounts to *being* a desire), or else there must be some other state present and necessary for motivation, so that the two representations are not themselves sufficient, contrary to the pure theory. This further state will have to have the direction of fit of a desire, and so the pure theory will have collapsed into Humeanism. Using the version of the distinction outlined above and applying it to the particular case at issue, aren't we going to have to admit that the second representation is a state that aims to cause its own content to be true, and isn't that just the admission of the Humean asymmetries that we were trying to avoid? In classic Humean terms, that the agent has a certain desire is a reason for him to make the content of that desire true. The second representation functions – *must* function – in that way, and so it is just a Humean desire. What then could all the fuss have been about?

There is a misconception here which it is worth untangling. It is based on an ambiguity in the account of the second representation. In holding that it represents the world as it will be when and if the action is successfully completed, we might have meant to see its content as that of the subjunctive conditional 'If I were to act in such and such a way, this would be the result.' But we might also have meant that the content is simply the categorical future tense statement 'The world will change in this way.' I intended the first of these; it was only by doing so that I could make it at all plausible that the second representation was not a Humean desire. For if the content were simply 'The world will change in this way', then if that is to be seen as a belief there seems to be no remaining reason for anyone keen on that change to act, since the change is already down to occur anyway. So the second representation would have to be seen as a desire if this is its content, contrary to my general intention. Better by far is to say that the second representation represents the world as it will be, not *tout court*, but in a way conditional on my action.

On the account I intended the second representation is not a desire, since its presence is not a reason for the agent to make its content true. The agent is not trying to make a subjunctive conditional true (there are more ways than one of doing this). He is acting with the intention of making the consequent true. So the pure theory remains distinct from its Humean rival. The only states necessary for action are the two representational states, and both of these have the same direction of fit, that of a belief; in fact, nothing is lost by thinking of them as beliefs.[12]

A second attempt to collapse the distinction between the pure theory and its Humean rival takes its start from our response to the first. We held there that the agent, in being motivated by the second representation, is not trying to make that representation true; its content is a subjunctive conditional, and he is acting with the intention only of making the consequent of that conditional true. But now the Humean sees his chance. Surely that intention, which we have just agreed exists, is a Humean desire. It is a state with a content, whose role is that it motivates the agent towards making that content true.

The answer here is to distinguish between intention and motive. The agent's intention is, shall we say, to make money. He takes it that he does not have enough money, and that if he invests in Consolidated Butter Mountains he will have enough (or more nearly enough, at any rate). According to the pure theory, these two representations constitute his motive for acting; they are what motivate him. In doing the action which they motivate him to do, he acts with the intention of making money. But that intention is not what motivates him. Intentions do not motivate, according to the pure theory. In this they are like desires (and emotions); the desire is the agent's being motivated by the relevant representations, and so is the intention.

This move, which is really nothing more than the assertion that when we said that a desire was not a state that motivates but a state of being motivated we meant what we said, is the crucial one in defence against the most direct attack, which claims that action is inconceivable without there being two states, one with each direction of fit, to provide the motivation. Philip Pettit and Michael Smith are aiming to express that thought in the following remarks:

a simple argument suffices to show that an agent acts, and more generally
an agent has a motivating reason to act, only so far as he has an appropriate desire.

1   Having a reason to F, specifically a motivating reason to F, is having
    a goal: say, the goal that p.
2   Having such a goal is being disposed, given appropriate beliefs, to act
    so that p.
3   And being so disposed is desiring that p.

From (1), (2) and (3) it follows that having a reason to F necessarily
involves the presence of an appropriate desire.[13]

Of course, as this conclusion is here expressed, I have no reason to
quarrel with it. For I admit the need for a desire as an independent
existence, and I am even willing to allow that such desires do have the
second direction of fit.[14] It is when Pettit and Smith express their real
view as that 'every action is the product of belief and desire'[15] that I
want to object. What I am in the business of denying is that the desire
must be (a part of) what motivates the agent; it seems to me that Pettit
and Smith have no warrant for their assumption that if the desire is
necessarily present, it must be a motivator.

4   METAPHYSICAL UNDERPINNINGS

These different ways of trying to discover Humean structures in a theory
which is avowedly set up in opposition to Hume seem to me to be
evidence of a kind of mental straitjacket from which it can be very hard
to escape. It is as if one knows that Hume *must* be right somehow, and
so one continues to search for ways of showing how any rival, no
matter how unconciliatory in appearance, is in fact just another way
of putting Hume's point. This leads me to look for a diagnosis of the
attractions of Humeanism in the theory of motivation, and there is one
not far to seek. The position we are trying to motivate is the one which
runs the eventual distinction between directions of fit, namely the view
that there are two sorts of mental state, those caused by their own
content and those which aim to cause their own content. Now suppose
that we think of mind and world as radically distinct existences which
are none the less able to interact, in the sense that the world can
impinge on the mind and the mind can impinge on the world. We need
these two sorts of impinging if we are to make sense of ourselves as
agents who can act in the light of knowledge (or at least justified belief)
about the world in which we are acting. Impinging is a causal relation,
and we have it already that, for there to be rational agents in the sense

given, such agents must have some states which are caused in them by the independent world and some states which cause them to change that world. It is just obvious that no collection of states of the first sort could be sufficient to motivate a rational action, since no such states have the status of being a reason to change anything.

What we have here is a position grounded on Cartesian metaphysics. The central idea is one which starts from the thought that mind and world are radically independent and therefore conceives of the natural world as intrinsically inert. The inertness of the world can be conceived in two ways, according to the Cartesian distinction of the operations of the mind into those of the understanding and those of the will. A world which is inert to the understanding is one which of itself contains no significance or meaning. Significance, if it exists, is something absent from the independent world. Where it exists, it is not proper to that world but consists in an added relation to a mind. When we find that significance in an event, this is either our gift to an event which did not have it before or else our recognition that some other mind has bestowed a significance on it by an act of will. Equally, a world which is inert to the will is one which of itself contains nothing important or relevant to action and choice. What is important in the world, what stands as a reason for action, is only so because of a relation to a Cartesian will conceived as a free and undetermined chooser. When we find an event important, this is either our gift to it or else our recognition that another mind (God's, this time) has bestowed an importance on it which is distinct from and alien to its own nature. Nothing matters but thinking and choosing makes it so.

Given this extraordinarily attractive picture, one can understand how it is that one comes to feel that there can only be two directions of fit, and, indeed, there cannot be any one state which has both. We know in advance that any state which appears to have both is an impostor, and can be disentangled into separate component parts. We also know that for there to be action there must be a state of each sort; in particular, there must be a desire present, for rational action is inconceivable without a state which motivates one to make the world be the way it conceives of it as being.

What I take this to show is that it is impossible for a radical opposition to accept the importance which Humeans ascribe to the notion of direction of fit and attempt to make their own use of it. The real thrust of that notion stems from the other side, and if we unwisely take it to be a significant tool we are very unlikely to be able to construct the radically opposed view that we are after. Given a Cartesian metaphysic, the notion of direction of fit is compulsory and Humean use of it

inescapable. The question is which direction of fit the second representation has, and we are faced with an unenviable choice. Either we say
it has only one, and are told that in that case our theory is only a
notational variant on Hume's: or we say it has both, which we are told
is effectively inconceivable: or we say it has neither, and are told that
this means it is no more that a creature of the imagination. With a
different metaphysic, however, we may be able to paint a different
picture so long as we do not try to express ourselves in Cartesian terms,
and so do not get caught in this way.

5   Motivating beliefs v. facts as reasons

The point now is to show that the pure theory is already committed to
a non-Cartesian metaphysic (and to show that the notion of direction
of fit is constrained by that picture so that without it it falls away). To
make this point I need to stand back from something I have up till now
allowed without scruple, namely that if it is not desires which motivate,
it must be beliefs. But when I speak of a belief motivating, I mean in
general to be understood as saying that what motivates is the matter of
fact believed, not the believing of it. In a sense I agree with Hume that
belief is inert, since to find the source of motivation you have to look
through the belief to the fact believed. One's reasons, after all, lie in the
nature of one's surroundings, not in the fact that one believes those
surroundings to be this way rather than that. It would in fact be odd
for a belief (in the sense of a believing) to be a reason or to motivate
– odd, though not impossible, as when the fact that I believe this cliff
to be dangerous is a reason for me not to attempt the climb, whether
the belief is true or not, for the belief itself is likely to unsettle me and
make the climb more hazardous. But here what motivates is the fact
that one believes, which is still a fact. Even when the motivating belief
is false, it is not the believing that motivates but the way we mistakenly
take the world to be.

Given this, we need to see through all the talk of beliefs that intrinsically motivate and see that this really means that there are facts
which intrinsically make a difference to how we should act. But to talk
about such facts is already to abandon the Cartesian picture of the
independence of mind and world. Admitting a conception of a belief as
intrinsically motivating is admitting a conception of the world under
which the world is *not motivationally inert*.[16] A world which is reason
for one choice rather than another is a world in which Cartesian polarities
have lost their grip. But the notion of direction of fit gets its life from

those polarities. So any attack on the pure theory whose source lies in those polarities is one against which no further defence is needed.

In making this point so far, I have been speaking as if facts motivate. I would have done better to have spoken of facts as reasons. Thinking in terms of facts as reasons rather than in terms of beliefs as motivating states is a further move away from Humeanism. The idea here is that if we talk about motivation and motivators, we are in danger of placing ourselves within a *causal* enquiry into the *source* or *spring* of action – the sort of enquiry that leads us to the claim that belief is intrinsically inert. This sort of talk about motivation has a natural Humean origin. It *can* be read in a non-Humean way without ceasing to be causal, but the safest way of doing that is to speak of facts as reasons rather than of beliefs as motivators. There are certainly mysteries about how facts can *be* reasons, but they are not the same as the worry that belief needs some help in motivation. We can see the need to keep these two thoughts apart when we sense the awkwardness of the idea that facts (*mere truths*) can provide motivation for those who don't notice them; for a good example, take the remark of Nagel's quoted at the beginning of chapter 1:

> On this view the motivation must be so tied to the meaning, or truth, of ethical statements that when in a particular case someone is ... morally required to do something, it follows that he has a motivation for doing it.

It would be far less outlandish to write 'it follows that he has a reason for doing it, or that there is a reason for him to do it', taking this as a 'reason-for-him' of which he is sadly ignorant (an external reason, in Williams' sense).

As I have said, the pure theory should be wary of claiming for its representations any particular direction of fit, if this amounts to an acceptance of the theoretical importance of the notion of direction of fit; for this brings back into play polarities which it rejects.[17] But there is no great harm in admitting that these representations (which can perfectly well be counted as beliefs, though not now Humean beliefs) have the direction of fit of belief and not that of desire. In the terms in which that distinction is drawn both are states whose nature it is to be caused by their own content. But there is another way of running a distinction between two directions of fit (one which I take to be much more significant) in terms of which our representations have both. For our beliefs stand both as representations of the world and as reasons to change that world. Similarly, the idea of a fact which is intrinsically motivational is one which sees that fact as relating to the world in two ways at once. It is true to (or part of) that world, and a reason for changing it.

This is not the old sense of 'having both directions of fit', but it is a sense that the pure theory can happily give, in its own terms, to a thought which encapsulates the radically anti-Cartesian and anti-Humean nature of the account of motivation it offers. It sees the distress I have caused her by my remarks both as a fact about the world and as a reason to change it, without needing therefore to introduce Humean asymmetries to account for the distinction between two roles the distress can play.

6 NON-PURPOSIVE ACTION

The time has now come to stand back from the restriction I have so far laid on the pure theory, in considering first its account of purposive action. I did this in order to tackle the Humean opposition head on – to make the cognitive theory work for the area in which Humean theory is traditionally strongest. It was in that spirit that the story about two representations was written, with the accompanying suggestion that what really motivates in such a case is the gap between them (rather than some desire, for example). But there are, of course, actions of other types, and some of these are not well coped with by the two representations story. That story must therefore be set aside as right in its place but not right for all action.

In moving away from that story I am not abandoning any essential part of the anti-Humean position I have been struggling to construct. The really important elements of the story so far have not been the distinction between two representations, but the notion of an intrinsically motivating state, the account of the place for desire in the pure theory, the refusal to accept and work with the standard distinction between two directions of fit (though I offered my own distinction here, in terms of which both representations had both directions of fit), and the refusal to admit even the existence of Humean beliefs and desires. None of these is in any way threatened by the suggestion that not all actions are motivated by a suitable pair of representations.

So why should we accept that suggestion? Two types of non-purposive action seem to need a different analysis. The first is the case where there is something I want to be doing rather than to have done. When I want to go for a walk, I am not motivated by the gap between my present static state and the future state in which I shall have returned. I am not

interested in how the world will be when and if my action is successfully completed. What motivates me is how things will be while the
action is still going on.

Now it would be possible to insist that this situation can be squeezed
into the structure of the two representation approach. We could say
that what motivates me is the gap between my present static state and
a possible future ambulatory state. I don't want here to argue either in
favour of this move or against it. It may turn out to be satisfactory or
it may not. Perhaps if it were the only sort of counter-example to the
two representation story, one would try harder to catch it under the
original umbrella. But there is a second sort of counter-example, for
which that sort of stubbornness seems much less plausible.

Take a case where, in response to your distress, I express my sympathy on your bereavement.[18] Am I motivated by the gap between how
things now are and how they will be when I have finished my halting
condolences? I would be if, for instance, I saw myself as trying to
console you, in such a way that if you do not end up consoled, I have
failed. Some expressions of sympathy are of that sort, but not all
are. Sometimes one just wants to express one's sympathy (or thinks
one ought to). Here there seems to be no second representation of the
right sort in sight. Nor are we likely to suggest that what motivates me
is how the action will be while I am doing it. I am not interested in
doing a bit of sympathy-expressing. So this sort of case is different from
the first. It seems to be one in which what motivates me is a *single*
representation, namely that of your distress – a representation which
seems to call for my expression of sympathy as the only acceptable
response.

Again, I must admit that it would perhaps be possible to force this
scenario into a two-representation story. But I see no need for the
cognitivist to insist on doing so. Expressive actions of this sort do not
stand as any sort of counter-example to cognitivism in the theory of
motivation (or of reasons, as I should now say). What they may show
is that the two-representation story cannot cover all cases, but this can
happily be admitted so long as we retain the essential elements of the
anti-Humean story listed above.

Are these further examples related to moral motivation? Are we
perhaps to say that all moral motivation is of the second sort? I did
eventually express the second counter-example in moral terms. But this
is no reason to insist that the purposive/expressive distinction, or any
other, is related to the moral/non-moral distinction. Many examples of
moral motivation fit best into a two-representation picture. For instance, I may take it that a wrong has been done and that if I act I can

rectify it. Others may best suit a one-representation approach, as perhaps the need to apologise for an unintended slight.

This point reveals a flexibility in the two-representation form of the pure theory. There is a temptation (of Humean origin) to suppose that of the two representations the second is the one that really drives (or leads). This is the residue of the thought that of a belief/desire pairing it is the desire that is really doing the business. But there is no reason to accept it. Sometimes the second representation is the more significant, and sometimes the first is. I may be motivated by the thought that things are terrible, so that almost any change will be for the better. I may be motivated by the thought that a great good is in prospect, though there is nothing so very bad in things as they are. Similarly, either representation may be a moral belief – or both. There is no reason for cognitivists in ethics to tie their flag to any one mast here. Flexibility is our watchword.

NOTES

1   This remark should be modified in the light of the discussion of non-purposive action in the final section of this chapter. It may be that in many cases of lust what motivates is not the gap between before and after so much as what the action will be like while one is doing it. This does not affect the view of desire being expressed in the text, but only challenges the implication that all action motivated by lust is purposive.

2   They are independently intelligible in both the strong and the weak senses identified in chapter 1, n. 19.

3   I am reminded here of Alvin Goldman's concept of causal level-generation; see Goldman (1970), ch. 2.

4   Another analogy from the theory of action: the role of a volition in action theory as described by Davis (1979), ch. 2. A volition is conceived of as part of a bodily action; the action is the volition's causing the bodily movement. So the volition is not the cause of the action.

5   The style of this remark is like that of Berkeley's attack on realism, when he claims that if realism were only possible it would be true. See Berkeley (1710), §22.

6   This fact is concealed by the ways in which these matters are commonly discussed, for instance by saying that desires motivate *eo ipso*. For a good example see McDowell (1981), p. 154.

7   The introduction of the notion of an intrinsically motivating state is the ground for my earlier claim that desires as the pure theory conceives them are independent existences, which some may have wished to dispute. The evidence that they are independent existences is their ability to bear phenomenal properties. The explanation of their being independent is that the

relevant beliefs can exist without them, not being essentially motivating.

8   I am very bad at examples. I owe this simple one to Elijah Millgram.

9   See Anscombe (1957), p. 56.

10 I do this because I get flustered when in the shop and forget what I intended to buy. However, since I often forget the list as well, writing a list does not leave me much better off.

11 See Searle (1983), pp. 8, 15; Stalnaker (1984), p. 15; Smith (1987). For criticisms of extant attempts, with constructive suggestions, see Humberstone (1992).

12 This is why I cannot agree with the view of Wallace (1990) that the notion of a direction of fit is not central to the debate between Humeans and rationalists.

13 Pettit and Smith (1990), p. 573.

14 This admission should not be taken to be very significant. The real point is that though I accept that desires as I see them are in the business of causing the truth of their own content, this fact is not important to my theory. It just emerges at the end that this is how things are; no damage would have been done to the theory if things had been different, because it has no *need* for any state of this sort. The Humean opposition, by contrast, puts the existence of a state with this direction of fit in centre stage; if there were none such, the theory would collapse. So there is an enormous difference in focus here. There is also the difference that on my theory these states do not motivate.

15 Pettit and Smith (1990), p. 572.

16 This phrase is lifted from McDowell (1978), p. 19.

17 I am grateful to Candace Vogler for helping me to see this.

18 Jay Bernstein and Nick Bunnin forced me to face up to examples like this.

3
In defence of purity

1 FURTHER PROBLEMS

In this section I defend the pure theory against three further forms of attack, which all concern the difference between what the agent does and does not choose. Since these attacks are all Humean in spirit, my discussion of them will be run in terms of purposive action and of beliefs as motivating states rather than facts as reasons, despite the remarks at the end of chapter 2. There is of course a danger of confusion in this procedure, but I think it necessary if the Humean counterblast is to be represented in the strongest light.

First, then, one might ask what the difference is between those conditional future beliefs which do motivate and those which don't. One has at any time a vast number of beliefs about what would ensue were one to act, only a few of which make the right sort of difference to what one actually does. Some such beliefs motivate, then, and others don't. What is the difference between these?

Humeanism takes itself to have an easy answer to this question. There is no intrinsic difference between beliefs of these two sorts, but there is the extrinsic difference that lies in the presence or absence of a suitably related desire. A belief that motivates, then, is one attached to a suitable desire. What can pure cognitivism say that could be as persuasive as this?

The first thing is to be sure that the sort of desire here appealed to is indeed necessarily a Humean one. Not just any old desire will do; my pure cognitive theory accepts the necessary existence of a desire wherever motivation occurs, though it holds that the desire is never what motivates. Why can't the pure theory borrow Hume's clothes here and simply join in the claim that the difference between motivating and non-motivating considerations lies in the presence or absence of a suitable desire? The answer to this question lies in the role of desire in the pure theory: since the presence or absence of the desire just consists in the presence or absence of motivation, we cannot look to the former to explain the latter. Matters are supposedly different for Humeanism. This might be because the desire is conceived as an independent existence; since it is independent, its presence has explanatory powers.

But we should be careful before admitting this. Despite Humean tendencies, we should not so easily admit that desires are mental states whose presence needs no explaining. Many desires need a sort of explanation which can only be given by specifying what they are desires for – by an account of their intentional object. But if we do this we immediately lose the apparent advantages of Humeanism. For the explanation of the desire will be given in terms of the agent's conception of the thing desired, which is just the sort of thing that cognitivists want to talk about. The only way to avoid this return to the cognitive is to base one's explanation of motivation on desires which need no explanation (or at least no intentional explanation) – desires which we accept as part of the way things are. These are presumably the four Fs (feeding, fighting, fleeing, etc.), or some limited expansion of them.

But now take an instance of an action explained by appeal to one of the four Fs: avoiding an oncoming car. Our agent acts in one way rather than another. What advantage does Humeanism have over the pure theory here? The pure theory asserts that there is no difference *in style* (such as one having some oomph and the other not) between the representation that motivates and others that don't – no intrinsic difference, that is. To understand why one motivated when the other didn't we need and can only look to differences between their intentional contents. If this will not explain the matter, nothing will.

Suppose that we find that no intentional characterization of the relevant contents will in fact explain the matter. We do not improve the situation by introducing a new element which itself cannot be explained, but must be taken as a brute 'given'. The four Fs merely play within Humeanism the role of that which puts a halt to rational explanation. We appeal to one where we feel that the powers of rational explanation have run out too soon. We reach a point where we say that people just are motivated by this sort of consideration, in a way that cannot be further explained (except in other ways, such as by appeal to evolution). We introduce a brute and inexplicable desire to make this point. But the pure theory is in no worse a position. It admits that at this stage all we can say is that people just are motivated by thoughts of food, safety, etc. It merely claims that we make no advance in asserting that the motivation is generated by an inexplicable desiring rather than by something inexplicably desired.

In this way the pure theory sticks to its view that it is the *content* of the relevant representations that explains the role they play in motivation.

The second question I want to face is what explains why an agent makes one choice rather than another in a case where he is tempted by both. Here we have two 'afters', one of which does in fact motivate him to action and the other of which is also seen by him as a reason to act, but not such a strong reason as the first. The pure theory will explain why he sees matters in this way by appeal, ideally, to the content of the two representations, i.e. to the claim that things *are* this way. Or if it is held that he is somehow looking at the matter askew, still it will be claimed that given the world as he views it, we can see why he comes to prefer this action to that.

But there is a further difficulty to face in this case. What is it for a consideration to motivate unsuccessfully? What is the difference between one which doesn't motivate at all and one whose motivation is defeated? A tempting move is to appeal to subjunctive conditionals. Roughly, the idea would be that a belief which motivates unsuccessfully is one which would lead to action if the agent did not have some other motivating belief on which he *is* acting. But is this idea true? Quite apart from perfectly general worries about analyses in terms of subjunctive conditionals,[1] there seems to be real room here for counter-examples – of cases where though this consideration does motivate and is defeated by another, it would not motivate in the absence of the other. Sometimes this can be captured by pointing out that a defeated consideration can still contribute to the action, as where the risk which would in other circumstances stand as a sufficient reason for not doing the action stands here as a reason for doing it more circumspectly, when defeated by a consideration which makes the risk worth taking. But a consideration can be defeated in a way that prevents it from making any difference of this sort to the eventual outcome. In such cases, can we conceive of counter-examples of the form given above? A case that occurs to me is one where my love for my chronically ill wife is a reason for me to take a job in Peru which would pay well enough for me to be able to afford private long-term medical care for her, a reason which is however defeated for me by my desire to express my love for her by nursing her myself. Were I, however, to lose the desire to nurse her myself, this would be because I no longer love her, and so it would not be the case that if I ceased to desire to nurse her myself I would be motivated to go to Peru. Here we have a defeated reason which would not motivate (would not be a reason) if it were not defeated. What can we say about this? What is the difference between this sort of reason and no reason at all?

The Humean can answer this question, it seems. A Humean desire which would be absent if it were not defeated is not impossible to conceive, and breaches no Humean constraints. We might wonder how exactly the Humean is to characterize the desire that is necessarily defeated when present. Surely all that can be said is what we already know – that the agent is motivated by this desire but not strongly enough to act. The pure theorist can say something pretty like this, namely that the agent is motivated by this representation but not strongly enough to act. Why is this any worse than what the Humean can muster? The answer must be that it is because the ability of a Humean desire to motivate is essential to it, so that we have no difficulty in conceiving of this state as motivating even when it never wins. No such answer is available to the pure theory. It would be no good appealing to what is admittedly true on the pure theory, namely that the agent has a desire for the action which he will never be sufficiently motivated to perform. For the presence of this desire, conceived as the agent's being motivated, is explained by and cannot explain the difference we are trying to capture. It is just not clear what resources remain to us here.

What we are looking for is a constitutive difference between the two cases, not an explanation of how some consideration might come to play one role rather than the other. The pure theorist, who wants to say that there is no *further* intrinsic difference between the two cases than the one already given, still has to say what that difference amounts to.

One possibility is to play clever with the subjunctive conditionals. We might say that in the example above, though it is true that I *would* not be motivated to go to Peru if I were not more motivated to stay at home and nurse my wife, still I *might* decide to go to Peru if, for instance, I became physically unable to nurse her but still able to earn enough in Peru to pay for professional nursing, while loving her deeply from afar. We might try to say that some such structure as this would be available in every case of a defeated reason, since a contingently defeated reason will pop up again somehow or other. There will be no defeated reasons which are incapable of being on the winning side, and so it remains open to us to define the status of some consideration as a reason by appeal to its ability to win, as in our original suggestion. This view is vulnerable to the provision of a counter-example, since we can hardly claim to have seen that there *can't* be one. But nor have we seen clearly that there *can* be one.

But even if this answer could be got to run, it would still leave us with the need to distinguish between a defeated reason and a consideration that is not a reason. For surely it is true of any belief that in certain circumstances it would motivate. Have we been able to claim more than this for our defeated reason?

I think the answer here is to distinguish between two sorts of subjunctive conditional. The first speaks of what would or might happen with diminished motivation; the second speaks of what would or might happen in different circumstances. In different circumstances, anything is possible: any belief is such that it might motivate, in this sense. With diminished motivation, only beliefs which already motivate are still left motivating, though some have dropped out. Applying this to the example of Peru, we see that originally three considerations motivate me: my love for my wife, my desire to express that love by nursing her myself, and the thought that I can earn enough to pay for professional care by going to Peru. We agreed that if I were to lose the second, this would be because I had lost the first. But we can still ask what would happen if I retained the first and the third. (This is what I mean by diminished motivation.) And the answer is that I would go to Peru. So this is the account of what it is for a consideration to motivate unsuccessfully. With diminished motivation, it would win. It may be hard to see quite how to run this distinction using the technical apparatus of possible world theory, but there is intuitive clout to it all the same, and it is this that the pure theory will be appealing to.

The third of the three problems is the easiest in one way and the hardest in another. Suppose that there are two distinct representations present to me, each one sufficient for me to act in these circumstances, and each standing as a reason for the same act as the other. What is the matter of fact which makes it the case that the first of these is in fact the one that motivates me and the second is not?

The first reply that occurs to me here is that nobody knows how to handle questions of overdetermination in causal theory. There is nothing about the pure theory which makes this hard question harder for it than for any other approach. Certainly, Humeanism is in no better a case here, and it might even seem to be in a worse position since it has to suppose that of two desires both driving the agent in the same direction, one may be 'operative' and the other not. I doubt that this makes sense, even when we detach it from the pseudo-hydraulic metaphor in which I have expressed it. (Try conceiving of the matter in Newtonian terms.) So though the question is certainly a hard one, it cannot form the basis of an attack on the pure theory.

There is, however, a second reply which I find interesting. As it stands, the question makes an unjustified assumption, namely that the identity of an act is independent of its motivation, so that one and the same act can be done for different reasons. If this assumption is straightforwardly false, so that a difference in motivation necessarily makes a difference in act, my third question evaporates. And my present view is that the assumption is false. We do, of course, naturally speak of repaying the money to escape further trouble rather than out of a sense of shame or simply because we see it is the right thing to do. But I hold here that the act in question differs as a *moral* object according to which of these did in fact motivate it, and that we should not say that a person who pays his debts out of duty does the same thing as one who pays them out of fear.[2]

If this is right, the third question evaporates. But this is not quite the end of the matter, for another question rises phoenix-like from the ashes (sorry about the mixed metaphor here). Even if the identity of the act is determined by the motive, we should still ask what matter of fact makes it the case that I am engaged in the first action-motive pair rather than the second. What makes it the case that I am paying my debts rather than saving my skin, when each motive is equally strong in me? What we have here is, of course, no longer quite the same as a normal case of overdetermination, since we do not have one object with two sufficient causes.

It is no good appealing here to what the agent says. First, her willingness to describe herself as saving her skin is not the matter of fact we were seeking but an effect of it, and so something which is at best evidence as to which action she is doing. We were not seeking evidence, however. Our question was constitutive ('what makes it the case that. . .?'), and the matter of fact in virtue of which her answer is true is not her willingness to give that answer.

Nor will it help to concentrate on the causes of her choice. Suppose that there were some cause of her being motivated by this representation rather than that one. This will not serve to answer our question. That question is constitutive, not causal, and so an answer that shows us the causes of her being motivated in this way rather than that does not tell us what it is for her to be so motivated.

It seems to me that we have reached bedrock here. The only possibility is that there is no further matter of fact in virtue of which she is motivated by this representation rather than that one. All we can say about the matter is what we have already said, namely that this representation is the one that causes the action, and that is not – or, in our new terms, that she is doing this action rather than that one. This is, so far as we can see, a bare truth.

2 MORAL AND NON-MORAL REASONS

What is the difference between moral and other reasons? One possible answer is that they have different subject-matter or content, but I think that this answer is not sufficient in itself and that anyway it is not available to the pure theory. We have, after all, agreed with McDowell that one's reason for doing the action is never that it is right (just as one is never given the reason by being told that it is right). The reason lies in more mundane features such as the worry you will cause your parents if you don't get in touch with them soon, and the ease with which you could pick up a telephone. So it seems to me that moral reasons don't differ from others in content; they differ rather in style. What then is this supposed difference in style?

The classic answer to this question is that moral reasons generate categorical imperatives. But there is a problem here for the pure theory, which is that though it may indeed give a sense to the idea that moral imperatives are categorical, it only does this by appealing to its claim that they are purely cognitive, and it will say the same about every other reason as well. Only a hybrid theory which takes moral reasons to be cognitive and others not has any chance of showing that moral imperatives are distinctive in being categorical. Pure cognitivism will just have to see all imperatives as categorical or none.

This criticism opens a can of worms, namely the exact sense in which we should allow that moral imperatives are categorical. So far we have worked simply with the idea that an imperative is categorical if it 'applies regardless of inclination',[3] and it is this which is causing the present problem. Let us stand back from that definition for a moment and consider the idea of a categorical imperative directly.

In doing so, there are two possibilities which we should bear in mind. The first is that there may be no such thing as a genuinely categorical imperative. The second is that prudential imperatives may be categorical – or some of them may be anyway, for instance 'You should look after your health.' Some may insist that this is a moral imperative, but there is at least room for the idea that it is a categorical prudential imperative.

There are three adjacent distinctions which have nothing to do with the distinction between hypothetical and categorical imperatives, and which one should not allow to clutter one's mind. They are those between: (1) paramount and non-paramount reasons; (2) external and internal reasons; (3) cognitive and non-cognitive reasons. I will run through these in order. To hold that moral reasons are paramount is to hold that a moral reason of any strength is a better reason than (is 'stronger than', in that sense, and so outweighs or rather ought to outweigh) any reason of any other sort. I reject this view because I think moral reasons are only morally paramount – but horticultural reasons are horticulturally paramount, and so on. But whether right or wrong, the view is quite distinct from any claim that moral reasons generate categorical imperatives. We can see this by looking at Kant. He holds that moral reasons are paramount because he holds (a) that moral reasons appeal uniquely to our rationality, and (b) that rationality is paramount. But these views are separable. If one took the view that our humanity was as important in us as our rationality, abandoning (b), one would see the matter differently and perhaps allow that non-moral reasons are sometimes better reasons than moral ones.

The second distinction concerns Williams' notion of an external reason (which I discuss in Appendix I). The question whether there are external reasons is the question whether it can ever be true to say that some consideration is a reason for her to act when there is no possibility of getting her into a state in which she would be motivated by that reason. One might claim that moral reasons are external in this sense; they are reasons for someone to act even if she doesn't and couldn't recognize them as such. Wiggins writes 'we think that categorical requirements such as moral requirements apply to you even if you ignore them and try to renounce every concern whatever.'[4] He may here be expressing the idea that moral reasons are external reasons. But this is nothing to do with whether moral imperatives are categorical or not. Even if there were no external reasons, there might yet be categorical imperatives. The distinction between categorical and hypothetical imperatives could perfectly well be drawn within the class of internal reasons.

The third distinction can indeed be drawn within the class of internal reasons, and so is suitable as far as that goes. But it is still not identical with the categorical/hypothetical distinction. To suppose otherwise is to hold that purely cognitive reasons generate categorical imperatives, while non-cognitive ones generate hypothetical imperatives. This is effectively one version of the hybrid theory, and we have already seen the problems it raises. It will only work if moral motivation is the only purely cognitive sort of motivation, or if all other cognitive motivation generates categorical imperatives as well. The first horn here is surely blatantly false, and the second is simply not available for the pure cognitive theory, because it would deprive the categorical/hypothetical distinction of any content. It is definitely a last resort, since it draws no distinction in style between moral and other reasons.

We can say more than this. As well as failing to draw the relevant distinction, the cognitive/non-cognitive distinction is manoeuvring in the wrong area altogether. Cognitive reasons, conceived as the internalist conceives them, appear vulnerable to the possibility of accidie. Now there may be an answer to the problem posed by accidie, and in 2.2 I offered one which appeals to the notion of an intrinsically motivating state. But the question whether moral imperatives are categorical is nothing to do with that problem. Even if moral accidie occurs, moral imperatives may still be categorical.

The way to move forward here is to remember the words of Kant: 'the categorical imperative would be one which represented an action as objectively necessary in itself apart from its relation to a further end.'[5] Wiggins echoes this, talking about the hypothetical: 'The requirement is hypothetical upon an aim, and what it says is required ... it only says is required by the pursuit of that aim.'[6] He seems to read this as a gloss on his earlier remark 'A categorical requirement applies regardless of inclination.' Now we would be wise to distinguish the idea that categorical imperatives apply independent of inclination (which is anyway multiply ambiguous) from the idea that the actions they recommend are necessary apart from any relation to a further end or aim (which is also ambiguous). The crucial distinction is between 'independent of desire/inclination' and 'independent of any further end/aim'. Pure cognitive theories maintain that all reasons are of the first sort, but they do not therefore maintain that all are of the second sort. To confuse the two, as Wiggins does, is yet again to adopt a Humean presupposition, namely that all aims are to be analysed in terms of Humean desires ('inclinations'). Kant, too, makes this mistake. Accepting Hume's account of aims, he is forced to place categorical imperatives within the space of pure rationality where there are no aims of that sort at all.

Pure cognitivists, by contrast, reject this picture and offer a cognitive theory of aims. They can then claim that there are two sorts of moral reasons, original and derived. Original reasons come in two forms. The first represent *actions* as required independent of any relation to a (further) aim or end; the second represent certain *aims* as required. When an action is represented as required in this way, it is called an end in itself. Derived reasons represent actions as required by a required aim. (Kant failed to notice that means-end reasoning occurs in moral thought as well as elsewhere.) Both original and derived reasons generate categorical imperatives, but the latter only do so because of their relation to the former.

There remains a problem concerning the nature of required aims, or of an action which is an end in itself. Many of our actions are ends in themselves. I might lie in the sun in order to cure a nasty skin complaint, but I might also do it for its own sake. (This is compatible with saying that there are some aspects of it which I particularly enjoy.) Won't it then be the case, on my account, that my reasons for lying in the sun generate a categorical imperative – one which applies 'apart from its relation to a further end'? No, it won't. Those reasons don't generate an imperative of any sort; there is no 'should' or 'ought' in them. The distinction between categorical and hypothetical imperatives only applies to those reasons which generate imperatives. Since my reasons for lying in the sun don't generate an imperative, *a fortiori* they don't generate a categorical one. Lying in the sun is an end in itself and one which I do have, but not one which I ought to have.

The nub of the distinction between moral and other reasons, then, is the unsurprising idea that moral reasons represent actions either as required in themselves or as required for a required aim – that in original moral reasons there is an underived *ought*. And the main difficulty for any such view is the idea that there are non-moral requirements just like this – that some non-moral aims are not optional, even though they are morally optional. Of course, horticultural and tennis-playing aims are optional. But the suggestion is that some prudential ones are not. For instance, the imperative 'take thought for the morrow' specifies a required aim, namely one's medium-term well-being. Should we agree that this aim is not morally required – that it is a non-moral aim? It would be wrong to think that *because* it is a prudential aim, it is therefore a non-moral one. A consideration can be prudential in the sense that it is concerned with the agent's own well-being, without being prudential in the other sense that recommendations that stem from it gain their force from their tendency to promote that well-being. Taking thought for the morrow is a prudential requirement in the first sense, but not in the second. In the second, it is a moral requirement.

I have been trying to capture the distinctive style of moral reasons by talking of requirements. But we should remember that this sort of talk can seem very strong. There are weaker and stronger moral reasons, and it may seem implausible to speak of all as equally *requiring* us to do the specified action or adopt the specified aim. I agree, and think it would be better in the end to think only of the strongest moral reasons as requiring. Less strong ones *demand* without requiring, perhaps, and yet weaker ones only *call for* the relevant action or the adoption of the relevant aim.[7] These are the terms in which I shall be speaking in what follows.[8]

3 SILENCING AND VIRTUE

John McDowell gives a quite different and very interesting answer to the problem discussed in the last section. He writes:

> The suggestion, so far, has been this: one cannot share a virtuous person's view of a situation in which it seems to him that virtue requires some

action, but see no reason to act in that way. The following possibility is still open: one sees reason to act in that way, but takes the reason to be outweighed by a reason for acting in some other way. But part of the point of claiming that the requirements of virtue are categorical imperatives may lie in a rejection of that possibility.

The rejection might stem from the idea that the dictates of virtue always outweigh reasons for acting otherwise. But I believe a more interesting ground for it is the idea that the dictates of virtue, if properly appreciated, are not weighed with other reasons at all, not even on a scale which always tips on their side. If a situation in which virtue imposes a requirement is genuinely conceived as such, according to this view, then considerations which, in the absence of the requirement, would have constituted reasons for acting otherwise are silenced altogether – not overridden – by the requirement.[9]

Both moral and prudential reasons are here conceived as purely cognitive motivating states. The difference between them, for McDowell, lies in the notion of a *requirement*. Reasons of prudence are never requirements, but moral reasons are; we think of these as peremptory demands on us which brook no shilly-shallying. So this is the difference we need between reasons of prudence and moral reasons. It is not just that what prudence requires one to do, morality may require one not to do. Rather morality generates requirements and prudence cannot. Now why cannot these requirements be outweighed? This should not be because they are actually stronger than other reasons here present. That would merely mean that they won't or shouldn't be outweighed, not that they cannot be. The only possible explanation for their invulnerability must be that there can be no other reasons present to outweigh them. And this can only be because the other potential reasons have all been silenced.

If there can be moral requirements in this sense, we must make room for the virtuous person, who is able to discern those requirements for what they are. It would not be attractive to hold that the real structure of moral reasons is one which our humanity prevents us from noticing. So to reject the notion of the virtuous person is to reject this account of moral reasons as uniquely able to silence any opposition.

Here McDowell has introduced two new concepts, that of the virtuous person and that of moral requirements which silence opposing reasons. He claims that the idea that moral reasons generate categorical imperatives includes the idea that for the virtuous person they silence opposing reasons and so eliminate any possibility that something other than the right action be done.[10] In this he goes way beyond anything that either Nagel or Kant would say. Nagel, whose central topic is prudence, takes it that reasons of prudence can always be defeated by opposing reasons; those who see them clearly may still not act on them, but prefer another action supported by different and maybe less good reasons. Even though the prudential reasons are beliefs which need no support from an independent desire, they can be overwhelmed by strong contrary desires – as in unprotected sex despite the risk of AIDS. So Nagel leaves room for prudential weakness of will (quite apart from allowing that there may be moral reasons which are stronger than any prudential reasons, and so *should* win the day).

Kant allows that moral reasons, even when perfectly conceived, can be opposed by other reasons which may or may not win the day. He admits the possibility of moral weakness of will. In this respect McDowell is more extreme than Kant. Kant says that in purely rational beings moral reasons will always win, not because such beings have a better grasp or a clearer perception of them, but simply because they lack inclinations to put on the other side. Beings like ourselves, however, who are imperfectly rational, being within the sway of inclination, can recognize our duty perfectly well and still fail to do it. When we do, the fault lies not in our perception of the reasons but in ourselves.

So McDowell goes beyond anything we can find in others. But we should surely question his (admittedly tentative[11]) suggestion that part of the point of claiming that moral reasons generate categorical imperatives lies in rejecting the possibility that they be outweighed by opposing reasons. For the topic of weakness of will is just a different topic from that of the nature of a categorical imperative. There is no reason to suppose that an imperative which is categorical (either in the sense given or in any other sense) will be invulnerable to weakness of will. Take a case where there are moral reasons on either side. The stronger reasons should win, but might not; there is such a thing as moral weakness of will, and if so it cannot be the case that moral reasons as such are invulnerable to weakness of will. Take a different case where there are weak moral reasons and much stronger non-moral ones; maybe the moral ones ought to be defeated by the opposition, but they are still categorical imperatives for all that.

So I don't think it can be right to link the idea of the virtuous person for whom opposing reasons are silenced to that of a categorical imperative. But this fact (if it is a fact) does little to diminish the independent interest of the ideas of virtue and silencing, which are worth discussion in their own right. In the rest of this section I discuss them in that spirit, suggesting reasons why they cannot play the role McDowell assigns to them.

This story about silencing is not the only feature of the virtuous

person. Such a person is conceived of as someone who has been perfectly trained, and thereby equipped with a full range of sensitivities to
the sorts of considerations that can matter morally. These sensitivities
have no content of their own. They are not independent desires which
training implants in us, but simply the ability to recognize whatever
morally relevant features we come across for what they are, case by
case. This virtuous person is not conceived of as someone equipped
with a full list of moral principles and an ability correctly to subsume
each new case under the right one. There is nothing that one brings to
the new situation other than a contentless ability to discern what matters
where it matters, an ability whose presence in us is explained by our
having undergone a successful moral education.

Anyone who has read Aristotle's *Nicomachean Ethics* will discern
the Aristotelian style of this account of virtue, both in its refusal to see
moral judgement as the subsumption of a new case under a previously
formulated moral principle and in its stress on the role of moral education.[12] And there is a further Aristotelian element in the idea that,
unlike the prudent person, the virtuous person necessarily acts without
regret or struggle. To regret what one does because it lacks something
that an alternative action would have provided, or to have to struggle
to get oneself to do what one knows to be the right thing here, shows
that the reasons in favour of doing the right thing have not succeeded
in silencing in one the reasons against. The virtuous person, therefore,
is not subject to regret or to struggle. This does not mean that we do
not value those who struggle to subdue contrary inclinations and succeed;
we may even value those who struggle and fail, since they are presumably
to be preferred to those who don't struggle at all. But we see a better
state than that of continence, a higher order of virtue which we dignify
by talk of *the* virtuous person.

It would also be wrong to think of the virtuous as inhuman in their
indifference to things that normal people have to drag their attention
away from, such as pleasure and pain. It is true that to be virtuous may
require that one does not see the pain one will suffer oneself as a reason
not to make the sacrifice, or that one does not see the profit one will
make as a reason to cheat or steal. But this does not mean that one is
insensitive to pain, or unaware of what a profit is and of what one
might do with it. McDowell expresses the point in the case of temperance,
which here stands simply as one of the virtues which the virtuous person
will have:

> The temperate person need be no less prone to enjoy physical pleasure
> than the next man. In suitable circumstances it will be true that he would

enjoy some intemperate action which is available to him. In the absence of a requirement, the prospective enjoyment would constitute a reason for going ahead. But his clear perception of the requirement insulates the prospective enjoyment – of which, for a satisfying conception of the virtue, we should want him to have a vivid appreciation – from engaging his inclinations at all. Here and now it does not count for him as any reason for acting in that way.[13]

I think it is important to admit the power of this conception of the virtuous person. But I none the less have the gravest difficulties with the use that McDowell makes of it. I have already argued that the sense in which all moral reasons generate requirements is not well captured by talk of the virtuous person for whom all opposing reasons are silenced. The notion of silencing should not be used in the analysis of the sort of requiring (or demanding) that all moral reasons do. But there is an alternative possible use of it, in the analysis of moral reasons of maximum strength.[14] We might say that such reasons, and only such reasons, silence their opposition, and express this by saying that only such reasons generate requirements – others merely recommend, or something like that. This is a new and more elitist notion of a requirement. But I reject this use of silencing as well.

This is not because I have problems with the notion of silencing. In fact, I accept that silencing can occur, and indeed may be common. Here is a trivial example of silencing, of the sort that persuades me that silencing itself is not a phenomenon that we should boggle at. I like the taste of chocolate, but one way or another I have got myself to a state in which the fact that I would enjoy this chocolate were I to eat it no longer counts as a reason to eat it. This reason has got silenced. But that which has silenced it is not and is not conceived by me as being a requirement.

Next, I am not convinced that there cannot be reasons of prudence which silence opposing reasons (including moral ones, sometimes). To give an example of what I mean here, suppose that an assailant breaks into my house in search of my gold, which I hand over, and then to cover his escape starts to take my 8-year-old daughter away with him. I realize that there is a very strong possibility that I will not see her alive and unharmed again. But as my assailant leaves, I see my one chance. There is a hammer lying unnoticed behind the door, and I have a chance to grab it and try to hit my enemy on the head. I do this. As I bring the hammer down, do I consider the question how hard I am justified in hitting this person? It may be that morally speaking I have no right to hit him harder than is necessary to frustrate his present purpose. But I have no inclination to judge the weight of my blow with any nicety, and anyway I have no experience in these matters. The nearest I have got to this before is playing squash. I take it, and in my view rightly take it, that reasons of prudence silence reasons of ethics in this case. I hit my enemy as hard as is compatible with reasonable accuracy. Notice that the claim is that the opposing reasons are not merely overwhelmed; they cease to count as reasons in the circumstances. The prudential reasons stand here as silencers. I see that I *have* to act this way, and any natural or moral repugnance must be fought down.

Third, McDowell seems to have left no room for the idea that one can fight down an opposing desire just because one recognizes the presence of a moral requirement (i.e. a moral reason of the strongest type – a complete moral reason). This is not the same as fighting down an opposing desire because one recognizes the existence of a strong moral reason which fails to amount to a requirement, because in such a case there is an element of balancing which is presumably not present when we are dealing with requirements. And I see no good reason for ruling this idea out in advance.

Further difficulties concern the question whether there can be opposing requirements, and if not why not. I will face this issue as squarely as I can in chapter 7. For present purposes, it should be enough to say that if there can be opposing requirements, neither can be such that it silences opposing reasons. Indeed, we particularly want to avoid saying in these cases that it is a virtue of a position that it silences the opposition; where what opposes it is itself a requirement it would be less than morally perfect to lose sight of either. On the other hand, I do not think it sits well with McDowell's general approach to hold that there cannot be opposing moral requirements – but this is more a matter of the feel of the approach than any explicit assertion on his part.

My conclusion for the moment is that though silencing does indeed occur, it is not peculiar to moral reasons. Silencing need not be done by a requirement, and requirements need not silence. What does this tell us about the virtuous person? I have no objection to the weak view that a virtuous person is someone in whom opposing considerations are silenced when they should be, and not when they shouldn't. Such people are conceived as sensitive to the nature of the reasons they face, and if the reasons silence the opposition, that is how they should be conceived.

I have been arguing that the notion of the virtuous person raises problems of its own, and that it is not necessary to use it to make sense of the idea of a moral requirement, if that is an expression of the view that moral imperatives are categorical; nor should we expect it to help us distinguish moral from prudential reasons. In the next section, I turn to a second reason for talking of virtue in this way, and argue that this reason is a confusion which weakens rather than strengthens the theory it is intended to support.

4   SILENCING AND WEAKNESS OF WILL

I now return to the topic discussed in 2.2. There I defended the pure theory against what I thought of as a standard argument which appealed to the principle that a cognitive state which might on some occasion be insufficient for action could never be sufficient elsewhere. My answer to this objection turned on the notion of an intrinsically motivating state, and thus eventually on the idea that facts can be intrinsically reasons for action. But McDowell sees this matter quite differently from the way I do, and the remainder of this chapter is a discussion of the differences between his response to the argument and mine. He accepts the crucial move in the argument – that if a cognitive state is anywhere sufficient for action, it is everywhere sufficient and so it must be impossible for a person in that state not to perform that action. This acceptance leads him to suppose that cognitivism is impossible without the notion of the virtuous person.[15]

The story goes as follows. The virtuous person's conception of the circumstances is one which could not be shared by someone who does not see exactly the same reason to act. For where opposing reasons are silenced, all who share the silencing conception must surely act in the same way; they have no reason left to do anything else. Now the virtuous person's conceptions are cognitive, and in fact any cognitive state which is itself sufficient for action must be one which cannot be shared by those who do not see the same reason for action. For, McDowell argues, a state which is sufficient for action on one occasion must be so wherever it occurs.[16] So the fact that it can be present elsewhere without generating an action shows that it is not capable of doing that on its own, and must be in need of help from somewhere. But the help cannot come from further beliefs, since the addition of further beliefs would not solve the problem, which would merely repeat. So the help must come from a desire. But this simply shows that, contrary to our original supposition, the motivation from which we started was not cognitive but Humean. So non-Humean motivation is only possible if we have a cognitive state which cannot be present without generating an action. But the only such state would be one which did not overwhelm but silenced opposing reasons, for only such a state would be invulnerable to the growth of stronger and stronger reasons against. So only the virtuous person is capable of non-Humean motivation, and the rest of us are reduced to living with Hume.

What this means is that, like that of the continent person, the motivation of the prudent person must be Humean, contrary to the position from which McDowell at least intended to start. This is so, at least, unless there is an analogue of the virtuous person in the realm of prudence – a person for whom all but the winning prudential reasons are silenced. But this leaves the virtuous person very much out on a limb. It would be a far more attractive position to hold that everyone, virtuous or otherwise, is capable of purely cognitive motivation. But McDowell seems to have prevented himself from holding this. This is all because he accepts that a state which is anywhere sufficient for action must be everywhere sufficient for action.

I think it is clear that McDowell has here accepted too much of the Humean map. It is because he accepts the Humean notion of an essentially motivating state that he finds himself arguing that there must be states which silence opposing reasons. Effectively, he ends up attempting to put his virtuous person's cognitive conceptions in the box with Humean desires. As I have argued, this is an unnecessary mistake, and I have a tentative suggestion about how it is that McDowell came to make it. I ascribe it to his adoption of the hybrid theory. For once one admits the possibility of Humean desires and Humean beliefs, one has a paradigm of motivation, represented by the relation between Humean desires and action, and what he tries to do is to get cognitive motivation to fit that paradigm.

It is worth pausing to contrast the position McDowell has got himself into with the much weaker position available to those who find the notion of silencing interesting in its own right, but who don't want to use it in McDowell's way. One could suppose that the phenomenon of silencing exists, but that it is not peculiar to ethics, nor relevant to the distinction between cognitive and non-cognitive motivation. As such, it would merely represent an addition to our list of ways in which reasons can relate to each other – a list whose main purpose is the discomfiture of over-simple theories. But by linking the idea of silencing to the problems of how to distinguish moral from non-moral reasons and of how to make room for weakness of will within a cognitivist perspective, McDowell disqualifies it from playing that useful role. We now have it that since moral reasons generate categorical imperatives, they issue in requirements which silence the opposition for those who correctly conceive them. Only such persons are motivated cognitively. Those for whom the opposition is not silenced are subject to Humean motivation. And this has the peculiar consequence that there can be no such thing as cognitive motivation in the prudential realm, since if there were it would silence opposition, which would be impossible if prudential and moral reasons are at all capable of conflicting (which surely they are). With this result, the only way to preserve the hybrid theory is to abandon altogether its historical roots in Nagel's work on prudence, and to see the area of ethics as the only one within which cognitive motivation is possible.

5 PARTICULARISM AND THE PURE THEORY

The final point I want to argue in this chapter is that McDowell should have no problem in accepting the general structure of the position I have been working out, because it is essentially the same as a position he adopts elsewhere. It is an analogue in the theory of motivation of something he finds plausible already, namely the rejection of generalism in the theory of reasons and in particular the rejection of the claim that moral judgements are universalizable. If I am right about this, the suggestion that cognitivism requires the notion of the virtous person must collapse completely.

To make the analogy plain, I need to re-express the position already outlined. Instead of thinking of one's mental set as divided into two parts, motivating states and pure background, we divide it into three parts: motivating states, active background and inert background. The active background consists of states without which the motivating states would have been different, and in a sense should also include those states here absent but whose presence would affect the motivating states. The inert background consists of states which have no effect of that sort here. Now this tripartite distinction in moral psychology is the image of a similar distinction in what I call the metaphysics of moral properties – the study of the way in which underlying properties combine to generate moral properties which result from or exist in virtue of them. The idea is that the logical behaviour of reasons will turn out not to be distinct from that of morally relevant properties. We can see a second tripartite distinction, in the case of some right action, between:

1 Properties in virtue of which that action is right.
2 Properties whose presence or absence affects or would affect the way in which the properties of the first sort make the action right.
3 Properties which have no effect of that sort (inert background here).

The properties of the second sort are the active background here. Now the phenomenon I want to appeal to is the fact that a property F of one action may be a reason for me to do that action, even though the F-ness of another action may be morally indifferent or even count as a reason against doing it. To give a schematic example which I have used elsewhere, the fact that an action will give pleasure can be a reason for doing it or for approving of it when done. But it can also be a reason for disapproving of it. If I tread on a worm by mistake, my action is perhaps morally indifferent. But if I tread on it with pleasure or to give you pleasure, my action is the worse for it. We should not say, as I once heard Professor Hare argue, that there is at least this to be said for the action, that it gave me (or you) pleasure, though of course we must condemn the action overall because the value derived from the pleasure is overwhelmed by other disvalue.

What we see here is that changes in the attendant circumstances can alter rather than merely overwhelm the moral tendency of a particular property. This is just like the ability of other mental states (the active background) to alter rather than to overwhelm the motivation of a motivating state. It is the crucial respect in which the logical behaviour of reasons is like that of morally relevant properties. Now you may not be persuaded by my schematic example here. You may feel, as will any generalist in ethics, that there is still room for the thought that particular properties have general moral tendencies which are not themselves affected by the circumstances which attend them in different cases, but rather set in some sort of balance with the general tendencies of the other properties there present, so that our eventual decision goes with whichever side predominates. This is Ross's position, for instance. His notion of the prima facie is expressly designed to keep this sort of balancing generalism going in the face of apparent difficulties. I do not take myself to have shown here what is wrong with that position; I reserve that attempt for chapter 6. My point here is rather that the view I have been suggesting is one which is peculiarly tempting for theorists like McDowell, in virtue of the moral particularism associated with the attempt to work out what is sometimes, though unhelpfully, called a perceptual model for moral knowledge. Particularism is at its crudest the claim that we neither need nor can see the search for an 'evaluative outlook which one can endorse as rational as the search for a set of principles'.[17]

Underlying this particularism cannot be just the view that no set of principles will succeed in generating answers to questions about what to do in particular cases. Ross, who stands here as the classic generalist, knew this perfectly well and allowed for it in his account of the move from our knowledge of prima facie duties (which are what moral principles express for him) to our judgements about duties proper, particular decisions about what we ought to do here, which are according to him never more than probable opinion. Particularism, if it is to go beyond this, must give a stronger sense to the thought that the moral relevance of a property in a new case cannot be predicted from its relevance elsewhere. The claim I have made about the way in which attendant circumstances can vary the moral relevance of a property seems to me the leading thought in the construction of this stronger particularism. And if this is so we have a model here which fits well what we want to say in showing that moral beliefs are intrinsically motivating states without needing to show that they motivate in the same way on every appearance.

The rejection of universalizability is part and parcel of the rejection of generalism in the theory of reasons. The doctrine of universalizability holds that if we judge one action right, we must judge any other relevantly similar action right.[18] An action is said to be relevantly similar if, roughly, it shares with the first all the properties which were reasons why the first action was right. It is clear that the particularist will deny this on grounds which should by now be familiar, namely that what is sufficient here need not be sufficient elsewhere. Circumstances elsewhere may conspire to overwhelm or defuse the ability of those properties to render their bearer right. The defender of universalizability is likely to reply that in that case what made the first action right was not just the properties mentioned, but the combination of those properties and the absence of any countervailing considerations. But we have seen this reply before and rejected it. The reasons why it fails are the same as the reasons why the notion of an intrinsically motivating state does not collapse into that of an essentially motivating state. I conclude that McDowell's particularism gives him sufficient reason to adopt my method of defending cognitivism, rather than appealing to the notion of the virtuous person.

Of course, all this would be of no importance if particularism itself were unsound. In the next three chapters I try to lay out the arguments for particularism. Meanwhile I can claim only that there is an internal coherence in the combination of the pure theory and particularism. This coherence is itself no direct argument in favour of either. The matter is similar to something we saw in the development of non-cognitivism. We were offered two distinctions, one in the philosophy of mind between belief and attitude and the other in metaphysics between fact and value. There was a tendency to defend either by appeal to the other, without recognizing that there is really only one distinction here, appearing now under one guise and now under another. But, though any argument of that sort would be unsuccessful (since there are not two things here, one to argue from and the other to argue to), these moves did reveal a satisfying internal coherence in the position they expressed. All I have been trying to achieve so far is the same sort of coherence for the position I favour.

NOTES

1 For the source of these worries, see Shope (1978).
2 I have borrowed this view from Joseph (1931). Joseph attacks the meta-physical picture in which the action somehow stands between motive/intention and consequences. He maintains that if things are carved up in this way, there is nothing of moral import left for the action to be.
3 This phrase comes from Wiggins (1991), para. 3.
4 Ibid., para. 1.
5 Kant (1785), p. 78.
6 Wiggins (1991), para. 3.
7 For an interesting discussion of demands, see Mandelbaum (1955), ch. 2.
8 All these suggestions need to be tempered in the light of the discussion of non-insistent reasons in 8.3–4 and 12.2, and in any case they are preliminary. Remarks in metaphysical style in 7.2 will place things in a slightly different light.
9 McDowell (1978), p. 26. It is worth stressing that the idea that, for the virtuous person, moral requirements silence opposing reasons is one which McDowell considers in this passage merely as an attractive possibility, one which gives a pleasing edge to the notion of a moral requirement. I say this because I am about to enter into a sustained attack on the way McDowell uses his conception of a virtuous person, though in no way do I want to reject it altogether. I think it is both interesting and productive.
10 With this conception of silencing, McDowell *may* have an answer to the problem of accidie, which I said in chapter 1 was effective against his form of cognitivism. I meant that remark to apply to the theory which McDowell shares with Nagel, so as to allow the possibility that the introduction of silencing makes a difference on this point. Whether it does make that difference will depend on whether a consideration that silences others, and so is to that extent active in the agent's mind, must necessarily motivate. Might a consideration not succeed in silencing the opposition but still be rendered unable to motivate by something else (such as depression)?
11 And tentatively ascribed: there is a quite different interpretation of McDowell's views on the relation between moral reasons and silencing, which I consider next.
12 This claim is, I fear, an exaggeration.
13 McDowell (1978), p. 27.
14 It may even be that this second use is closer to McDowell's real intentions. See McDowell (1978), p. 29, where he says 'There can be less exigent

moral reasons, and as far as this position goes, they may be overridden.' The problem is that I am not convinced that this remark is consistent with other things he wants to say in this area, as I try to explain in the next section.

15 These thoughts can be found in section 3 of McDowell (1979). The long train of thought which follows is the second way in which McDowell may have come to link discussion of moral reasons as categorical imperatives and requirements that silence opposing reasons. To put it briefly: if moral reasons sufficient for action are cognitive, they are categorical imperatives (in the weak sense). But if they are cognitive, and sufficient for action, weakness of will is impossible. So weakness of will is impossible. But how can it be impossible? – because opposing reasons have been silenced.

16 See McDowell (1979), pp. 333–4.

17 McDowell (1985), p. 122.

18 This notion of universalizability is familiar from Hare (1963). I discuss it in much greater detail in chapter 5. Hare (1981) adopts a completely different notion of universalizability, which I discuss in Appendix II.

4

Why particularism?

1 HOLISM IN THE THEORY OF REASONS

The leading thought behind particularism is the thought that the behaviour of a reason (or of a consideration that serves as a reason) in a
new case cannot be predicted from its behaviour elsewhere. The way in
which the consideration functions *here* either will or at least may be
affected by other considerations here present. So there is no ground for
the hope that we can find out here how that consideration functions *in
general*, somehow, nor for the hope that we can move in any smooth
way to how it will function in a different case.

In my view, this holistic view of the behaviour of reasons has an
obvious initial attraction. And it can be supported by examples. I gave
a schematic one in chapter 3 (Hare and the worm). But meatier ones
can be produced. They will be examples in which the *natural* thing to
say is that a consideration is functioning in one case as a reason in
favour of doing the action, but in another is either no reason at all, or
even a reason against.

Here is a simple example of the first type. I borrow a book from you,
and then discover that you have stolen it from the library. Normally the
fact that I have borrowed the book from you would be a reason to
return it to you, but in this situation it is not. It isn't that I have *some*
reason to return it to you and more reason to put it back in the library.
I have no reason at all to return it to you.

Of course one can dispute the intuitions I am appealing to here. But
do we feel that those intuitions must be wrong, or merely that in the
present case things aren't the way I say they are? The particularist may
dispute the instance, but will take it that there are plenty of better
examples.

For an example of the second type, I offer a family game called
'Contraband', in which the players are smugglers trying to get contraband

material past a Customs Officer. The game requires them to lie; if one doesn't do plenty of lying, it spoils the game. That an action is a lie is commonly a reason not to do it; here it is reason in favour. Less domestically, that we did this last time can be a reason for doing the same this time, but sometimes it will be a reason for doing something different. Whether it is so or not will depend on other features of the case.

There is a special type of example of this sort, which constantly recurs in discussion. That an action is fun is a reason in favour of doing it – normally. But sometimes it is a reason against. Roy Hattersley provides a good example:

> I have long supported whoever it was who said that the real objection to foxhunting is the pleasure that the hunters get out of it . . . If killing foxes is necessary for the safety and survival of other species, I – and several million others – will vote for it to continue. But the slaughter ought not to be fun.[1]

The fun involved makes the action worse in this case. Perhaps pleasure and fun are different. But then the same point can be made about pleasure. If I take pleasure in your discomfiture, this is not a redeeming feature of the situation. It seems that the way in which pleasure and fun function as reasons is logically dependent on the nature of the activity we are enjoying. Consider the suggestion that we have more reason to have public executions of convicted rapists if the event would give pleasure both to the executioner and to the crowds that would no doubt attend.[2] Surely this pleasure is a reason against rather than a reason for; pleasure at a wrong action compounds the wrong. (This is the special feature of examples of this type.) Since I recommend a particularist understanding of the rightness or wrongness of the action, I recommend a particularist approach to the rightness or wrongness of any resulting pleasure.

With this point we can introduce a defence of particularism against a common charge. Isn't it always bad knowingly to cause pain? Isn't an action always the worse for the pain it causes? I doubt it. First, if someone deserves pain, the infliction of that pain can hardly be diminished in value by the pain inflicted. Second, suppose that I know that Satan is grieved (pained) by every right act. He ought not to be pained by this sort of thing, and the fact that he is does nothing to diminish the value of each right action, nor create anything of a (defeated) reason to hold back. This is an example of mental pain. Perhaps it is physical pain that is always a reason against. (Why?) But suppose that when he gets upset in this way, it aggravates his old war wound. Does that change the situation so that now there is a (defeated) reason to hold back when there wasn't one before? I think not. This is another instance of the sort of holism that drives particularism in the theory of reasons.

The most extreme possibility, in the way of examples, is that one and the same consideration can function on both sides in the same case. I sent an article to a philosophical journal some years ago, taking it that the fact that I had already had two articles published there on the same general area was some reason for them to publish the third in the series. The editor persuaded me tactfully that it was a greater reason for them not to. This need not be taken to mean that it was no reason for them to publish. If we insist that it does mean that, what is driving us? We might be supposing that nothing *could* function in that Janus-like way. But what could be our reason? One possible explanation is an implicit theoretical commitment to generalism in the theory of reasons – to the view that a reason functions everywhere as it functions anywhere. With that commitment in place, we are not going to find any example convincing. But here is another one of the same type, which I owe to David Bakhurst. Take a case where the fact that an action is against the law is a reason against doing it. It might also be a reason for doing it, if this sort of behaviour is one which should not be regulated by law. Probable responses to this example are, first, that the thought that the illegality of an action is a reason against it is a generalist thought; second, that if the action ought not to be illegal, its illegality cannot be a reason against doing it. Both of these responses seem misplaced to me. To the first, we can say that there was no commitment intended to the view that illegality is a standing reason against an action, only that it is one here. To the second, we can say that someone who experiences a tension in the situation – a tension driven by the fact that the action is illegal – is not necessarily wrong to see that tension as due to the fact that the illegality is functioning in two ways at once. If anything prevents this, it is theory.

The general picture I want to promote here is that *pre-theoretically* particularism is a perfectly natural view with obvious attractions. It is adherence to theory of some sort that upsets the apple cart, and causes us to abandon our initial particularist intuitions. Of course, if the theory concerned were good, intuition would have to yield. So in the next two chapters I try to show that the theories that are probably at issue here are not good ones. But the point for the moment is that if we could give an account of the way in which reasons behave that allowed them to work in the way they certainly *seem* to in these and many other examples, we have a strong incentive to do so.

2   APPROACHES TO MORAL JUDGEMENT

If moral reasons function in the variety of ways that particularists suppose, we may presume that moral judgement should allow for this fact. Our account of moral judgement should show that such judgement is able to cope with the holism of reasons. So any view that supposes that the essence of moral judgement lies in the move from one case to the next is bound to come unstuck, because it focuses on the wrong place. Of course, we are going to have to say something (or more than something) about the way in which our judgement in a new case is informed by our moral experience. But we must be careful to retain the sense that considerations may not be functioning here as they have previously done, and so not allow ourselves to be driven too easily to fit what we say here to what we have said on other occasions. Or rather, the sort of fit at issue should be a particularist sort. Consistency can be understood in more than one way. As the generalist understands it, it means coming to a view about the moral relevance of particular features under which they function as reasons in the same way on each appearance. As the particularist understands it, consistency is a different and less demanding constraint. The primary focus of particularism is the particular case, not surprisingly. This means that one's main duty, in moral judgement, is to look really closely at the case before one. Our first question is not 'Which other cases does this one best resemble?', but rather 'What is the nature of the case before us?' Of course, a comparison with other cases may help us to decide how things are here, just as a long experience of car engines may help us to diagnose the fault this time. But this decision or diagnosis is still essentially particular. It would be surprising if a long experience in garages were no help to the mechanic; it would be surprising if a long and varied moral experience did not serve to sharpen one's sensitivity for the future. But in neither case is one's first question what one can say here that is consistent with what one has said elsewhere. The crucial question is how things are in the case before us.

This means that for particularists the demand for mere consistency is fairly easy to satisfy. It is far harder to satisfy the need for *coherence* in a moral outlook. But we should not pretend that the need for coherence is the same as the need for consistency, as one leading form of generalism tries to do. Nor need the demand for coherence (however that is to be conceived in this area) be a generalist demand. The coherence of an overall outlook can be questioned in the following way without generalist motivation. 'Here you think the fact that she was unhappy functions as a reason in one way, and there you took it to function in quite another. To me they seem to be functioning in much the same way both times, so that I can't really see how you can distinguish in the way you do. What is the relevant difference between the two cases?' This challenge can always be made within the constraints of particularism, and there must be an answer to it if one's position across the two cases is to emerge as coherent. (Its consistency was not at issue.)

Whatever account we give of the coherence of a moral outlook, our account of the person on whom we can rely to make sound moral judgements is not very long. Such a person is someone who gets it right case by case. To be so consistently successful, we need to have a broad range of sensitivities, so that no relevant feature escapes us, and we do not mistake its relevance either. But that is all there is to say on the matter. To have the relevant sensitivities just is to be able to get things right case by case. The only remaining question is how we might get into this enviable state. And the answer is that for us it is probably too late. As Aristotle held, moral education is the key; for those who are past educating, there is no real remedy.[3]

Particularism claims that generalism is the cause of many bad moral decisions, made in the ill-judged and unnecessary attempt to fit what we are to say here to what we have said on another occasion. We all know the sort of person who refuses to make the decision here that the facts are obviously calling for, because he cannot see how to make that decision consistent with one he made on a quite different occasion. We also know the person (often the same person) who insists on a patently unjust decision here because of having made a similar decision in a different case.[4] It is this sort of *looking away* that particularists see as the danger in generalism. Reasons function in new ways on new occasions, and if we don't recognize this fact and adapt our practice to it, we will make bad decisions. Generalism encourages a tendency not to look hard enough at the details of the case before one, quite apart from any over-simplistic tendency to rely on a few rules of dubious provenance.

3 SWITCHING ARGUMENTS

A switching argument is an attempt to determine what to say here by appeal to what we say about something else. Some switching arguments are of course sound. But the particularist allows far fewer to be sound than does the generalist. We have already seen some disallowed:

1   This feature counts in favour there: so it must count in favour here.
2   This feature is relevant there: so it must be relevant here.
3   This feature determines the issue there: so it must do so here.

But there are far more. Here are some:

4   If this action were not F, it would be wrong; so one of the things that makes it right is its F-ness.
5   If this action were less F, it would be better; so its F-ness must detract from its overall value.

The particularist supposes that all these argument forms are attempts to *force* us into a view of the present case by appeal to some feature of another case, or some comparison between this case and that. And the response to moves of that sort is invariably sceptical; they all attempt to pre-empt the authority of the present case.

We can be conciliatory here. Of course it often happens that our judgement here is enlightened by a comparison between the new case and others in our experience (or outside it; the reading of novels can similarly cause a change of view). There is no reason for the particularist to dispute this, or attempt to minimize its significance. All that the particularist is saying is that this is enlightenment, not coercion. Switching arguments should not be used in the attempt to *drive* us from case to case.

The discussion of this point so far has been abstract. An example might help. Take the case of pain again. There is a common view that pain is intrinsically bad, and so that any action that involves the causation of pain must be the worse for it. This is not itself a switching argument, but it may be supported by an appeal to one of type 5 above. Here is an example. My daughter trod on a sea-urchin on holiday a few years ago, and we caused her considerable pain (not entirely with her consent) in extracting the spines from her heel. Was the pain we caused her something which made our actions worse than they would otherwise have been? Here is a switching argument which says that it was. Had there been available a painless method of getting the spines out, we would and should have adopted it. We would have been wrong to continue digging in her heel with a needle, because of the pain. Surely this shows that as things were our actions were the worse for the pain they caused?[5]

I don't think it does show this. What we should say about cases like this is that a feature which would have made this sort of difference had there been any alternative choice need not necessarily make it if there is no alternative. It seems to me quite consistent to say that as things stood our action was not the worse for the pain it caused, though that pain should have led us to choose another method had one been available.

I do not mean to suggest that switching arguments are good elsewhere, but no good in ethics. I think they are dubious everywhere. For two good examples of non-moral arguments of type 4 above, I am indebted to Marc Lange:

> If this neuron were not firing, I would be blinking
> So the role of this neuron is to stop me blinking

> If there were no gravity, the balloon would keep going up
> So the balloon's being stationary is due to the operation of gravity.
> (It's actually due to relative densities.)

If such arguments are unsound elsewhere, why should they be sound in ethics?

4 MORAL PRINCIPLES

If there is a holism of reasons, as the particularist supposes, the prospects for substantial moral principles look bleak. For in one way or another such principles seem committed to the view that the properties that feature in them play the same role on every new appearance. And this is true, not just for what one might think of as ordinary principles such as 'Do not lie', but for the sort of principles that moral theorists seem especially interested in. Here I have in mind the attempt to construct a moral theory by proving true one or many crucial principles such as the Principle of Moral Indifference (that all count for one and nobody for more than one) or the Utilitarian Principle (that the right action is the one that has the best consequences for human welfare). Sometimes the list of principles is longer, as in Baier;[6] sometimes shorter, as in Sidgwick.[7] But either way, there is something unrealistic about the whole enterprise.

I devote the next two chapters to a far more detailed investigation into what I see as the two mainstream forms of generalism. The purpose of this is to show that they provide us with no reason to abandon our particularist intuitions. Particularism clearly raises questions for us to which we need to provide answers; what philosophical position does not? But I hope to show that the enormous weight of the generalist tradition in fact rests on very little.

In doing that, I shall be expressing in detail the particularist suspicion that moral principles cannot play any of the roles that generalism assigns to them. But particularists need not be too aggressive on this point. It seems wise for particularism to allow *some* role to moral principles, somehow conceived, rather than simply announce that everyone is completely mistaken about them and their importance in ethical thought and education. It is the job of a philosopher, so far as possible, to give an account of our practice rather than to tell us that we all ought to be doing something else. To the extent that this cannot be done, it is normally a fault in the philosophy rather than in the practice. So particularism needs to provide some account, within the constraints which it accepts, of what is a very common practice of somehow appealing to general truths and previous cases in the course of reaching a moral judgement, and in the justification of one when reached. I think that there is a way in which particularists can make their own sense of this practice, which will also show how we are able to learn such principles from experience, and how they are able to survive conflict.

The suggestion I want to make here is that a moral principle amounts to a reminder of the sort of importance that a property *can* have in suitable circumstances. It seems to me that this suggestion makes good sense of a number of puzzles in moral philosophy, in a way that is perfectly compatible with the spirit of particularist arguments against generalism in the theory of practical reasoning. So my suggestion will not be a new form of generalism. It is an account of what moral principles tell us, which is not available to the generalist. First, however, I turn to the puzzles which this account of moral principles will solve.

To start with, those in possession of a large list of principles, so long as they do not misunderstand their proper role, are at an advantage when coming to a decision in a particular case. They want to be sure that they do not miss the importance or relevance of any relevant property. A panoply of moral principles, understood in the way I suggest, can function as a sort of checklist for this purpose. It will not be a complete list, of course, for we can give no sense to the idea that we might now have finished the list of moral principles or of properties that can make a difference sometimes. But our approach allows for that and explains it. There is no limit to the number of properties which can on occasion be important. But of course some are more commonly important than others,[8] and some are commonly more important than others; and therefore some properties should be viewed as more 'central' than others, i.e. as having a natural right to figure early on in one's list of principles. This centrality does not entail that the properties mentioned in the leading principles are always more important than those mentioned elsewhere. But it does create some order in what would otherwise be a bewilderingly random list of properties which can matter in suitable circumstances. So the account I offer makes its own sense of the use of moral principles in reaching decisions in a new case.

It can make sense of the appeal to the importance of a property in justification of a choice or judgement already made. In answer to the question 'Why did you do that?', one may mention a property which one took one's action to have, by saying perhaps 'It was the only honest course.' This is not an explicit appeal to a principle, and we have already seen how a particularist should account for such a reply. But if we suppose that one were to add 'and it is important to be honest', we have the sort of explicit appeal to a principle that would be predicted by the present account of principles. It is not suggested, of course, that honesty is the only important property, only that honesty *can* be important and that it was here.

Second, our account gives an answer to the main question in moral epistemology. I assume that we must find a way of saying how our knowledge of a moral principle can be derived from what we can see in a particular case. I take this form of empiricism in ethics to be the only one which can make sense of our feeling that particular cases must be able to function as some sort of a test for moral principles. This need not be a very direct test, any more than the sense in which scientific theories are testable by particular cases is direct; but only an empiricism of this sort leaves us with a chance of showing that moral principles are not immune to the behaviour of particular cases. Now it seems to me that a particular case can reveal the importance that a property *can* have. It may bring this home to us and force us to recognize it when before we denied the impossibility of such a thing. I have in mind here the example of an adolescent who maintains that good manners are hypocrisy; this position is vulnerable to the occurrence of a case which brings it home forcibly how important good manners can be. So on my account ethics is empirical. Moral principles are learnt in and from particular cases.

The account also gives us some understanding of the appeal to imaginary cases to help us decide what to do about a case before us. I think there are unrecognized problems about this common practice.[9] They derive from the fact that an imaginary case seems to be far too thin to establish anything like what we are after, namely a decision there which we can transport to the actual case before us. And the difficulty is only compounded by the fact that the imaginary case, if it is to serve its purpose, must be one in which we don't face the complexities and problems that we are finding in the actual one. (Why otherwise would we think it possible to make any progress by shifting attention to the imaginary case?) This difference between the actual and the imaginary should be a bar in the way of any easy inference from one to the other, unless we can somehow tell in advance that the difficulty of the actual case is not relevant to its moral features, but just an isolated – or isolable – epistemic feature. But to know that, we would have already to have the sort of understanding of the actual case we were trying to use the imaginary one to achieve; the cart has come before the horse. How can an imaginary case help, if essentially we have to make up our minds about the moral make-up of the actual case *before* we can come to a view about whether the imaginary case is after all a reliable guide? I take there to be genuine problems here, but I also think that the account I give of moral principles provides at least part of the answer. An imaginary case might be an abbreviated sketch of a situation where a property can be seen to be important: where the importance it can have is revealed. I think this especially effective as an account of what is going on in some of the parables in the New Testament, or in the morals attached to Aesop's fables. And if the account is right, it makes good sense of the idea that an imaginary case is one in which whatever one is looking for is somehow easier to see, without this being a stumbling-block in the way of a move from that case to the actual one. Of course, we have learnt less from the imaginary case than some might have hoped, but we have at least learnt something.

The fourth, last and most technical virtue of the account is that it gives a good sense to the idea that moral principles, if true, are necessarily true. Traditionally, this idea amounts to one of three things. The first is the useless idea that if this action is right, then any action similar to it in all non-moral respects is right. There is necessity here; supervenience, which is what is at issue, is to be expressed in modal terms. But it is, I think, the wrong sort of necessity; it seems to offer a modal inference rather than a necessarily true moral principle.[10] The second thought is not uselessly true, but grotesquely false. This is that if this action is right because of its F-ness, then any action that is F is necessarily right. Whether the necessity here lies in the inference rather than in the conclusion, this thought is false for reasons which should by now be familiar. Whatever may be the case here, other properties may conspire to interfere elsewhere. (At its weakest, this is simply the idea that moral principles are defeasible.) The third thought is that if a property is morally relevant in one case, it necessarily has the same relevance wherever it recurs. I am not convinced that the necessity here is other than inferential. What if there never was a case in which the property was morally relevant? But, waiving this, we know already that particularism cannot accept this third thought because of its insistence that relevance is contextually grounded. One main reason for this insistence is the appeal to epistemology. How could we learn from what we can discern in a particular case that a property has the sort of relevance here which is necessarily repeated elsewhere? Everybody here faces the same difficulty, that of showing both how the truth of a moral principle can be discerned in a particular case, and how what we are there discovering is a necessary truth. I think that my account of moral principles can do this, without falling into the trap of making the necessity lie in an inference from what is observed rather than in the truth observed. For the suggestion is that we can see in a particular case the sort of importance that a property *can* have, in suitable circumstances. What we are observing here is already modal, and if our observation is correct there cannot be a situation in which our property *could* not have that importance if the circumstances were suitable. Hence what we observe, if true, is necessarily true.[11]

I think, then, that the account of moral principles as reminding us of the importance a property can have in suitable circumstances solves several outstanding problems in moral theory. So it is important to see that it is compatible with the constraints of particularism, though of course it represents particularism in a conciliatory rather than an aggressive mood. Although we are able to observe, in a given case, the importance that a property can have in suitable circumstances, the particularist can still insist that no notion is available of a sort of circumstance in which it *must* have that importance. The particularist's strictures on the possibility of inference to the nature of a second case from what we see in the first are not violated by our account. This is the main reason why the epistemological problem is easier for the particularist than it is for the generalist, since the particularist wants to insist that the results of observation are less powerful than the generalist needs them to be. There is no substitute for the kind of detailed attention to each new case which an appeal to principles might lead us to shirk.

I end this chapter with a wonderful diatribe from George Eliot, Patron Saint of Particularists:

> The great problem of the shifting relation between passion and duty is clear to no man who is capable of apprehending it: the question, whether the moment has come in which a man has fallen below the possibility of a renunciation that will carry any efficacy, and must accept the sway of a passion against which he had struggled as a trespass, is one for which we have no master key that will fit all cases. The casuists have become a by-word of reproach; but their perverted spirit of minute discrimination was the shadow of a truth to which eyes and hearts are too often fatally sealed: the truth, that moral judgements must remain false and hollow,

unless they are checked and enlightened by a perpetual reference to the special circumstances that mark the individual lot.

All people of broad, strong sense have an instinctive repugnance to the men of maxims; because such people early discern that the mysterious complexity of our life is not to be embraced by maxims, and that to lace ourselves up in formulas of that sort is to repress all the divine promptings and inspirations that spring from growing insight and sympathy. And the man of maxims is the popular representative of the minds that are guided in their moral judgement solely by general rules, thinking that these will guide them to justice by a ready-made patent method, without the trouble of exerting patience, discrimination, impartiality – without any care to assure themselves whether they have the insight that comes from a hardly-earned estimate of temptation, or from a life vivid and intense enough to have created a wide fellow-feeling with all that is human.[12]

Perhaps Eliot is not as precise as a philosopher would wish in the characterization of her target here. My next two chapters each consider a 'man of maxims', in the attempt to show that the generalist alternative to particularism is on much shakier ground that is normally supposed.

NOTES

1 The *Guardian*, 21 April 1990.
2 The example is from McNaughton (1988), p. 193.
3 See McDowell (1979).
4 For fun, here are two damning exposés of generalist bad faith, taken from Cornford's account of academic committees: 'The *Principle of the Wedge* is that you should not act justly now for fear of raising expectations that you may act still more justly in the future – expectations which you are afraid you will not have the courage to satisfy. A little reflection will make it clear that the Wedge argument implies the admission that the persons who use it cannot prove that the action is not just. If they could, that would be the sole and sufficient reason for not doing it and this argument would be superfluous. The *Principle of the Dangerous Precedent* is that you should not now do an admittedly right action for fear you, or your equally timid successors, should not have the courage to do right in some future case, which *ex hypothesi*, is essentially different, but superficially resembles the present one. Every public action which is not customary, either is wrong, or, if it is right, is a dangerous precedent. It follows that nothing should be done for the first time'. (Cornford, 1908, p. 15). Cornford is making these points in pursuit of his view that 'There is only one argument for doing something ... that it is the right thing to do' (1908, p. 14) – a view on which I have commented in 1.4.

5 See Goldstein (1989).
6 See Baier (1958).
7 See Sidgwick (1874).
8 In conciliatory mood the particularist might admit that some are always relevant, regardless of other circumstances. But I see no reason to allow oneself to be pushed in this direction.
9 I try to lay these out in Dancy (1985).
10 And anyway, as we shall see in 5.2, supervenience does not provide us with useful moral principles.
11 This is just an example of the inference from Mp to NMp in S5; but I make no claim to be a competent judge of the suitability of S5 for the formalization and evaluation of ethical inference.
12 *The Mill on the Floss*, end of Bk 7, ch. 2.

5
Against generalism (1)

1 RESULTANCE

I need to start by distinguishing two relationships which it is very easy to confuse, resultance and supervenience.[1] I begin with resultance. This is the relationship which we are talking about when we say that one property of an object exists 'in virtue of' another or some others. For instance, we may say that a thing has the property of squareness in virtue of its possession of some other properties. A dangerous cliff is dangerous in virtue of some other properties it has, perhaps its steepness and the friability of its surface. A table has the property of being a table in virtue of other properties, and so on. We often express this relationship using the word 'because'. The square object is square because of the relative lengths and number of its sides, and the angles which they subtend to each other. The cliff is dangerous because of its steepness and friability, and so on. There will be different sorts of resultance, as the examples I have already given indicate. Sometimes there is only one way for an object to get a resultant property, as in the case of squareness. Squareness results from the same packet of properties every time. But there are different ways of getting to be dangerous, and different tables are tables in virtue of different properties. Crucially, of course, we will be wanting to say that moral properties such as being right or bad are resultant properties, and that there are different ways in which different actions get to be right.

Resultance of this sort is an endemic feature of our conceptual scheme, or indeed of anything recognizable as a scheme. It resists analysis; or at least I know of nothing by way of analysis that looks even remotely plausible. All we can do is to gesture towards it. But this does not make me suspicious of it, though of course in the absence of analysis one has to be specially careful not to confuse different relationships which can all be expressed using the word 'because'.

A resultant property may itself be a property from which (probably with the help of others) a further property results. As a relationship, resultance occurs at many levels; the properties in virtue of which this is a table may themselves exist in virtue of other properties, and the properties in virtue of which this action is wrong may include its unkindness, which itself results from further properties. So there is such a thing as a resultance tree. But it should be clear that this tree is restricted in its application to the particular case; it is the resultance tree for *this* property of *this* object *now*. The tree for the same property of a different object will quite probably be different, because the way in which that object gets to be F (where F-ness is a resultant property) will probably be different from the way in which this one got to be F. This means that there is a certain temptation to see what we might call the 'resultance base' for this property here as *what it is* for this object to have that property. If we make this move we have adopted a sort of 'token identity' theory of resultance, according to which the resulting property is *constituted* here by this resultance base and there by that one. It should be recognized, though, that in making this move we do not see the resultance base as a flat list of properties, but as a structured shape in which those properties are placed here. It matters how they are related to each other; the resultance tree has or is a structure every aspect of which makes a difference, though of course not all are equally important.[2]

This is what one might call the metaphysics of resultance. But it is important to notice that the epistemology of resultance need not follow the metaphysics. We might take it that if one property results from others, we cannot discern that property directly, but must work to it through a recognition of the presence of the properties from which it here results. But the epistemological direction has in fact no need to follow the metaphysical one. The property of being a table is a resultant property, but one can certainly notice that something is a table first, before one takes in the particular features that its tableness results from. The weakness of a chess position is a resultant property, but an expert can see at a glance that the position is weak before turning to work out the various respects in which it is weak, which are the properties from which its weakness results.

I now turn to some abuses of the notion of resultance. The first of these is a classic argument of Hume's:

> But can there be any difficulty in proving, that vice and virtue are not matters of fact, whose existence we can infer by reason? Take any action allow'd to be vicious: Wilful murder, for instance. Examine it in all its

lights, and see if you can find that matter of fact, or real existence, which you call *vice*. In which-ever way you take it, you find only certain passions, motives, volitions and thoughts. There is no other matter of fact in the case. The vice entirely escapes you, so long as you consider the object. You never can find it, till you turn your reflexion into your own breast, and find a sentiment of disapprobation, which arises in you, towards this action.[3]

This argument is an abuse of resultance because it takes a resultant property (viciousness), asks you to look hard at the properties from which it here results, asks you if you discern another property like those, and then announces that because you do not, there is no such property as viciousness in the object. The fact is that Hume is asking you to look in the wrong place. The viciousness is not another property by the side of those properties from which it results. They *are* that viciousness there, according to the theory of resultance. The vice consists in those properties and the way they relate to each other. So if you find the vice hard to discern, a good method would be to consider the resultance base here, and to consider it in the right way. Hume insists that the vice be a separate property (metaphysically and epistemologically), and then announces, quite rightly, that there is no sign of any such property. But this is just to ignore the fact that moral properties result from natural ones in the sense given.

To support this diagnosis I offer an analogy. The property of being a table is a resultant property, and one can ask about it just the same questions as Hume asks about vice, with as much effect. Here is a piece of crude mimicry:

> But can there be any difficulty in proving, that whether something is a table is not a matter of fact, whose existence we can infer by reason? Take any object allow'd to be a table: This one, for instance. Examine it in all its lights, and see if you can find that matter of fact, or real existence, which you call *its being a table*. In which-ever way you take it, you find only certain shapes, sizes, textures, and colours of its component parts. There is no other matter of fact in the case. Its being a table entirely escapes you, so long as you consider the object. You never can find it, till you turn your reflexion into your own breast, and find a certain sentiment of respect-for-tableness, which arises in you, towards this object.

I take this argument to rest on a misconception of the relation between the property of being a table and the other properties which make this object a table. Like Hume's argument, it directs our attention in the wrong direction and then holds that since we did not see what we were looking for, there was nothing there to be seen.

The second abuse of resultance consists in assuming that those who lack the concept of some particular resultant property can acquire it from others by noticing the base properties present when the resultant property is attributed to different objects, and working from there. This is not the assumption that this is the only method of acquiring the relevant concept: only that it is a method which is always available. Nor is it the claim that the resultant property can only be discerned via a more direct recognition of the resultance base; someone committing the second abuse of resultance need not make that mistake. Start rather from the idea that the resultance base, in the particular case, has a certain shape; the interrelationships of the various properties are important. Now we can suppose easily that each property in the resultance base is discernible by those who lack the concept of the resultant property as well as by those who have the concept. But what we should not assume is that the shape taken by the resultance base is one which must be discernible by those who lack the concept. Nor should we assume that the resemblance between different resultance bases as we move from one case to another is one which could be visible to those who lack the concept. It may be, that is, that there is no way of this sort into the concept from outside, since the relevant shape or similarities may only have point for those who can already see their point, i.e. those who share the concept already.[4] A concept may be naturally shapeless in this sense.

If there are concepts like this, an obvious candidate will be any concept whose point is given by some human interest or concern. Creatures that lack that interest or concern will lack the perspective from which it makes sense to group the properties in a resultance base together, or from which the similarities between different resultance bases are discernible. So the moral concepts, which seem to be paradigm cases of the sorts of concepts here at issue, will not be ones which can be acquired from outside by creatures who lack the relevant concerns. For them, as for other such, the base is not able to be disentangled in the way required from the higher-level concept, so that one could work to the one through a grasp of the other.

The third abuse of resultance is the expectation that moral principles can be extracted from individual cases of resultance. We might hope that, given an example of a wrong action, which we understand well enough to be able to specify its resultance base, we can immediately get from this the moral principle that all actions that match that specification are wrong. But this would be a mistake for two reasons. The first is that we are in danger of having one moral principle for each case. Each wrong action is wrong in its own way, and our principles, if we expect to reach them by this route, will just be a list of the cases we have so far encountered. Here we have quite lost the sense that a principle can be extracted from one case and applied to others. Second, there may be an action which matches our specification of the resultance base in the first case but which is not wrong. This sort of point will recur incessantly, but the idea is that the resultance base contains only those properties in virtue of which the action is wrong (those which make the action wrong). There is no guarantee that wherever those properties are present, no matter how much the new action may differ in other respects, it will be wrong too. It may be that there is present in the new case a countervailing property strong enough to turn the tables, as it were, which was absent in the first case. This does not mean that the absence of the countervailing property should have been included in the original resultance base. The action's not having a property strong enough to make it right is not a property in virtue of which it is wrong, though it is something required of it if it is to be wrong. Not having a countervailing property is something without which it would be right and with which it is bound to be wrong; but it is not what makes it wrong – that is done by more ordinary things like being unkind or cruel.

The fourth and final abuse of resultance is to confuse it with something very different, namely supervenience: to which I now turn.

2 SUPERVENIENCE

Like resultance, supervenience is a pervasive feature of our or of any conceptual scheme. But unlike resultance, supervenience can be defined. We speak of a property or of a group of properties supervening on another group of properties. So we say that this moral property supervenes upon certain natural properties, or that moral properties in general supervene upon natural properties. A property P supervenes upon properties of the class [C] if and only if:

If one object has P and some properties of class [C], then any object with exactly the same properties of class [C] as the first will have P, and have it to the same degree and in the same way, and:

If an object has P and some properties of class [C], then it cannot change in respect of P (lose P or become more or less P) unless it changes in respect of some properties in class [C].

Note that I here make no assumption that where a property P supervenes upon properties of class [C], no object can have P without also
having some properties of class [C]. This is because I want to leave
room for the thought that the mental properties supervene upon neural
properties, even though there might conceivably be disembodied objects
that have thoughts and suffer.

There are two important ways in which supervenience differs from
resultance. The first is that supervenience is not concerned with the
particular case. It is a relationship between classes of properties, not
between whatever members of those classes happen to be present in the
case before us. No sense is given to talk about the properties on which
some supervenient property supervenes here.[5] At best we can speak
of the members of the subvenient class here present; but there is no
relationship other than that of resultance between those members
specifically and the property that supervenes upon the class. To think
otherwise is to confuse resultance with supervenience. So when we think
about particular cases, we are almost certainly thinking about resultance;
when we think in general terms, we are almost certainly thinking about
supervenience.

The second difference between resultance and supervenience is that
no token identity theory or constitutive account of the relation between
supervening and subvenient properties is at all tempting. There is no
prospect of identifying goodness with the class of properties on which
it supervenes (the class of natural properties, probably), nor somehow
with the sets of members of that class that collectively belong to the
various objects that are instances of the supervenient property. The only
identity theory that tempts is the one we have already seen, namely the
one which concerns resultance.

There are, however, several respects in which supervenience resembles
resultance. In epistemological terms they are the same. There should be
no sense that a supervenient property cannot be discerned directly, so
that we have to work to such a property through the members of the
subvenient class here present. Second, supervenience is of no use in the
project of generating moral principles from particular cases. What
we get out of supervenience is the truth that any object exactly similar
to this one in natural respects must share the moral properties that the
first one has. But the relevance of this truth is far too restricted for it
to play the sort of role normally assigned to a moral principle. For we
are told nothing about any case except those exactly similar to the first.
At best, this is of little use, since there will be few such cases. But there
is the danger that there will be none, for the rather annoying reason
that it is impossible for any two objects to share all their natural

properties. There is then a danger of triviality in the announcement that any object exactly similar to the first in natural respects must share its moral properties, since we know in advance that this claim, though true, is true only by default. I have to confess that though I think that supervenience claims are not trivially true in this sense, I know of no effective method of saving them from triviality. But this does not trouble me very greatly, since my general view is that thoughts about supervenience, though true enough, are not of much use. I think that resultance is the interesting concept, once one keeps it apart from supervenience. That the moral properties supervene upon the natural ones is entailed by the idea that a moral property cannot exist on its own, but must result from some other (probably natural) properties.[6] So we get to supervenience from resultance, but it is still resultance that leads.

A final respect in which supervenience resembles resultance is that the subvenient base may be naturally shapeless in the sense given earlier. As John McDowell says, 'however long a list we give of the items to which a supervening term applies, described in terms of the level supervened upon, there may be no way, expressible at the level supervened upon, of grouping just such items together ... Understanding why just those things belong together may essentially require understanding the supervening term.'[7]

So much for the relations of supervenience and resultance. Now the first point against generalism is that nothing like a moral principle can be extracted from particular cases by means of either of these relations. Neither shows us how to move from what is contained in a particular case to a principle which can apply to a range of cases which resemble the first one in limited ways. I take this to be comparatively uncontentious. So I now turn to look at two further accounts of how that sort of move works.

3   UNIVERSALIZABILITY

The first of these is Richard Hare's notion of universalizability. This should be carefully distinguished from a Kantian notion of universalizability. For Kant, moral judgements are univerzalizable in the sense that to decide that an action is right, I have to determine that my maxim could stand as a law for all rational beings; I have to show that all rational beings *could* act on this maxim. For Hare, by contrast, I have to determine not that all (relevantly similar) others could act in the way I am acting, but that they *should* do so. Kant does not ask that we prescribe that others should act as we are acting; Hare insists that we should so prescribe. So it is important here to put aside any Kantian thoughts, and concentrate on Hare's form of universalizability.

Hare holds that moral judgements are universalizable in this sense: a person who makes a moral judgement is committed to making the same judgement of any relevantly similar situation. A situation is relevantly similar to the first if it shares with the first all the properties that were the person's reasons for his original judgement.[8] So if we come across a case which resembles the first one in those limited respects, we are compelled to make the same judgement or to retract our first judgement. In this sense each judgement creates a moral principle. Where our reasons for approval were features F1–Fn, our judgement establishes for us the principle 'All actions that have F1–Fn are right.'

There are two ways of attacking this doctrine. The first is to try to refute it on internal grounds; the second is to undermine its motivation, so that one begins to see that there is no reason to hold it. In general, I have been more tempted by the first, while John McDowell has taken the second; but they are clearly consistent. The attempt at an internal refutation starts by pointing out that, as expressed, the doctrine of universalizability is clearly false. I cannot possibly be obliged to make the same judgement wherever that limited set of properties recurs. For there may in a new case be a strong reason against the judgement which was not present in the first case – a defeater, as we might call it. This defeater may have been present all along; in the first case it was not enough to defeat the reasons in favour, but it is present to a greater degree in the second case, and there it is strong enough to defeat what would otherwise be good enough reasons on the other side. For instance, the first action is kind and generous but a bit thoughtless. We approve of it for its kindness and generosity, not for its thoughtlessness. The second action is just as kind and generous, but grossly thoughtless. We may now wish to disapprove of this action, but the doctrine of universalizability, as first formulated, prevents us from doing so unless we revise our opinion of the first action.

Defenders of universalizability may at this point change their account of relevant similarity. Instead of asking that the second action resemble the first only in respect of the reasons in favour of our judgement there, they may broaden the universalizability base and ask that they resemble each other in terms both of reasons in favour and of reasons against. This will clearly dispose of the original problem, but it is vulnerable to new sorts of counter-example. For instance, suppose a man knocks a woman down with his car and puts her into hospital. When he pays for special care for her, visits her and so on, we approve of his (subsequent) actions. They are expressions of regret and an attempt to make amends so far as possible, and these facts are our reasons for approval. We are not therefore committed to approving of another person who behaves in exactly the same way, but whose ultimate purpose is to seduce the woman away from her husband. And we cannot escape this point by saying that the fact that the first person had no ultimate purpose of seduction was among our reasons for approval. First, this was not and need not have been among our reasons. Second, the aim of someone who suggests that it must have been among the original reasons is to insulate the first judgement from counter-examples of this sort. But that aim is doomed to failure. There are just too many potential defeaters for the absence of each one to count among our original reasons, and the general absence of a defeater is not to be thought of as one of the reasons why we judge the first action right. It is a condition in the absence of which we would not judge the action right, but that is not the same as saying that its presence is something for which we judge the action to be right. (We saw this sort of point earlier in the discussion of resultance.)

The defender of universalizability may attempt to broaden still further the account of the universalizability base, so as to require similarity not only in all respects that were either in favour of or against the original judgement, but also all respects whose presence or absence would have affected that judgement to any degree. Now what is going on here is that the original conception of the universalizability base, which was rather narrow, is getting progressively larger. Eventually it will grow to coincide with the supervenience base, i.e. it will cease to exclude any of the natural properties. And the question is whether a stable stopping point can be found short of this trivializing result. One thing we should notice on the way is that the moral principles generated by thoughts about universalizability are becoming progressively less use, since as the universalizability base grows the number of actions relevantly similar to the first diminishes correspondingly. So there is a cost to the universalizabilist in this sort of defence. But this does not mean that the defence is impossible.

What is interesting now is why we should insist that some such defence is there to be found. It is as if one feels that something like this must be right, and it is only a question of getting the details to fall into place. Thinking in this way, one will probably find the sorts of criticisms I have been raising merely annoying; in no sense is one's confidence that some version of the doctrine of universalizability is true at all damaged. This is the point at which the attack on the doctrine of universalizability turns from an attempt at internal refutation to an attempt to discredit the motivation of those who find the doctrine so convincing.

4 SUBSUMPTIVE RATIONALITY

What is that motivation? There is an underlying conception of rationality at work here. Rationality requires consistency in judgement and
practice; this we can all agree. But what is contentious is the specific
form that Hare imposes on the abstract requirement of consistency. For
him, to be consistent just is to subsume particular cases under general
principles in the same way. (In fact, this is all that rationality *can* amount
to within the constraints of his approach.) This is what 'going on in the
same way' *is* here. Given this view of consistency, if we want to claim
that our moral practice (including linguistic practice) is rational, there
must be some general principles underlying our moral judgements. For
otherwise we will lose the possibility of consistency, and without that
our moral practice will be no better than the choice of chocolates after
dinner. There will be nothing in one choice which constrains later choices,
no sense in which we can say that if you make one choice today and
the opposite one tomorrow you are being inconsistent. Hare rightly
wants to avoid this annihilating result, and takes it that the only way
to do that is to see our moral judgement as constrained by general
principles each of which needs only one judgement to set it up.

This *subsumptive* conception of rationality is at best optional, and
its rigidity makes it implausible. It ignores the vast variety of practical
problems and circumstances in which difficult choices have to be made,
trying to drive us in what may seem a very simple-minded way from
one case (which may be very easy) to another which happens to resemble
the first in some limited way. In fact, given the variety of cases that our
principles should somehow equip us to face, they are more likely to be
of practical use to us if they are somewhat open-ended. A principle of
this sort might say 'Other things being equal, it is better not to lie'; or
we might have 'If an action sufficiently resembles this wrong action,
it will be wrong too.' But principles of this type would simply not be
equipped to serve the purposes of Hare's conception of the sort of
consistency required for rationality. That sort of consistency required
us to be *driven* from case to case on pain of contradiction. Only hard-
edged, codified principles with no fudge clauses or room for manoeuvre
in them could drive us in that way. So the sort of implausibility I find
in Hare's conception of what principles are like is one which is required
if they are to serve the purposes for which they are set up.

There is a further objectionable feature of Hare's conception of moral
rationality, which is that though he gives some account of the rationality at issue in the move from a judgement about one case to one about

another, he gives (and can give) no account of the rationality of any individual judgement. The *internal* rationality of a judgement grounded in good reasons is something about which he has prevented himself from speaking. This is specially damaging, because it seems odd to feel bound by rationality to make a judgement here that coincides in some way with one made previously, when the previous one can itself lay no claim to rationality. Unless the first judgement was rational, how can it be rational to feel bound by it? Particularism, as we have seen (and will see in greater detail), can do better than this.

We can all agree that if there is to be such a thing as rationality in moral judgement, we need to give an account of the 'must' that drives us from case to case. We need to give an account of what is at issue when we take it that, given what we have said before, we *must* say this here. This is beyond dispute. What can be disputed is the form that Hare gives to this requirement: the sort of 'must' he takes to be at issue. Hare's 'must' is one which binds on pain of contradiction; it is a 'must' with a very hard edge. Against it one can make two points. The first is that it is unnecessarily hard; Hare is seeking for a 'must' that is too strong. This point I have already made, though of course it needs to be supplemented by an account of a weaker 'must' that is still strong enough. The second is that if you are afflicted with a sense that a 'must' of this strong sort is really required, you are setting yourself an aim that is unattainable, for the vertigo which you are hoping to expel cannot but recur.

Both of these points are due to Wittgenstein. I take the second first. Opposed to the sense that a hard, logical 'must' is required, if there is to be such a thing as rational consistency, is the claim that though there is a 'must' in the case, it is one which we need judgement to discern. In judging that the new case is relevantly similar to the previous one, we are expressing a sense that we are bound to make the same judgement of the second as we made of the first. But we are not bound on pain of contradiction, only of failure of judgement. The classic example is that of the person who, on reaching 100 in a series that began 2, 4, 6, 8, 10, 12 . . . , feels that he *must* continue 102, 104. . . . The sense that this is the only rational continuation is not supported by the thought that there is some contradiction involved in continuing any other way. But suppose that one felt that this is not enough; if it is really true that this way of going on is required, and the others are forbidden, then there must be some demonstrable incoherence in all ways of going on but one. One would say, perhaps, that there must be a rule here which all other ways of going on break, and there is, namely the rule 'add 2'. But the problem about this direct appeal to a rule to avoid any need for judgement is that the question what is and what is not a correct application of the rule is as much a matter of judgement as the apparently simpler question whether one should put 102 next in the series. We have not escaped the need for judgement but at best relocated it. So the sense that if there is to be rationality there must be something more than judgement, something which grounds the sense of 'must' when one judges that given what one said there one must say the same here, is a sense which once admitted will never be satisfied.

If this is right we must rest content with something less than what Hare purports to provide. Our account of consistency will not be one which takes our sense that in this new judgement we are carrying on as before (so that to make any other judgement would be inconsistent) to be fragile unless it is supported by a general principle in the way Hare envisages. Instead we see that sense as robust enough not to need outside support. By this we mean that while Hare's principles could in theory be operated and imposed on us by an outsider, who uses the principle as an independent benchmark by which he assesses our consistency in the operation of a practice which he does not directly understand, by contrast the reason why we are right to think that the next number in the series must be 102 is not one that could be understood by someone outside the practice. For when asked we can only reply 'the next number must be 102 because so far the series has gone 2, 4, 6, 8, 10, 12, and so on.' This 'reason' is not the sort of independent reason that someone in the grips of the subsumption theory of rationality takes us to need, but it is a reason none the less and is the only sort of reason available. No tighter reasons can be provided. In this way we have to learn to live with a sense of vertigo, though if we still feel the vertigo this shows that we have not yet escaped from a sense of insecurity that is based on an illusion. If we can only dispel the illusion the vertigo must fall away with it.

5   SUBSUMPTION AND NON-COGNITIVISM

I started by arguing that the subsumption theory of rationality is optional, but moved gradually to arguing that it is not an option. It is still enormously attractive to proponents of non-cognitivism in ethics. There is a standard argument for non-cognitivism which stands or falls with the subsumption theory.[9] It is often suggested that objective moral values or properties are explanatorily redundant, since we can perfectly well explain moral choice as an affective response to an independent reality which contains no such values or properties. The sort of response we are talking about will be rationally coherent, since it is subject to the demands of consistency, in the sense that the same response is to be made to items of the same natural sort.

This popular argument makes a questionable assumption, which we have already seen elsewhere. It assumes that the group of items to which we respond in the same way has a natural shape – a shape expressible in a vocabulary available to those who see no sense in the sort of response we make to those items. It supposes this because it presumes that the items to which we respond will have natural similarities which are independent of any relation to our response, and which render our response a rational one. If they are independent in this way, they must be recognizable by someone from outside who does not share the distinctive concerns which give point to the response.

It should be clear that if we do not make this assumption, or if it is invalid, the argument collapses. And we have already given notice that nothing in the facts of resultance and supervenience gives any ground for the assumption. What is more, the assumption looks very implausible indeed in ethics. There are many different possible resultance bases for each ethical predicate, that is, many different ways in which an action can come to satisfy that predicate. From our vantage point as active practitioners of moral thought, we are in a position to see similarities between the different actions that the predicate groups together. But those similarities are not natural ones; they require the focus of the moral predicate to mediate them. Here we have a *natural shapelessness*, in a way that undermines the argument for non-cognitivism completely.

It is important to note how strong this position is intended to be. Neither natural grouping nor concern is independently intelligible. The shape of the resultance bases is invisible to those who lack the concept of the relevant concern. But the concern also has not got enough determinate content to *explain* the choices that are made. It is not that someone could come to grasp the concern and then work out how someone with that concern would see this or that state of affairs. To have the concern is no more than to see situations in a certain way. The choices *give* content to the concern. So one cannot work from the choices to the concern, nor from the concern to the choices. Otherwise the concern would be playing the role of a universal principle, from which we move to our views about particular cases by something alarmingly like subsumption. The strong position is necessary if we are to rule out this possibility.

One might suggest that non-cognitivism does not need the argument that values are explanatorily redundant, nor the assumption that moral properties have a natural shape.[10] But without that assumption (and if we make that assumption we are going to find the argument virtually irresistible), it is not clear how non-cognitivists are in a position to conceive of moral practice as rational. Natural shapelessness, if it exists, undermines the only account of rationality available to them. For in taking moral judgement away from the realm of the cognitive, where natural similarities are thought of as grounding consistency in the use of natural predicates, the only way to see moral thought as able to be consistent or inconsistent is to relate it back to (no doubt complex) natural similarities.

I take it therefore that Hare's non-cognitivism forces on him an assumption that is unnecessary, that has no coherent motivation and that makes demands which if once seen as valid will be impossible to satisfy. But I have offered no direct argument against the possibility of a better successor to the original doctrine of universalizability. All I have done is to suggest that the apparent need for such a thing is based on an illusion, and that the only real reason for supposing that a successor can be found is the fear that unless one is found, moral judgement will be shown to be non-rational.

6　A DIFFERENT ARGUMENT

I now consider a different style of argument against universalizability put forward by David Wiggins, in elaboration of suggestions made by Peter Winch.[11] My general view will be that this argument is interesting but inconclusive since it leaves unimpugned one central aspect of the use to which Hare wants to put the universalizability of moral judgement. Wiggins (after Winch) considers the thought that in a hard case I may judge that it would have been wrong for me to have done an action which it was not wrong of the agent to do. The example he discusses (which is Winch's)[12] is that of Melville's *Billy Budd*, in which Captain Vere decides to have Billy Budd executed for mutiny on what he knows perfectly well to be a trumped-up charge made by the master-at-arms. Wiggins suggests that I may judge that it would have been wrong for me to have done that, but that it was not wrong for Vere to do it. One is immediately tempted to explain this, if one agrees with it at all, by appealing to 'relevant differences' between oneself and Vere. And it is true that there are such differences; they include such things as the life, position and character of the agent. But such differences do not play the role which this explanation envisages, because they are not 'deliberatively admissible' for the agent though they are for the non-agent judging from outside. The agent (Vere) does not deliberate from his life, position and character, since the question for him is just what sort of life, position and character he is willing to have. But we can consider such matters as fixed in asking whether he made the right decision. For instance, we might say that for a naval officer in a fleet that is particularly vulnerable to mutiny, the choice that Vere made is the right one. But for Vere the question was rather 'Should I be the naval officer for whom this would be the right choice?' So such matters are deliberatively admissible for us in assessing Vere's choice in a way that they are not for Vere. This makes room for us to judge that Vere made the right choice, even though we think that we would have been wrong to make that choice. In a way (though I am not sure that Wiggins would want to put it this way) the question we ask as potential agents is not the same question as the one we ask as outside judges of the choices of others. Different things are held fixed. This generates a sense in which the agent's perspective is primary, for the agent faces a question which nobody else faces and the agent's answer is unimpugned by the fact that others judge correctly that they would have been wrong to give that answer.

I think, with Wiggins, that this argument of Winch's is very interesting. But it only attacks part of the doctrine of universalizability. That doctrine has it that if I judge myself right to perform this action for reasons R1–Rn, then I must first judge myself right to perform any action that has features R1–Rn, and second judge anyone else right to perform actions with features R1–Rn except where I can appeal to relevant differences between myself and them. The argument which Wiggins brings out attacks the second half of this, but not the first. It only attacks the first if the perspective of the agent is restricted to that of the person who is considering acting now. We might suggest that in comparing this action here with an action which I did some time earlier, I am moving from the agent's perspective to that of an onlooker, since I play the role of onlooker for actions, even those of my own, which lie at some temporal distance from the present. If this were right, it would not be the distance that makes the difference exactly, but the fact that an action which I once did or which I might do is not one on which I presently occupy the special perspective of an agent. We might support this by arguing that facts about my life, position and character are probably deliberatively admissible when I assess my own past actions in a way that they would not be if I were somehow still occupying the position of the agent. But even if we grant this interesting but contentious point, there remains some part of the doctrine of universalizability that escapes our net. We held first that universalizability cannot drive us from thoughts about what others are right to do to thoughts about what we are right to do. Then, by restricting the perspective of the agent to actions whose time is now, we held that universalizability cannot drive us from thoughts about what it was wrong of me to do then to thoughts about what it would be wrong of me to do now. But this restriction revalidates moves from what it *was* wrong of me to do to what it is wrong of others to do, since the perspective of the agent is now limited to the present case. And we never found anything wrong with the final use of universalizability, to take us from what we think wrong of one person to do to what we think about the relevantly similar actions of another, when those two people are not us and we occupy the position of an onlooker with respect to both. If we want to upset these uses of universalizability, we will have to return to the attack on the subsumptive conception of rationality on which any use of universalizability relies.

7   Universalizability as a Weapon

Part of the reason why people are reluctant to abandon universalizability is that with it they would lose certain argument forms to which they are attached and to which they can see no alternatives. The first sort of argument that would go would be one which attempts to isolate a feature as 'morally relevant'. A good example of such an argument is given by James Rachels.[13] Suppose that we want to know whether killing someone is, in itself, worse than letting them die. Rachels uses the following method to find out the answer. He considers two examples. In the first, Smith stands to inherit a large fortune if his six-year-old cousin should die. One evening while the child is taking a bath, Smith creeps upstairs and drowns him in the bath, taking care that everything is arranged to look like an accident. In the second example, Jones stands equally to inherit a large fortune from his young cousin. He creeps upstairs to drown his cousin in the bath, but as he reaches the bathroom door the child slips and knocks his head on the side of the bath, falls into the water and drowns all on his own with only a minimum of faint kicking. Jones stands by to help out should it become necessary, but the child dies without needing help (as it were).

Rachels asks whether we think worse of Smith than of Jones. Of course, Smith killed his cousin while Jones merely let his cousin die, but this seems to make no difference. They are, within the limits of precision of which moral thought is capable, equally evil. So far I have no real quarrel with Rachels' procedure. It is the next move that I want to question. Rachels takes himself now to have established that because these two examples differ only in one respect, he has isolated (working as it were by Mill's method of difference) the respect in which they differ and established that this respect is not morally relevant. And by this he means not just that it is not morally relevant here, but that it is not morally relevant anywhere. The distinction between killing and letting die thus emerges as without moral content.

It is not the conclusion that I doubt here so much as the method. Suppose that I argue in a similar way for the opposite conclusion. I have an awkward choice to make. I can either kill one innocent child or let two die. Clearly, I ought to let the two die, despite the fact that twice as many deaths result. But this must be because we throw into the balance, to compensate for the fact that more children die, the greater wrongness of killing than of letting die. So, since this is the only feature that can explain our judgement, we seem to have established that killing is in itself worse than letting die, contrary to what Rachels' examples purported to establish. He argues that the distinction makes no difference here, and so can make no difference anywhere. I argue that the distinction makes a difference here, and so must make the same difference everywhere.[14]

Of course, there are plenty of perfectly sound methods of arguing where the same method can generate opposite results from different data. But this is a peculiar case. For if one application of the method is correct, the other must be totally misconceived. But if the other is totally misconceived, so must the first one be. My diagnosis of what has gone wrong here is that Rachels has forgotten that moral relevance is sensitive to context in a way that his method cannot capture. According to me, it could be the case that the distinction makes a difference in the one case and none in the other. It is a mistake to think that a feature is either relevant everywhere or relevant nowhere. The same feature may be irrelevant in one case and make all the difference in another. This is just like the way in which intrinsically motivating states work. Sometimes they motivate, and sometimes their ability to motivate is defused or reversed by some other feature of the case.

If this is right, we can see another sort of argument which must be rejected. In discussions of animal rights, racism or feminism there is commonly an appeal to the inability of some suggested characteristic to make any moral difference. Suppose, for instance, that the human race is the only one gifted with a power of speech or with the ability to think abstractly. We may imagine someone trying to say that this justifies all sorts of preferential treatment for humans and all sorts of dubious practices towards animals. But to arguments of this nature it is often replied that no such feature could be morally relevant. Considered in isolation, how could the ability of humans to think in certain structures make a difference to what it is morally permissible to do to them? And how could the greater size and strength of men make a moral difference to how they should be treated compared with women (to change the example)? But if the attempt to reject universalizability is not misconceived, these arguments, despite their popularity, will have to be rethought. One cannot establish that some feature is incapable of proving morally relevant in this sort of way in advance, either by the sort of appeal to intuition that we see here or by arguments like that of Rachels.

Of course, as well as these more disguised moves, any argument such as Peter Singer's defence of animal rights which are explicitly formulated in terms of universalizability will have to be put aside too. No doubt many of those arguments can be reformulated to escape their dependence on the doctrine of universalizability, which turns out to be more a matter of presentation than of substance. My purpose here is merely to show that there is something important at stake in the attack on or the defence of universalizability. In losing it we lose a weapon which I think we are better off without.

In the next chapter I turn to consider a rather different account of the nature and role of moral principles.

NOTES

1 This is the theme of my 'On Moral Properties'; see Dancy (1981).
2 There will be much more in this vein in chapter 6.
3 See Hume (1739/40), Bk III, pt I, sec. I, at pp. 468–9.
4 This is one of the main points of McDowell (1981).
5 None the less, this sort of talk is very prevalent in the literature, both among moral theorists (who should know better) and among epistemologists.
6 In general I think that we come to know that a property or class of properties supervene upon some other class of properties because we recognize particular cases in which properties of the first sort result from properties of the second. It is interesting that this is not true for the supposed supervenience of the mental on the physical.
7 McDowell (1981), p. 145.
8 See Hare (1963), ch. 2. I am here discussing Hare's earlier work, and his earlier use of the term 'universalizability'. In Appendix II I relate my criticisms to Hare's later work in Hare (1981), in which he uses the term 'universalizability' to mean what I mean by 'supervenience'.
9 For a classic presentation of the argument, see Mackie (1976), pp. 17–19. For McDowell's reply to this argument, see McDowell (1981).

10 See Blackburn (1981).
11 See Wiggins (1987), pp. 166–84, and Winch's paper 'The Universalizability of Moral Judgement', originally published in *The Monist* and reprinted in Winch (1972).
12 Wiggins' discussion is mainly concerned to dissipate misunderstandings of Winch's point which weaken it severely, such as those in an otherwise admirable article by S. Guttenplan; see Guttenplan (1979/80), esp. p. 74.
13 See Rachels (1975).
14 I find a point similar to this in Philips (1987).

6
Against generalism (2)

1 THE THEORY OF PRIMA FACIE DUTIES

The attack on Hare's doctrine of the universalizability of moral judgement hinges on features peculiar to Hare, or at least on features which not all theories in the area need to share. If there were a cognitive theory which still allows the existence of general principles, but disowns the subsumptive theory of rationality and refuses to countenance the idea that the shape of the relevant base must be recognizable by those who lack the concept of the higher-level property (i.e. the idea that the higher-level property can be disentangled from the lower-level ones), it should be immune to any criticism that we have so far made. The only objection we make directly to the possibility of general moral principles was based on the holism of reasons, discussed in 4.1. But this is just a sharper way of making the familiar point that given the complexity of moral life it is going to be impossible to codify any moral maxim in a way that will render it invulnerable to the vagaries of future situations. Effectively, any moral principle that is going to be some use is going to have to cover a variety of different situations, and in doing so it must give an incomplete description of the situations it is intended to cover, leaving unspecified those areas in which they are allowed to differ. But in doing this it leaves itself open to the possibility that there will be a situation which resembles the others in the respects that are specified, but differs elsewhere so markedly that though they are indeed wrong, it is not. So uncodifiability is a problem, but only for those theories, such as Hare's, which require codifiability if they are to work at all.

Now there is indeed a fairly well worked-out theory which has the features needed to escape what we have said against Hare, so that even if our attack on Hare's form of generalism is felt to be effective, we need completely new arguments in order to complete the defence of particularism. This is Ross's theory of prima facie duties. This theory is cognitive, non-subsumptive and non-disentangling. It has no problems about codifiability and fails to be impressed by the search for a hard, logical 'must'. But it is still a generalist theory of moral thought and reasons, in a way that particularism is concerned to escape. I will run through these points one by one.

Ross's position, often called intuitionism, holds moral thought to be cognitive; it sees moral attitudes as beliefs rather than as desires. Interestingly, however, Ross is an externalist in the theory of moral motivation. He accepts the need for an independent desire if moral thought is to lead to action.[1] Ross adopts this position because he accepts the broad outlines of Hume's theory of motivation. And it was his adoption of externalism which caused the greatest trouble for his intuitionism. It was held against him, quite reasonably in my view, that it was absurd to suppose that there are moral facts of the matter the recognition of which has in itself no tendency to motivate in any direction at all. And his account of moral cognition came to appear more suspicious than necessary because of the inertness of the facts to be cognized.[2] This makes his externalism hard to understand. Why did Ross not see the non-Humean option? I think that the answer can be found in my earlier discussion of motivation. I held there that cognitivism in the theory of motivation (which I saw as the combination of a cognitive theory of moral judgement and internalism in the theory of motivation) requires us to abandon generalism (the view that what matters somewhere must matter in the same way on every recurrence). The reason for this claim was that generalism is fatal to the attempt to suppose that a purely cognitive state can be 'sufficient for action' in the sense which generalism gives to this phrase. This means that anyone who is a generalist and a cognitivist, as Ross is, must be an externalist. The triad of internalism, generalism and cognitivism is inconsistent.

To show the exact way in which Ross's theory is non-subsumptive, I am going to pay careful attention to a short passage in which he sets out his position:

> What comes first in time is the apprehension of the self-evident prima facie rightness of an individual act of a particular type. From this we come by reflection to apprehend the self-evident general principle of prima facie duty. From this, too, perhaps along with the apprehension of the self-evident prima facie rightness of the same act in virtue of its having some other characteristic as well, and perhaps in spite of the apprehension of its prima facie wrongness in virtue of its having some third characteristic, we come to believe something not self-evident at all, but an object of probable opinion, viz. that this particular action is (not prima facie but) actually right.[3]

There is a lot packed into this passage. To understand it one needs to be familiar with what Ross means by 'intuitive induction'. This is contrasted with induction in a more familiar sense, which is normally called enumerative induction. With enumerative induction the accumulation of instances is important to the increase of probability of one's conclusion. With intuitive induction the accumulation of instances adds little or nothing. When we learn the validity of a logical principle (*modus ponens*, say) by being shown an example, we can often see the validity in that example alone. Further examples are not necessary for this process; if required at all, they play quite a different role from that played by the increase in evidence in enumerative induction. They direct our attention towards the phenomenon we are being shown, rather than give us more evidence to suppose some conclusion to be true.[4]

We are now in a position to express Ross's moral epistemology, i.e. his account of how we come to know and use moral principles. According to Ross, we start from a particular action in which we recognize that some feature is one in virtue of which this action is prima facie right; what we are recognizing is that the feature is a reason to do the action. We probably recognize other features, some as reasons not to do the actions (properties in virtue of which the action is prima facie wrong), and others which are more reasons for doing it. So far everything we have noticed is restricted in its application to the case before us. But we come immediately to see that the property which made this action prima facie right must have the same effect wherever it occurs. What we notice here is that our reason is, must be, a general reason. In noticing this we are engaged in intuitive induction. We move to knowledge of a general moral principle from knowledge of the difference a property makes in a particular case. What we know is self-evident to us, not in the sense that one only has to consider it in order to recognize its truth, but in the different sense that nothing is necessary for its recognition other than what the particular case contains.

Note that Ross never claims that we know moral principles by intuition, in the sort of way that is often suggested, to his detriment, by unsympathetic critics. His account of how we come to know them is essentially empiricist; their truth is revealed to us in experience, since nothing more is necessary for their recognition than what the particular case contains.

So far we have seen two stages of the process. Stage 1 was where we discern the difference a property makes in a particular case. Stage 2 was where we see that it must make that same difference everywhere. There is a third stage, however, to which we move without going through the second. This is where, considering all the properties which here make a difference, we come to a view about which side the preponderance of reasons lies on. Ross says that the recognition that one's reasons are general reasons plays no role in this move. This is what the words 'From this, too' mean in the passage quoted; but he is more explicit in his later book, where he writes:

> Now it seems at first sight to follow from this that our perception of the particular duty follows from the perception of a general duty to relieve human beings in distress. And, generalising, we might feel inclined to say that our perception of particular duties is always an act of inference, in which the major premise is some general moral principle ... Yet it will not do to make our perception of particular duties essentially inferences from general principles ... Do we, without seeing directly that the particular act is right, read off its rightness from the general principle, or do we directly see its rightness? Either would be a possible account of what happens. But when I reflect on my own attitude towards particular acts, I seem to find that it is not by deduction but by direct insight that I see them to be right, or wrong. I never seem to be in the position of not seeing directly the rightness of a particular act of kindness, for instance, and of having to read this off from a general principle – 'all acts of kindness are right, and therefore this must be, though I cannot see its rightness directly'.[5]

Ross goes on to admit that there are occasional exceptional circumstances where we do 'apprehend individual facts by deduction', both in ethics and elsewhere. But he does not take this to detract from the truth of his general thesis, that our knowledge of what to do in a particular case is not reached by subsuming the case under any general principle.[6] So Ross's theory is non-subsumptive. Moral principles play no epistemological role.

There is no suggestion in Ross that those who lack the relevant moral concepts should still be able to see the natural shape of those concepts, i.e. see the practice of moral thinkers as a way of going on as before. Ross is not committed to the idea that the natural base can be disentangled from the moral superstructure in any way. So he avoids the implausibilities associated with that idea.

He also has no problem with codifiability, because of the different account he gives of the content of a moral principle. Instead of telling one that all actions of a certain sort are wrong, as Hare's principles do, lending themselves to refutation by complex cases which despite being of that sort are not wrong, Ross's principles do no more than specify a property as being one which counts generally in favour of (or against) any action that has it. This is a much more convincing account of what a moral principle says. And it gives a quite different picture of what a counter-example to a moral principle would look like. Instead of being an example where the principle tells us to do one thing and we think we ought to do the opposite ('Do not steal'), it would be an example where, though the principle tells us that some feature counts in favour of any action that has it, we think it either makes no difference at all here or else that it does make a difference, but counts in the opposite direction. (I tried to give examples of both these types in 4.1.)

I find this account of moral principles altogether more true to life than the sort of account we find in Hare.[7] It is clearly a generalist account, in that it maintains that what is a reason here must be the same reason everywhere. But it lacks all the weaknesses we were able to point to in Hare. So we need new arguments, not just because we want to be particularists (at least I do), but because we want to be internalists and cognitivists. As I suggested before, that combination is not available to a generalist.

2   THE NOTION OF A PRIMA FACIE DUTY

Ross's notion of a prima facie duty is clearly the keystone of the whole story, and in a way one can hardly believe that any one notion could possibly do all that is required of it for the theory to work. It plays the following roles:

1   It tells us what moral principles say.
2   It shows how moral principles can conflict in particular cases without the truth of either being impugned and so gives a much better account of what a counter-example to a purported moral principle would look like.
3   It shows how we learn our moral principles from what we discern in particular cases.
4   It shows that a generally relevant property is related to a particular case.
5   It shows that a property relevant in one case is relevant in the same way everywhere.
6   It shows how contributory reasons are related to one's overall decision.
7   (?) It shows the rationality of regret for a defeated reason.

In discussing the extent to which the notion of the prima facie is able to achieve these things, I shall be concentrating on items (4) and (5).

My original exposition of Ross's theory took the notion of a prima facie duty for granted, explaining it by the use of phrases like 'counts in favour of' and 'is some reason for'. But Ross aspires to explain what these phrases are getting at, not just to appeal to them; and rightly so. His official definition of a prima facie duty runs like this: 'I suggest "*prima facie* duty" or "conditional duty" as a brief way of referring to the characteristic ... which an act has, in virtue of being of a certain kind, ... of being an act which would be a duty proper if it were not at the same time of another kind which is morally significant.'[8]

I have several criticisms to make of this attempt.[9] It is not unimportant that the account *assumes* the notion of the 'morally significant', without which it would not even get going. If one tries to take that notion out, we get the merely circular definition which is what we have above, but ending 'if it were not at the same time of another kind which makes it prima facie right or prima facie wrong'. It is more important that Ross's definition tells us only what effect 'being a prima facie duty in virtue of property F' has when F is the only morally relevant property the action has. It has nothing to say at all about what it is like to 'be a prima facie duty in virtue of property F' in any other situation. And of course the case where an action has only one morally relevant property is extremely rare, if indeed one can be found at all. What has gone on here is that Ross has, at best, picked out a *consequence* of the phenomenon he is interested in.

To substantiate this criticism, let us ask how well the notion of the prima facie, so defined, succeeds in playing the various roles listed above. What we see at best is that Ross achieves what he is after in a merely technical sense, but quite unsatisfyingly. What we have learnt is that the moral principle 'It is wrong to steal' tells us that if being theft is the only relevant property of an action, it will make the action wrong. This would tell us how we might learn the truth of a moral principle (3). We see that this property matters here, and immediately see that wherever it is the only relevant property, it must decide the issue. This is what I call a technically correct account. When we turn to (4) and (5), we get a similar result. What matters here must matter in the same way everywhere (5), since in every case it will be true that if this property were the only one that mattered (even if it is not the only one that matters here) it would decide the issue. Similarly, a property which is generally morally relevant is one which is relevant in the same way to each case where it is present (4). Again, there is a kind of technical correctness here. But the property is relevant only in the very thin sense that if (counter to the facts) it were the only one that mattered here, it would decide the issue. This is admittedly true in every case, but it is hardly a satisfying account of what it is for a property to be morally relevant in a given situation, nor of how a moral principle can apply in the same way to quite different circumstances, which is what we really want to know. For it fails completely to tell us how the property is behaving *here*, only how it *would* behave in a quite different (and very rare) situation. Essentially, the theory turns our attention away from the interesting questions about the behaviour of reasons when they are together, and tries to get away with talking only of their behaviour in situations which don't really happen, when they are present alone.

When we look for an account of moral conflict (2), we find that what it is to face a moral conflict is to be in a situation which has two properties, each of which would decide the issue were it the only relevant one, and which would in that case decide it in different ways. Yet again, the theory works technically, but the result is not at all satisfying. For nothing has been said about conflict in this case, where the properties are co-present.

When we turn to (6) and (7), we find that the theory fails to work at all. A theory which focuses on the case where there is only one relevant property prevents itself from giving a genuine account of the relation between contributory reasons and overall decision except in that special case. And there is no room for an account of the suitable attitude towards a defeated reason, because there is no analysis given of a defeated reason. The theory only tells us about successful reasons, and those only when they are alone. Nothing is said about how two contributing reasons might combine to be together sufficient, where neither is sufficient on its own.

In general, it seems to me that though the epistemology offered by Ross's official definition is possible, it is just wrong. Is it true that what we notice when we notice that this property makes a difference here is that if it were the only relevant property, it would decide the issue? To the extent that introspection is allowed to have something to say to such questions (certainly Ross is not frightened of such appeals to intuition, though his intuitionism is only rightly so called because of the role of intuitive induction) I think it clear that it decides against Ross.

What is more, have we been offered anything to persuade us that a property which would win the day if it were alone cannot be completely inert in an ordinary case where it is joined by others? If this interesting possibility has been ruled out, it has been ruled out by definition. But surely something more substantial than that is needed to establish this important point.

However, the official definition of prima facie duty is not the only one to be found in Ross. There is a less formal account in terms of tendencies, which may seem more promising. Ross sometimes speaks of a property which makes an action a prima facie duty as one which *tends* to make any action that has it a duty proper. So here is a different definition of a prima facie duty: an action is a prima facie duty in virtue of having property F iff actions that have property F tend to be duties proper. One's first thought here is that talk about tendencies can only be cashed at the general level, in a way that would completely distort the role of moral principles as we understand it. The principle 'Stealing is wrong' would tell us, not that this action's being theft makes it the worse (or something like that), but rather that in general if an action is theft, it is overall wrong (or something like that). But it seems quite clear to me that the first of these could be true when the second is false. It might well be that a wrong-making property is normally accompanied by a stronger right-making property, so that though every action that has the former property is the worse for it, still most such actions are overall right, not wrong.

The thought that moral principles do not express anything of the form of a generalization, or anything that is the proper product of enumerative induction, can be supported in the following way. Suppose that we have a moral principle 'Do not do acts that have property F', and a generalization that tigers have tails. Some acts that have F may be right despite their F-ness, and in some of these cases (though not necessarily in all) the rightness will be reduced by their having F; they will be wrong *qua* having F, or the worse for having F, but still right overall. Moral principles are able, even when defeated in a particular case by countervailing considerations, to linger or have residual effects. But generalizations are not able to do this. A tiger that has no tail is not somehow one that has a tail *qua* tiger, or one which has more of a tail for being a tiger, even though for other reasons it has not got one overall.

What is more, the account in terms of general tendencies fails to provide satisfying answers to our seven questions. It does not show how we manage to learn the truth of a moral principle from what we see in a particular case (3); it does not fit Ross's empiricist epistemology at all. It fails to show that a property relevant in one case must be relevant in the same way everywhere (5), unless we accept as an account of relevance a theory which holds that the generalization 'Most men are taller than most women' is relevant to the height of all men under four foot six inches tall. For the same reason it fails to show how a generally relevant property is related to a particular case, since though a man who is taller than most women is an instance of the true generalization, he is not somehow made to be like that by falling under the generalization. The generalisation does not affect his height at all. What is more, nothing is said about conflict and the rationality of regret (2 and 7). An extremely fit smoker is not someone whose properties are in conflict, even though *qua* smoker one's life tends to be shorter than that of others, and *qua* extremely fit person it tends to be longer. If this is conflict, conflict is not an interesting phenomenon. And finally, the behaviour of contributing reasons is quite unlike that of probabilities, tendencies or frequencies (4 and 6). If women tend to go to the hairdresser more often than men do, and the rich tend to go to the hairdresser more often than the poor do, there is no probability that a rich woman goes to the hairdresser more often than a rich man. But if an action is the better for being kind and the better for being self-denying, there is some reason to suppose that if an action is both kind and self-denying, it is better than if it had merely been one or the other.

3   THE PROPENSITY THEORY

So the less formal account in terms of tendencies is a manifest failure. I once thought that this was the end of the matter, but I now see that there is a further way of understanding Ross's unworked out talk of tendencies, namely on the analogy not of the frequency but of the propensity theory of probability.[10] Here we are offered a notion of a 'tendency in a particular case'. The suggestion is like this. A solid object travelling in a certain direction has a tendency to continue in that direction at the same speed. Its having this is not to be understood as some sort of generalization about the behaviour of such objects; it is irreducibly a fact about this one object that it has this tendency. It has other tendencies too. If near a larger object such as the earth, it has a tendency to move towards it. If travelling through a dense medium, it has a tendency to slow down. It has all these tendencies, and what it actually does will be a function of its tendencies, computable in principle. A moral principle states that to have a given property is to have a tendency to be wrong (1). Tendencies can conflict in a particular case, as in the example given above where the object has a tendency to continue at the same speed and to slow down (2). We can in principle learn whether a property is a tendency of this sort from a particular case, though we are more likely to need a comparison of various instances; these instances will still not be playing the role of accumulating evidence as in enumerative induction (3). Each tendency plays the same role here that it does wherever it appears. There is no problem about seeing a property that is a tendency as being that tendency wherever it appears (4), and if it is a tendency in one case it must be so in all (5). So far things are looking good for this version of the theory of prima facie duties. If we want to upset it, we have three options. The first is to attack the propensity theory of probability directly. This is not in itself a very promising plan, largely because we would have to show, not that the theory fails to capture some aspect of the behaviour of the natural world, but that it is philosophically incoherent. Effectively the question is not whether or not it fails in physics, but whether or not it fails in ethics.

The second option is to attack the analogy. Difficulties may seem to arise for it when we ask whether there is sufficient flexibility in Newtonian physics, which is really our model here, to match all the various and subtle ways in which contributory reasons can gather together to make enough reason to act. There is no problem about ordinarily contri-butory reasons, each of which is not enough on its own to make the action right but which are enough together. If a ball is struck by two objects, neither of which would have been able to move it on its own, the combination may well succeed where each would have failed. Each object has a propensity to move the ball, but needs help from the other. But there seems to be no analogue in the physical model for the idea that two features, neither of which is itself (or alone) a reason to act, may each be reasons when in the presence of the other. Here neither feature is individually a right-making propensity; each contributes only when the other does. If this sort of situation can occur, the appeal to the propensity theory of probability will fail to capture some aspects of the behaviour of reasons.

Another respect in which the analogy seems to fail is that in the moral case the eventual overall property (rightness, say) is identical with the property which the strongest party *tends* to give the action. This seems not to be true in the physical case. There we can be more or less sure that the eventual behaviour of the object is not something that it has any tendency (of the sort we are talking about) to do. Take the example of a balloon thrust in a particular direction. It has a tendency to travel straight on, another to go directly downwards, another to rise (since it is lighter than air) and another to decelerate, travelling in its original direction. In fact it will not exactly do any of these things, but what it does do will be some function of these tendencies.

It is possible just not to be impressed by these disanalogies: to admit them but to carry on regardless. One way of doing this would be to say that in the ethical case there is only one polarity at issue, in the nature of things, whereas in the physical case there are very many. In ethics our action is being dragged by its various properties between the two extremes of right and wrong, whereas in physics there is up/down, slow/fast, left/ right (not really, of course) and so on. It is hardly surprising that there are disanalogies, then. We could have predicted, from the multi-polarity of physical tendencies, that the eventual behaviour of the object will not be in exact accordance with any of the tendencies it has, while it is necessarily true that the action will either end up right or wrong (or neither – are some of its properties tendencies to make it indifferent?). But the analogy is sound in the respect intended.

There is, however, a further way in which the analogy fails which we cannot so easily discount. This is that the epistemology of the physical case is quite different from that of the moral case. Ross holds that in moral judgement we are directly aware of the individual features as tendencies, i.e. we are aware of them as making some difference here and we are aware of the sort of difference they make. From this atomistic awareness we move to what is merely a probable opinion about the over-all rightness or wrongness of the act. The physical case is quite differ-ent from this. There we are aware only of the overall outcome, and infer the particular propensities by means of theory. We are not aware of the propensities as such at all.

One might try to reply again that this merely shows that the moral case is not similar to the physical one in all respects. All that is needed for the analogy is that there be metaphysical similarity between the two, not that they match epistemologically as well. But this reply now looks less convincing. One way of seeing Ross is as trying to combine a particularist epistemology with a generalist metaphysic. And this is just what is threatened by the disanalogy we are now considering. The physical model does not show us how to run this combination, since it fails to capture the required features. Nor can we easily alter Ross's position to keep the analogy in place, by saying that we are first aware of the overall rightness and wrongness of an action, and only later work out the nature of the particular tendencies which lead to that result. For this would be hard to square with Ross's insistence that our judgement of whether the action is right or wrong is never more than probable opinion, while our view of the tendencies of particular properties is know-ledge of self-evident truth.

It is also possible to attack this sort of generalism directly rather than to try to find fault with the analogy. In this vein one can point out that there are various contentious features of moral and other reasons which the new generalism cannot make room for. The first of these is the phenomenon of silencing. There seems to be nothing like this in physics, and nothing in the theory which could persuade one that silencing is even coherent as a possibility. The second such point is that there is no room in the theory for tragic dilemmas, conceived as cases where an action is both required and forbidden in a way that has neither side of the argument outgunning the other but still does not hold that the action is morally indifferent. We shall discuss this possibility in chapter 7, and there is of course the view to be taken into consideration that there is no such thing as a tragic dilemma in this sense. But for anyone who does not take this view, the present form of generalism is suspect. A third point of the same style is the idea that where an action has a point of a certain power to be made in favour of it, and another of rather less power to be made against it, it may eventually emerge that the action is right, and more right than one would have thought if one had merely subtracted the negative point from the positive one.[11] Ross, of course, need not say that the eventual result will be precisely computable as a function of the contributing reasons, but since he holds that each reason plays the same role on every recurrence he needs either to give an account of a way in which the defeated reason functions in such cases other than by subtraction, or deny that cases of this sort occur at all. The latter choice is not very promising, and it is not clear what resources the theory offers in promotion of the former.

A different move would be to argue that the propensity theory of probability is simply not a good model for generalism, since it is not itself committed to the claim that a propensity makes the same contribution on every recurrence. Perhaps there is nothing that prevents reversed or annulled tendencies, and if such things remain possible they are all that is needed to establish the particularist position. There is a matter of tricky detail here, since particularists need to decide the extent to which they want to say that a property brings *nothing* to an action, its contribution being determined only when it is present with others, or whether they only want to say that though there is a default position, a contribution which the property makes other things being equal, that contribution can be reversed or annulled by untoward circumstances. This weaker position is clearly the one which is going to be best suited by the idea that propensities in physics can be reversed or annulled. I do not know whether adherents of the propensity theory of probability would allow the possibility of reversal and/or annulment. I do know that there are some examples of reversal in science fiction, such as the way in which gravity can be reversed to achieve lift-off in H. G. Wells' *A Voyage to the Centre of the Moon*. And I do not think it outlandish to suggest that the Stealth bomber is coated with a substance which simply annuls the propensity of various waves to rebound from the surface of the aircraft. Whether they are or not, tendencies could be like this in nature.

So the mere possibility of the analogy with the propensity theory of probability seems to me insufficient to establish the new form of generalism.

4 THE NEED FOR GENERAL MORAL TRUTHS

So far we have been trying to attack generalism internally, as we started attacking the doctrine of universalizability. In that case, as in this, the internal attack was inconclusive, and there we turned to consider the motivation that lay beneath the theory, to see whether we could undermine that.[12] Unfortunately, we cannot say that the motivation underlying Ross's generalism is unsatisfactory, but we can say that it is non-existent, which I take to be a greater defect.

Why does Ross suppose that there are general moral truths? Not because he supposes that these play some role in our moral decision-making. His theory, as we have seen, explicitly holds that they play no role at all. Why then suppose that there are any such? Ross simply takes it as obvious that there cannot be such a thing as a stubbornly particular reason. He supposes it metaphysically impossible for a property to make a difference here without making the same difference everywhere. But this is an independent input, and it appears completely unmotivated. Ross seems just not to have noticed the possibility that reasons are holistic.

It is not that there are no reasons that could be offered, but rather that for most people the truth of generalism is a datum which underlies other things, so that any argument they offer for it is likely to beg the question since they have not seen the availability of the opposing position.[13] Thomas Nagel is a good case in point here, particularly since his realist position can be seen as a successor to that of Ross. The reason he offers is that objectification and generalism go hand in hand. The drive to think of values as objective emerges in Nagel's work as a search for a special sort of ethical view, consisting of: (1) a set of moral principles, which (2) treat all persons as of equal importance, and (3) on which all can agree, whatever their point of view.[14]

However, Nagel's view here involves a series of mistakes about objectivity. For Nagel, this is a matter of degree. The most objective point of view is the one which abstracts from one's subjective view every element that derives from the peculiarities of one's perspective, leaving only elements comprehensible to (or visible from, to continue the metaphor) a point of view which has no peculiarities at all. This notion of objectivity, about which I will be saying a great deal more in chapter 9, certainly produces the third element in the list of three above. But it does not validate the other two. Nagel supposes that an objective moral view will consist of a set of principles (item 1) because his model of objectification is physics, which is a generalist model. But the concern of physics with the objective world and its generalism seem to me to be simply distinct. Physics has both; but this fact alone does not render it a suitable model for ethics in this respect. Equally, I see no reason in advance why a perfectly objective view might not hold that only two people in the world really matter – Charles and Di, say. If this claim were false, it would not be because objectivity rules it out; it is false for different reasons.[15]

Nagel's view here is an instance of the triad which I earlier claimed to be inconsistent; he is an internalist, a cognitivist and a generalist. What is more, he is a generalist of the most extreme degree imaginable. He writes: 'If I have a reason to take aspirin for a headache or to avoid hot stoves, it is not because of anything specific about those pains but because they are examples of pain, suffering and discomfort.'[16] All I want to say here is that it seems to me crazy to suppose that a position as extreme as this can be motivated by an appeal to physics. And anyway, why deny that what gives me a reason to take aspirin is the way my head is hurting *now*? It is true that any other headache would have been a reason too or instead. But why suppose that this fact shows that the nature of this particular headache cannot be the reason it seems to me to be? That I might have had a similar reason without this headache is nothing to the point, unless we distort the matter by saying contentiously that I might have had *the same* reason with a different headache. If this means merely that I might have had a reason equally good, I have no quarrel with it, but it does not take us any of the way towards Nagel's sort of generalism. If it means that I might have had *this* reason with a different headache, I think that it is false.

Even if Ross's generalism is based on a mere metaphysical assumption, and Nagel's on a mere mistake, there may still be a solid metaphysical ground for generalism of some sort to be found. But what might it be? One would have thought that the question whether reasons are holistic or not has few metaphysical trappings. Of course, there are mistakes to be made here, against which I have already tried to warn. They involve the supposition that supervenience can establish the existence of general truths in a quite uncontentious way. But once we recognize that mistake and avoid it, what else drives us from the particular to the general?

The only answer I know is that particular moral truths will always need an explanation, and that the explanation can only be given in terms of general moral truths.[17] In answer to this, I want to agree that every particular moral truth will need and have an explanation, but deny that the explanation has any need to be run in terms of general moral truths. The explanation will be given in terms of the properties from which the thin properties of rightness and wrongness result. This has no need to be generalized. But is there perhaps something else here to be explained and which can only be explained with the sort of appeal to the general that I am trying to avoid?

Two possibilities suggest themselves. The first is that the properties of rightness and wrongness themselves need an explanation. I accept that this is so, but deny that it need or could be given in the sort of general terms envisaged. In giving part of my own explanation of these properties, as I shall in chapter 7, I try to show that it *need* not. We can see that it *could* not because general moral truths are expressed in terms of those properties and so cannot be expected to explain them.

The second possibility is that the possibility of moral truth itself needs an explanation. This is probably true. One could even view this book as part of the attempt to offer such an explanation. But surely, whether it is true or not, we can hardly suppose that the possibility of moral truth could be explained by appeal to instances of moral truths, general or particular. There is just no room here for the resort to the general.

A weaker but still sufficient move would be to say that though the explanation (of whatever we see the need to explain) will not itself appeal to general moral truths, still it is impossible to run the explanation if one does not admit the existence of those truths. We shall see in chapter 9 another example of this idea – that something can be necessary for the success of an explanation without pulling its own weight in it. But is it applicable to the case in hand? All I can say here is that though such a move is possible, I cannot see a version that has any chance of succeeding.

Where does this leave us? I argued in this chapter that Ross's form of generalism, even in unfamiliar dress, failed to achieve the tasks it set itself. But I did not dispute those tasks, which seemed to me to be correctly conceived as what a theory of moral reasons should be trying to achieve. We do need to tell some story about contributory reasons and their relation to the eventual overall judgement, and we do have to show the rationality of regret for a defeated reason. So if I am going to be able to recommend particularism I need to be able to show that it does better in these respects. This is the task of the next two chapters. In doing this my general strategy is to derive as much light as possible from two metaphors, the metaphor of shape and that of salience.

NOTES

1   See Ross (1939), pp. 226–8.
2   I argue this in Dancy (1991a).
3   See Ross (1930), pp. 32–3. The method of paying careful attention to Ross's text seems to me not to have been much followed by his critics. There is more in Ross than is normally allowed; I have great respect for him as a moral theorist.
4   Ross followed the use of the term 'intuitive induction' that is found in W. E. Johnson's *Logic*: see Johnson (1921) vol. 2, ch. 8. Johnson wrote (p. 192): 'it is characteristic of the propositions established by means of intuitive induction that an accumulation of instances does not affect the rational certainty of such intuitive generalisations.' There is an Aristotelian background to this concept, of which Ross was of course well aware. He explains it this way in the introduction to his edition of *Aristotle's Prior and Posterior Analytics* (1949, p. 49): 'How do we come to know [the law of contradiction]? By seeing, Aristotle would say, that some particular subject B cannot both have and not have the attribute A, that some particular subject D cannot both have and not have the attribute C, and so on, until the truth of the corresponding general proposition dawns upon us.' As far as this goes, we might seem to have merely a rather strange instance of ordinary induction, concerned with the discovery of general necessary truths by induction from a sufficient number of particular ones. But Ross adds: 'The general principle, in such a case, being capable of being known directly on its own merits, the particular examples serve merely to direct our attention to the general principle; and for a person of sufficient intelligence one example may be enough' (1949, p. 49). This remark muddies the water considerably. First, it is not agreed by everyone that general principles discoverable by intuitive induction are knowable in some more direct way as well; even Ross denies this when he comes to apply the theory of intuitive induction to ethics. Second, the remark above seems internally inconsistent; it suggests, rather patronizingly, that for a person of sufficient intelligence one example may be sufficient immediately after saying that no example is necessary.
5   See Ross (1939), pp. 168–71.
6   Here Ross is taking the view expressed by Aristotle in his claim 'ἐν τῇ αἰσθήσει ἡ κρίσις' (*Nicomachean Ethics* 1109b23). The stress here is on judgement as opposed to subsumption. The appeal to subsumption, and its attendant respect for principles, is that it minimizes the role of judgement. Ross's theory puts the respect for principles in another place, which is what makes it interesting.
7   It is an interesting question, to which I do not have a worked-out answer, whether the theory of prima facie duties could be espoused by a non-cognitivist. My hunch is not; but at the moment I see no way of showing this.

8   See Ross (1930), p. 19.

9   For more elaborate criticisms and stage-setting, see Dancy (1983).

10   For an account of this theory, see Mackie (1973), ch. 5. Robert Gay first made this objection to my original discussion of Ross, in Dancy (1983); see Gay (1985).

11   This is the sort of point that led G. E. Moore to talk of organic wholes.

12   As I said then, my habit has been to try to dismantle generalism from within, while McDowell's has been to try to undermine it from without. However, all his published remarks relate to codifiability, and the Aristotelian argument that particular cases will always escape the codifier's attentions is powerless against Ross. One is left to speculate what argument he would think effective against Ross (if any).

13   This is the only explanation I can offer of Susan Hurley's insistence that the business of ethics is to come up with a theory, in the sense of a set of true principles; I think this thought could be subtracted from her work to great advantage. See Hurley (1985) and Williams (1988).

14   See Nagel (1986). The three elements I pick out emerge respectively in the following remarks: 'The search for generality is one of the main impulses in the construction of an objective view – in normative as in theoretical matters. One takes the particular case as an example, and forms hypotheses about what general truth it is an example of' (p. 152). 'From the objective standpoint, the fundamental thing leading to the recognition of agent-neutral reasons is a sense that no-one is more important than anyone else.' (p. 171). 'The detached, objective view takes in everything and provides a standpoint from which all choosers can agree about what should happen' (p. 183).

15   I make these claims in Dancy (1988a).

16   Nagel (1986), p. 158.

17   See Brown (forthcoming).

7

Conflict, dilemma, regret

1 DEFEATED REASONS

In chapter 6 I suggested, against a version of Ross's theory of prima facie duties, that it failed to allow for various possibilities and complexities for which one might wish to find room in the theory of reasons. The first of these was the phenomenon of silencing. The second was the tragic dilemma. The third was the fact that the value of the whole may sometimes be determined in more complex ways than by simply adding and subtracting the values of any parts. In a way these three points all amount to one charge, which is that Ross's theory, no matter how one writes it, fails to give a satisfying account of the relations possible between defeated and defeating reasons. The simplest point of this sort is just to claim that the role of defeated reasons is distorted by Ross despite his valiant efforts, which I am keen to acknowledge, to do better here than his predecessors managed. Now defeated reasons are the normal result of moral conflict, where we face reasons of some strength on both sides of a disputed question, and so the question becomes what sense can be made of moral conflict by the sort of theory of moral reasons that I have been beginning to outline.

In attempting a theory of moral conflict, we want to show the role of reasons which do not win the day. In particular, we want to show the rationality of regret in cases where reasons are defeated. This idea that there is a place for rational regret comes in two forms. The first is where we have reasons in favour of both of two alternatives A and B. Those in favour of A are the stronger, and we choose A; but we feel that there is something of value that this choice lacks. In the second form (which may not in the end be distinct from the first), we are set to do an action which we take to be overall the right thing to do in the circumstances, but which we recognize to have some regrettable features.

It is possible for a moral theory to have great difficulty in coping with these two phenomena. For instance, a theory which was too simply additive might find itself holding, in a case of the second sort, that the role of the regrettable features was to diminish the rightness of the action we are set to do. But once this diminishing has been taken into account, there is no further way in which we can see the action as regrettable for having those features. The negative tendency of the features, if one can call it that, has been entirely used up already by the way in which they render the action less right than it would otherwise have been. But this means that regret is out of place, since there is nothing to regret.

It has been suggested that views like mine are vulnerable to similar charges. The position I am trying to work out is a combination of three elements: internalism, cognitivism and particularism. It is the cognitivism which Bernard Williams attacks here, urging that:

> It seems to me a fundamental criticism of many ethical theories that their accounts of moral conflict and its resolution do not do justice to the facts of regret and related considerations: basically because they eliminate from the scene the *ought* that is not acted upon ... Such an approach must be inherent in purely cognitive accounts of the matter; since it is just a question of which of the conflicting *ought* statements is true, and they cannot both be true, to decide correctly for one of them must be to be rid of error with respect to the other – an occasion, if for any feelings, then for such feelings as relief (at escaping mistake), self-congratulation (for having got the right answer), or possibly self-criticism (for having been so nearly misled).[1]

Now, why cannot the conflicting *ought* statements both be true? Presumably because the claim 'I ought to do A and I ought not to do A' is incoherent. But why should it be thought incoherent? One possibility is that it can be reduced by various manoeuvres to the form 'p and not-p'. But I doubt that this contradiction is at the root of the problem. The difficulty seems to me to stem rather from something like the thought that in making this claim one has made two opposing choices or decisions: here there are two conflicting *oughts*, to choose one is to decide *which* one ought to do, and this claim makes *both* choices, incoherently. But this cannot be quite right. First, weakness of will shows there to be a gap between the acceptance of an *ought* and any choice or decision. Accepting an *ought* is coming to a decision of a sort, but it is a decision-that rather than a decision-to. The person in conflict has decided that he ought to do both (or rather each one severally), but he has not decided to do both or either, and has as yet made no choice.

For this to be possible it must be the case that the *oughts* he is concerned with are not comparative *oughts*. At this stage he is dealing with *oughts* that are practical without being comparative. Of course, there are comparative ought-statements too, as when one asks 'Which of these two ought I to do?' When we reach that stage, even though our answer is a decision-that rather than a choice, it would indeed be incoherent to decide that I ought to do this rather than that and that rather than this. This incoherence seems to me unpuzzling, however; it is like the incoherence of deciding that this is heavier than that and that is heavier than this. Of these comparative *oughts* it is true enough that 'since it is just a question of which of the conflicting *ought* statements is true, and they cannot both be true, to decide correctly for one of them must be to be rid of error with respect to the other.' But it seems to me clear enough that the defeated non-comparative *ought* can remain true. There is no sense of error here, for otherwise the reasons against (of which there will always be some) will vanish as we make our decision; that may happen in the special case of reasons that silence any opposition, but cannot be true as a general rule.

Ross tried to capture this in his theory of prima facie duties, as Williams acknowledges, but he failed to retain the defeated non-comparative *ought* in its full vigour. The general idea is that the defeated *ought* has made its contribution by diminishing the overall rightness of the action we in fact choose. That this is not sufficient as an account can be seen in Philippa Foot's excellent example of the dangerousness of picking up a snake.[2] It is dangerous to pick up a snake, but it may be more dangerous not to pick up this one. The dangerousness of not picking up this one is not reduced by the dangerousness of picking it up (as Ross's account would have it), and to pick it up remains dangerous though not so dangerous as not picking it up. Here the opposing reason retains its full force, even though overwhelmed in the particular case.

2 SALIENCE AND SHAPE

It is all very well simply to say that, once we distinguish between comparative and non-comparative *oughts*, the cognitivist is not committed to supposing that the defeated non-comparative *ought* should be thought of as false rather than true. To persuade ourselves that this is really so, we need to flesh out the cognitive account: to give a picture which shows how it can be that the practical relevance of a defeated reason remains undisturbed. To this end, I want to lay out how I see the activity of giving reasons. My account is in conscious opposition to any subsumptive theory, and aims to show that rationality should not be seen exclusively as the comparative choice of the best (most probable/most profitable) alternative available.

Some of the properties of a situation are relevant to the question what one should do, and some are not. And even among those which are relevant, some are more relevant than others. These relevant features are *salient*; they stick out or obtrude, and should catch our attention if we are alert.[3] Some are more salient than others. Salience is a practical notion here (it may not be so elsewhere). To see a feature as salient is to see it as making a difference to what one should do in the case before one. Since there are normally several different salient features, related to each other in various ways, a full view of the circumstances will not only see each feature for what it is but will also see how they are related to each other. Such a view will grasp the *shape* of the circumstances. From saliences we move to shape. A situation has a shape in the sense that its properties have a practically related profile. There are the properties which are here non-salient; they are as it were on the valley floor. Rising from that level are the various peaks, major or minor, which are the properties which make a practical difference to the case.

When we come to give a description of the situation, the various saliences (i.e. the shape of the situation) make a difference to how we should go about it. It is not as if it doesn't matter where we start among the myriad properties here present. There is a right and a wrong place to start – many wrong places, in fact. What we are doing is telling the story of the situation, and our narrative has to follow the shape that the situation has. By the time we have mentioned every salient property, we have said enough to show how we see the situation and hence the reasons we find here for the action we do. But we might yet need to continue, for on occasion the salient properties are only able to be salient because of the presence of certain background properties. This is the structural position I referred to in 3.5; the properties I am talking about here come in the second of the three groups there distinguished.

A good analogy for the case of the moral description of a situation is found in the aesthetic description of a building. Suppose that I want to explain to someone how I see a particular building; we are both standing in front of it. No description worth the name would simply start from the left, as it were, and work its way along until it reached the last feature on the right. First, this would not be a description but a list of properties, which is quite another thing. The properties do not have a flat profile in the way that a mere list of them would lead us to suppose. They have a shape which the order in which they are mentioned (the narrative structure of the description) is intended to reveal. So the sort of description I am talking about is a form of narrative, and it can have the vices and virtues of narrative; features can be mentioned in the wrong order, and important relations without which the story does not make sense can be omitted, distorted or misplaced. In the case of describing a building, one might start with that feature which one takes to be central to the building's architectural structure (which I distinguish from its physical structure). Perhaps this building should be seen as basically a flat rectangle, against which certain other features stand but to which they are complementary. So this is the way in which a description of it should start. There are going to be plenty of features of the building that don't get in to this description at all, and a lot more that only play the sort of secondary role referred to above.

It is common to distinguish any description of this sort from a quite different activity, that of arguing for one's way of seeing the situation (or the building). In part this is because of the view that, at least in the moral case, justification can only consist in the subsumption of this case under some general principle which commands rational support in some way or other. Since description is clearly not intended to achieve any such thing, description is one thing and justification another. I reject this account of justification, and with it the distinction between justification and description. To justify one's choice is to give the reasons one sees for making it, and to give those reasons is just to lay out how one sees the situation, starting in the right place and going on to display the various salient features in the right way; to do this is to fill in the moral horizon. In giving those reasons one is not *arguing* for one's way of seeing the situation. One is rather appealing to others to see it (as the building) the way one sees it oneself, and the appeal consists in laying out that way as persuasively as one can. The persuasiveness here is the persuasiveness of narrative: an internal coherence in the account which compels assent. We succeed in our aim when our story sounds right. Moral justification is therefore not subsumptive in nature, but narrative.

The father who tells his child not to take the flowers from the next door garden because that would be stealing should not be seen as subsuming this action under the general principle 'Stealing is wrong' (or perhaps 'Do not steal'), but rather as pointing to the most salient feature of the situation (that the flowers belong to somebody else), which in this case gives sufficient reason for the child not to do it. Even if the father were to add 'and stealing is wrong', this need not mean that there is any subsumption going on. Rather, as I suggested in chapter 4, he is reminding the child of the sort of importance the fact that one's action would be theft can have.

As an aside, I would like to point out that I try to make this book fit the theory I here propound. I argue against the opposition to particularism, but I hardly *argue* in favour of my own position in any way other than that of trying to lay out its more salient features. The underlying assumption is that if people do not agree with one's view of a situation, and if one is here in the right of it (which of course one may well not be), the best way to win them over is to show them in detail what that view is and rely on its persuasiveness to attract them, rather than trying to browbeat them with principles of rational choice or judgement. One's own view, if there is anything to be said for it, will appeal to rationality in a different sense. And there need not be anything else to be said for it; there need be no *argument* that can be relied on to drive people from the opposite camp into one's own. Rationality here is not to be seen as essentially related to the ability to construct or respond to arguments. It is more like the ability to listen to and appreciate a story.[4]

It is at this point that one can see the distance between the conception of rationality which I am trying to bring out and any conception which sees the operation of reason as essentially comparative. To take an example, a utilitarian conception of rational moral choice must, I think, see it as the activity of comparing the likely products of different alternative actions. The choice of an action is rational if this action promises more utility than others do. No action is rational in itself; there is no room in the theory for such an internal or intrinsic notion of rationality. The rationality of choice is rooted in comparison. On my view, by contrast, though we need not be suspicious of the comparative activities of reason, the central role of moral rationality is to find a view of the situation and the demands it creates whose structure is internally persuasive in the sort of way that a narrative can be. We can assess a narrative for internal coherence in a way that does not yet involve comparing that coherence with that of others, and indeed we could hardly run such a comparison if we could not discern independently the coherence of each action by itself.

The metaphors of shape and salience lie at the centre of my approach. Obviously I am hoping to use them to underpin an account of defeated reasons, or of conflict in general. Before making that attempt, however, I want to make three additions to what I have already said. First, to see a consideration as a reason to act is to see it as salient. This does not mean that it will necessarily be salient in the same way in other cases. A particularist will hold that the salience of a feature is a matter of context; alter the context and what was salient may cease to be so or begin to play a different role in the story which captures the action's overall shape. So salience is not supposed to be general salience.

Second, though reasons for acting are salient considerations, so are the reasons against. The salient features should not be thought of as lying all on one side of the question. This is going to be important when we come to see how it is that the reasons against the action remain in the picture as reasons against rather than being somehow deprived of that role once they are defeated.

Third, moral reasons are just ordinary considerations such as his distress or the loss to her self-respect. The wrongness of the action is not a reason for not doing it; reasons for not doing it are more mundane features. This is in keeping with the claim that telling someone, even with authority, that the action is wrong does not give her a reason to hold back. The reason for holding back is the same as the reason why the action is wrong, namely the damage you will do to your friend's prospects (or whatever).

This raises a question about the so-called thin moral properties of rightness and wrongness, goodness and badness.[5] There are two possible ways of accounting for them within the constraints of the picture I am trying to build up. The first is to see them as resultant properties, discernible independently of the properties from which they result though presumably more ordinarily discerned by seeing how they emerge from the resultance base. If there is such a thing as salience, these thin properties will always be the most salient ones. So the resultance tree emerges as a salience tree. This view is the one which makes people charge intuitionism with inventing such a property as 'to-be-doneness', a property which is somehow tacked onto an action as the label 'Eat Me' was tied onto the side of Alice's cake. Though there are some misconceptions in this charge, which largely derive from failing to take the notion of resultance seriously, there is still enough content in it to make me look hopefully to the other alternative. This is to hold that the thin moral properties are not further properties just like the others. Instead of taking the thin properties as the final level in the resultance tree, we are to see an action's being right or one which ought to be done as identical with the *shape* of the circumstances – what it is about them which calls for just this action. To see the action as required by the circumstances is to see the situation as having a certain shape. To say this we do not need to abandon resultance. We just get a different picture of the resultance tree. The thin property results from (exists in virtue of) the properties that are salient here without being among those properties itself.

Here we are trying to tread a difficult path between saying that the thin property is distinct from the thicker ones from which it results, and saying that it is somehow identical with them (a non-naturalistic form of reductionism). The notion of shape enables us to do this. The shape which the thick properties adopt is not exactly distinct from them there, but it is not quite identical with them either. We could perhaps express this intermediate position by saying that the thin property is *constituted* by the shape of the thick ones in this case, in the sort of way that we began to speak in chapter 5. The idea of constitution is designed to give us the advantages of a token identity theory, though it should be remembered that the identity is between the *shape* of the resultance base and the thin moral property, not between the thick and the thin properties. It is a token identity theory rather than a type identity theory because the whole story is intended to be an expression of a particularist account of moral reasons.

3   DEFEATED REASONS AGAIN

I now turn back to the question what account we can give of defeated reasons. The problem is to show how it is that such reasons retain their full force in defeat. This problem arises whether the defeat is an easy one or not; there need be no real *conflict* at issue. Cases of genuine conflict raise problems of their own, which we shall consider later. What happens to defeated reasons-against on the picture I have been building up? Remember that one's conception of a situation shows it as having perfectly ordinary properties, but shows them in a certain shape. As far as this goes, the properties that are reasons against are present in the picture along with the rest. Of course, if they are less prominent than the reasons in favour, this is only to be expected; for we are talking about a case in which, though there are reasons against, they are dominated by the reasons in favour. But it is not to be thought that once we see the action as having a shape in which those reasons dominate these ones, somehow these ones are expunged from the picture altogether. They remain and retain their practical relevance. This can be seen from the fact that though they do not persuade us to refrain from the action, they may yet affect the way we do it. It is not as if the action is somehow given, the only question being whether to do it or not. The roles that reasons can play are more varied than that. For instance, I have to break some bad news to my sister. The distress I shall cause her is not sufficient reason for me to keep silent; as a reason against, it is defeated. But it still makes a difference to how I should break the news to her, when and where I should do it and so on. So it remains in the picture as a practically relevant consideration, even though it does not count among those features of the action which reveal why I do it. It is not a reason for doing it, but it is a reason for doing it this way rather than that.

As the reasons against grow in strength, we approach a situation in which there are two total views of the action, in one of which the reasons in favour are the most salient, in the other of which the reasons against stand out the more. No feature is expunged from either picture; there is no dispute about the facts, in this sense, but only about their shape. One picture has the facts in one shape, and the other has them in another. In choosing between these, the question is which picture is the more compelling. I see this question as analogous to the question which *narrative* is the more compelling. The two narratives are in conflict with each other, because though one can consider the situation as having either, one cannot take it actually to have both.

In a case where the reasons against are comparatively weak, it may be hardly possible to build up a picture which sees those reasons as the most salient features of the situation. But there must be at least the prospect of this. In a way, one can consider variations of the present situation in which these features occur, with others, as part of a picture which reveals the action as wrong. Or one can suppose that if this feature were present to a greater degree, it would be enough to persuade one not to do the action at all. The danger here is to avoid saying *merely* that the feature would make a difference in different circumstances, because this is close to an admission that it does not in fact make a difference here (where it is defeated).

This is the way in which I want to express the fact that in conflict, or more generally where there are defeated reasons, there is conflict between truths which retain a practical relevance even in defeat. How does this fare as a response to Williams' charge that cognitivist theories 'eliminate from the scene the *ought* that is not acted upon'? Those features which are reasons against do remain in the picture in the light of which one acts, and there is no reason to think that they have therefore somehow been turned into reasons in favour. The rightness of the action is parti-resultant – it exists in virtue of some among its features rather than in virtue of all, even though there are various different ways in which properties can make a difference. So not all remaining properties need be reasons in favour.

It is time for an example which will help us to see what is being claimed here, and will also help to assess the justice of Williams' charge; it is a case where I am deliberating what to do. Suppose that I am driving to the station to pick up my wife. It is 10.30 at night, and I am rather late. Would I be justified in breaking the speed limit? The station is not a very salubrious place for unaccompanied women at this time of night, I am awake, sober and alert, the street lighting is good, my car is in good condition and I know the road well. All these are considerations which incline me to think that the right course would be to break the law. But on the other side is the fact that in England at that time of night the pubs are closing and all manner of unsteady persons are coming out onto the streets, some of whom will no doubt be intending to drive home, making the roads much less safe than they would have been half an hour ago. What should I do?

I see myself as torn between two complete ways of seeing the situation. These two ways are not in conflict about any matter of fact, nor even on which considerations are practically relevant here. (A different example might differ on this point.) The only question for me is which matter more. On one view, my wife's isolation and the time of night stand out as the most prominent (salient) features; on the other, the probability of finding a drunk on the road dominates. I have to choose between these, and in making that choice I am coming to see that situation as having one shape rather than another.

It is worth stressing that the reasons against are not expunged from my overall picture. Suppose that I see my wife's isolation as the most prominent feature, and in the light of that accept that I ought to break the law this time. The incidence of drunks remains in the picture, and still matters. If there is an alternative route which, being slightly longer, will mean that I arrive slightly later but which does not take me through the city centre where most of the pubs are, I should perhaps take that.

We might now be able to resuscitate Williams' complaint against cognitivism's ability to account for defeated reasons. We originally wanted to say that the fact that the pubs close at 10.30 is a reason for keeping to the speed limit. But this feature of the situation only stands as *that* reason in a view of the situation which we have rejected. In the view we accept, it is merely a reason to take a less direct route to the station. As such a reason it is not defeated at all. So the feature which generates a defeated reason is not present as such in our actual view of the situation at all. Conceived as a defeated reason, it has to be thought of as an error, for it counts as that reason only if one misreads the situation as a whole.

Is this a problem? I think we should admit that this is the way we see the matter, but insist that we have not therefore distorted the role of defeated reasons. The fact that there are drunks around is the reason it is because of what other reasons are present with it. Its status as a reason, and the nature of the reason it is, derive from the difference it makes to how one should act in the circumstances. (Note the insidious presence of particularism.) Here, therefore, it is only a reason to take a less direct route, not a reason to stick to the speed limit. But in another sense it is a reason to stick to the limit, that is, in the sense that there is a reasonably persuasive picture of the situation in which this is a prominent feature, and in which it is functioning as a reason not to go above the limit.

The behaviour of this reason can be contrasted with that of the pain which I cause myself when shaving in the morning. This pain is only mild. Should we say that it is present as a reason not to shave? As things are, the difference it makes to my actions is that I shave more carefully. There is no remotely persuasive picture of the situation in which this pain is present as a prominent feature in a total view which justifies my not shaving. So this pain is not a reason not to shave, but in a sense the drunks are a reason not to exceed the speed limit.

The only remaining question, I think, is whether those defeated features are present as *oughts*. In raising his question, Williams assumes that this is what needs to be shown if one wants to capture the role of defeated reasons, and in my initial response to him I followed that assumption, answering in terms of a distinction between comparative and non-comparative *oughts*. But it now seems implausible to suppose that the defeated reasons remain present as *oughts*; instead they remain as *reasons*. On the picture I have ended up with there really seems, at least where the reasons against are weak, to be only one *ought*, which attaches itself to and emerges from the most persuasive story one can tell about the circumstances. Where the reasons against are strong, so that we can be said to face a genuine conflict, we might say that there are two potential *oughts*, since we have two pictures, on one of which we ought to act and on the other of which we ought not. These *oughts* are not to be identified with the successful reasons in favour or against. They rather express the growing sense that the picture concerned is persuasive. And in ordinary cases of conflict only one of them can be admitted, in the final decision. So in ridding oneself of the claims of one, one is ridding oneself of error; for one is rejecting the claim of one picture to be the right way of seeing the situation. But one is not in error in supposing that the features salient in the defeated picture are salient, since they will be salient also in the defeating picture. So those features, as I said, remain as reasons but not quite as *oughts*. So in a sense I claim both to have answered Williams' question and to have rejected the terms in which it was posed.

4 THE RATIONALITY OF REGRET

One of the ways in which Williams pressed his question was to ask whether cognitivism could show the rationality of regret. I need to show how the response already given succeeds here too, but it is wise first to ask what the phenomenon of regret is supposed to be. My general view here is that ordinary notions of regret are not quite what is at issue; rather 'regret' is a technical term for a proper attitude towards defeated reasons. The sort of regret we are talking about now is not the wish that one was not forced to make this choice, since it is in place even when one welcomes the need to choose. Nor is it a sense of compassion for the person who loses because of our choice, since there need be no such sense. Nor is it the wish that one had made the other choice ('regretting the choice one made'), since again there need be no such evidence of second thoughts. Nor is it to be identified with the creation of residual duties, as where by failing to keep my promise I create the duty to apologise as soon as I may. The regret concerned is rather an attitude to a feature that *explains* the creation of residual duties – that is the source of those duties. As such an attitude, it would not be sufficient to say that it is a certain sort of feeling; even if there is a feeling involved (which there sometimes isn't), the nature of the feeling (its phenomenology) is not what we are after here, since that explains nothing. What we have in mind rather is the sense that though one indeed made the right choice, still either there was something of value which this choice lacked and another alternative did not lack, or there was something of disvalue which this choice had and another alternative lacked. Whether this sense is ever, often, sometimes or even merely here accompanied by any feeling is not of importance. And in fact the sense concerned seems to me not to be what we normally refer to as regret, which is why I suggest that 'regret' here is functioning as a technical term.

If this is what regret is to be, what is required for us to show such a sense to be a rational response to one's own choice? Presumably what is needed is to show that it can be true, even though one made the right choice, either that there was something of value which this choice lacked and another alternative did not lack, or that there was something of disvalue which this choice had and another alternative lacked. If this can be true, and is true in the present case, then a sense that it is true – which we are calling regret – is surely a rational response to the situation. To show that this can be true, we need to say more about *lacks*, since it is the notion of a lack that is the pivot on which all this turns.

In discussing lacks it is common to distinguish between monism and pluralism in the theory of value.[6] Suppose that there were only one sort of value – a view often imputed to classical utilitarianism. Then actions could only be compared and assessed by reference to how much of that value they produced. An action which one was right to choose must be the one which of all available alternatives produced the most of that value. But such an action could not lack anything, by comparison with those alternatives. There being only one sort of value, anything good they had, it must have and more; otherwise it would not have been right to choose it in the first place. So monism of this sort can make no sense of lacks, and hence can make no sense of regret. Pluralism, on the other hand, which asserts the existence of irreducibly many forms of value, is all that is necessary if one is to make sense of lacks and therefore of regret.

There is much that is right here, but this position suffers from the fact that the distinction between monism and pluralism is not very sharp. We can see the problem by asking whether fully ordered vector theory is a form of monism. Samuel Guttenplan expresses cautiously the view that it is:

> It is not an unfamiliar thought that the values (moral or otherwise) we attach to things are, in some sense, incommensurable. Indeed some would think that only monistic prejudice supports the idea that claims such as [A is more valuable than B] are, in every circumstance of choice, true or false and, hence, that our values can be, in principle, completely ordered. Rejection of such an account is what ... pluralism ... consists in.[7]

The suggestion here is that full ordering, which amounts to the claim that in every case of choice the values between which one is choosing are either greater or less than each other or equal, is something which only a monist would accept. But this seems to me to be false. Fully ordered vector theory can be pluralist in the admission of many irreducibly different goods, and yet retain its insistence that of any two parcels of such goods either one exceeds the other or they are equal. There is a gap between monism and the sort of incommensurability that Guttenplan is talking about. What is more, that sort of incommensurability is the weakest sort I know. It amounts to saying that if there is no fact of the matter about whether the value of this exceeds the value of that, the values concerned are incommensurable. The problem with this is that any monist impressed with the phenomenon of vagueness will find himself committed to incommensurability of this sort.

There is a second form of incommensurability, which I find in the work of David Wiggins that Guttenplan was writing about.[8] Wiggins suggests that the mark of this sort of incommensurability is the combination of pluralism and the lack of compensation in kind. One might even say that for Wiggins one is not a genuine pluralist unless one accepts the lack of compensation in kind. What this means is that monists such as hedonists might accept that there are different sources of value (pleasure), but the mark of their monism will be that they suppose that a loss of value derived from one source can always be compensated by an increase of value from another source, since it is value of the same sort always. So here, if there is compensation, it is compensation in kind. A pluralist, on the other hand, holding that there are just irreducibly different sorts of value, will hold that the loss of one cannot be compensated in kind by an increase in another. Wiggins takes it that to accept this sort of incommensurability is to reject the vector theory of practical rationality, presuming that interesting pluralists are those committed to this sort of incommensurability. But again that does not seem to me to be so. Suppose that I look for wine, women and song in a holiday resort. I am a pluralist, and do not take it that these different values are in fact covert forms of the same value. I am considering taking a holiday with a comparative lack of wine but plenty of women and song (a teetotal form of Club Med. Choral Tour). I take the lack of wine to be compensated by a great deal of song. Here we have a lack which is compensated, but not compensated *in kind*. Surely the mere fact that the value of song is not the same as the value of wine does nothing to show that an increase in one cannot compensate for a decrease in the other. And what this shows is that the notion of a lack of compensation in kind is not definitive of any interesting notion of incommensurability. A fully ordered vector space has no incommensurability but lacks compensation in kind.[9]

The really interesting notion of incommensurability (and the really contentious one) is the sort that Joseph Raz defines as a case where there are two states of affairs such that neither is more valuable than the other, but they are not of equal value either.[10] Here there is no truth value gap, since all the relevant claims come out false. But at least we have reached a theory which is clearly at odds with fully ordered vector theory. It appeals to the most extreme of our forms of incommensurability, and introduces a genuinely partial ordering.

The question now becomes how far we have to move from simple monism and full commensurability if we want to make room for the sort of lacks required to make regret rational. The answer is the one suggested earlier, that even vector theory is perfectly able to show the rationality of regret, in the sense given earlier. To continue with the previous example, why should I not regret the comparative lack of wine (in that sense)? Obviously, I take it to be compensated, since I do not regret my choice; but I can still recognize what in any case is true, namely that there is something of value which this choice lacks and of which another choice would have had more. What this shows is that the question whether the vector space is fully ordered or not is not relevant to the question whether good sense can be made of regret.

It is possible to pursue the question whether a fully ordered vector theory is truly pluralist. If one does this, one is moving towards the view that the only true form of pluralism is one which denies full ordering. But the rationality of regret is established without appeal either to pluralism of this strong sort or to the attendant strong notion of incommensurability.

There are two aspects of regret: regret for an element of value which our choice lacks, and regret for an element of disvalue which our choice has. The second of these is shown to be rational, within the constraints of our approach, by the fact that the reasons against remain in the picture as salient features of the situation. The first is shown to be rational by the adoption of a form of pluralism which is committed only to Wiggins' intermediate form of incommensurability.

5 STRONG INCOMMENSURABILITY

To make sense of regret, then, we do not need to go so far as to admit the possibility of strong incommensurability. But the question naturally arises whether my approach does make room for incommensurability of this sort. For the remainder of this chapter I argue that it does. Of course, the suggestion is that this is a strength.

The interest of this matter is that with strong incommensurability of this sort we show the possibility of a tragic dilemma. Tragic dilemmas are those in which the agent has to choose between two actions, both of which are right in a way that makes it wrong to be indifferent which one is chosen. Normal dilemmas are those where the value of each choice is more or less the same as that of the other (this is perhaps what is meant by conflict), so that one is in the right whichever choice one makes. In this sense indifference is the rational response, though the sort of indifference at issue must be one compatible with sharp regret at having lost the value available in the other choice. In tragic dilemmas, by contrast, whichever choice one makes one does a wrong. This is because one's failure to make the first choice cannot be compensated (at all, let alone in kind) by one's having made the other. The question is whether there can be such cases.

The first thing to sort out is the sort of indifference at issue here. As I said, given the pluralist claim that there are irreducibly many goods, even in ordinary cases where the values are equal (but different) it would be irrational to be indifferent to the choice before one in the sense of not minding the loss of the value available to the choice one didn't make. So those pluralists who deny the possibility of strong incommensurability can deny that all choices between equal goods are proper objects of indifference. But we might suggest that the choice is indifferent in another sense, meaning that, where reasons have given out, it can be rational to decide by tossing a coin. One need not be indifferent to the result, but one may adopt this indifferent method of reaching it. None of this yet requires strong incommensurability; the whole story has been told within full ordering.

What is needed is a way of distinguishing this sort of choice between equal goods from cases of conflict where tossing a coin is not a rational method of reaching a decision. I think that the metaphors of shape and salience give us a way of doing this. We supposed that situations have a shape, and the shape of a situation reveals what action it calls for. In a case of conflict there are two ways of seeing the situation, one of which calls for one action and the other for the other. There are occasions, however, when one picture can be superimposed on the other, resulting in a single picture which shows the reasons in favour and those against (or those in favour of one action and those in favour of another) as equally salient. Indifference is justified in such a case because it is the same picture both times. But there are other occasions where this cannot be done, because the salience of one set of features is at odds with that of the other. There is competition for salience. This crucial difference means that there is now no picture that recommends the tossing of coins as a method of resolving a decision-making blockage. We can see this clearly in cases of the most extreme sort. To take the classic Sartrean example, from the point of view of national survival in the face of the Nazi threat, comforting one's ailing mother cannot be all that important. But from the point of view of family love, national duties pale into insignificance.

In the most extreme such cases, the dilemma is what it is because it involves the question what sort of a person one will be.[11] In the case of indifference nothing else in the picture changes when I look at the situation from the point of view of the person who is going to do the other action. In the tragic case, many things change. This makes more sense of the idea that in making my choice I am deciding who to be. For a choice of this magnitude, it would *clearly* be inappropriate to toss a coin as if it doesn't matter who one becomes, even though in a sense all reasons are already exhausted and no reason is able to count twice. What the reasons have done is to lay out for you *what* choice faces you.

But this does not mean that only existential choices involve tragic dilemmas. The structure of a tragic dilemma was merely that in some sense, whatever one does, one does a wrong; this is to be contrasted with ordinary choice between equally good alternatives, where whichever one chooses one is not doing a wrong. Existential cases are ones in which it is especially obvious why there is something at issue between the two choices that renders tossing a coin an inappropriate response to the exigencies of the situation. But more ordinary cases may still contain dilemmas that are tragic in the sense defined, so long as there is competition for salience. Here there is no one picture which captures the equality of the goods available.

Of course, just as in the ordinary cases the conflict exists between truths, so for there to be tragic dilemmas both pictures must in some sense be true. It would not be attractive to suggest that if you do not see the situation aright, you may find oneself in a dilemma which has you in its grips but does not really exist. This would have it that the whole idea of a tragic dilemma is a problem in moral epistemology, and some of the duties at odds in the case are bound to be only subjective (in the sense that you take them to be there, but they aren't). And this brings out the real interest in the notion of a tragic dilemma. It has it that the world may be morally nasty, not just that you may be unable to sort the matter out.[12] And for this to be true there must be opposing demands, in the face of which indifference, in the technical sense, is not an appropriate response.

So for there to be tragic dilemmas, it must be possible for the various features of the situation to have more than one shape at once. It seems hard to suppose that anything can have two shapes at once. My talk of shape makes this seem more outlandish than it really is, however. We should remember that the shape of a situation is conceived of as its practical relevance; it is the demands it places on action. In tragic cases the situation speaks with two voices. And in these cases we have the strongest sense in which reasons on the other side do not go away. They stay there, shouting loudly.

NOTES

1   This is from his 'Ethical Consistency', pp. 166–86 of Williams (1973), at p. 175. This paper is reprinted in Gowans (1987).
2   See Foot (1983).

3   I first found the notion of salience put to this sort of use in David Wiggins'
    papers on Aristotle's theory of action; see Wiggins (1976a) and (1979).
4   In all this I am very heavily influenced by John McDowell. See McDowell
    (1979) and (forthcoming).
5   I think that the idea of thin properties comes first in Wiggins (1976b); it
    is elaborated in Williams (1985), esp. chs 8–9. Thick properties are so
    called because they have more empirical content than the thin ones have.
    Generousness is a thick property; if you know that an action is generous,
    you know more about what it is like than if you merely know that it is
    good. The distinction between thick and thin properties is important to
    these two writers, because in their different ways they want to be more
    cognitivist (or realist) about the thick properties than they are about the
    thin ones.
6   See e.g. Stocker (1990).
7   Guttenplan (1979/80), p. 71.
8   Wiggins (1979).
9   David Gauthier helped me to see this.
10 See Raz (1986), ch. 11.
11 Here I take myself to be following the general lines of the discussion in Raz
    (1986).
12 This idea is expressed very forcibly by Thomas Nagel. See his 'War and
    Massacre' in Nagel (1979), pp. 53–74, esp. p. 74; this paper is reprinted
    in Scheffler (1988a). However, despite my general agreement with the thrust
    of his remarks there, I think that his more theoretical views on incommen-
    surability are heavily exaggerated. For a discussion, see Appendix III.

8
Supererogation

1 SHAPES AND THE SUPEREROGATORY

The idea that some actions are supererogatory raises awkward difficulties for the metaphor of shapes. Supererogatory acts are those which lie
'above and beyond the call of duty'. Such acts characteristically enjoy
a very high degree of value, probably more value than any other act
available to the agent. But in thinking of them as supererogatory, we
are thinking of them as actions which it is not wrong of the agent not
to do. The puzzle about supererogation is how there can be such acts
as these.

As I have expressed it so far, the concept of supererogation involves
a contrast between duty and value, suggesting to us that duty can give
out where value persists and grows. But in fact this is too narrow a
perspective on the problem. We should not focus too directly on the
notion of duty, since there may be actions which one *ought* to do but
which can not exactly be said to be one's *duty*. In saying that the agent
is not wrong not to do such an action, we are leaving behind the notion
of duty and working with a more general contrast between an action
which ought to be done and one which has value. This is a contrast
between the deontic and the evaluative properties of an action. Properties such as goodness, badness and evil are evaluative properties;
properties such as rightness and wrongness, and also that of being what
one ought to do, are deontic. Normally we would think that, as value
rises, the change in degree of evaluative property is attended by a change
in degree of deontic property; the more good one's action would do,
the more one ought to choose it in preference to others. But if there
are supererogatory actions, there can come a point where the value rises
while it becomes less rather than more true that one ought to do the
action.

This already seems peculiar, but my first concern is that the metaphor of shape appears to rule it out completely. Both evaluative and deontic properties are *thin* properties, in the sense discussed in chapter 7. When I first considered the notion of a thin property, I ended by identifying a thin property with the shape in which the thicker properties of the case presented themselves. But now we see that there are two different sorts of thin properties, the evaluative and the deontic, that the same situation can generate one of each sort (by both calling for a certain action and permitting one not to do it), and that the two can vary apparently independently. This places pressure on the notion of shape, because I seem now to be committed to holding that one situation can have more than one *sort* of shape at the same time. This looks very awkward, and the question is what to do about it.

2   DEONTIC AND EVALUATIVE PROPERTIES

Supererogation is not just a problem for me, of course. Everyone has to decide whether they want to make room for supererogatory actions in their moral theory, and many end by denying the possibility of such a thing, as we shall see. This is partly because the notion of supererogation involves something quite considerable in the way of a paradox. If we are not careful, it drives too much of a wedge between the evaluative and the deontic.

Contemporary interest in the supererogatory derives from the work of J. O. Urmson.[1] In his paper 'Saints and Heroes', Urmson starts from the traditional map:

> wrong – permissible – required.

He argues that this map is defective because it leaves no room for the idea of the supererogatory or saintly action. But he was not intending to say merely that the map should be extended in the following way:

> wrong – permissible – required – saintly.

Rather his intention was to undermine the map altogether, conceived as a general map of the moral terrain. The original map may be adequate for the deontic properties (though I think he would be chary of admitting even that). But it simply assumes that the evaluative ones go with the deontic ones, in this sort of way:

> wrong – permissible – required
> negative value –/– positive value.

This is the assumption that Urmson was really after. The suggestion he wanted to pursue was that the deontic and the evaluative vary completely independently so that

(1) an action which has no value can have a deontic property, and

(2) an action that has value can still lack deontic properties.

If I were to promise to perform some trivial action such as retying my shoelaces, this valueless act would acquire a deontic property; this is an example of an act with deontic but no evaluative properties. If a recruit were to throw himself on a grenade to save the lives of the rest of the platoon, this is an act with highest value, but no deontic property; there is no sense in which the recruit ought to have done it, for he would not have been wrong not to do it.

Urmson's general point was that traditional moral theories made no room for the discrepancy between evaluative and deontic properties, but for the present it is sufficient to see that the sorts of considerations he advances tend to separate the two sorts of properties in an unexpected way. Given this separation, we should look for an account of how there can be these two distinct forms of moral properties, and the answer that suggests itself is that the deontic properties are action-guiding while the evaluative ones are not. The evaluative properties concern the existence of value in the world, and the deontic ones concern what we should do to change things. This suggestion does not sit very happily with Urmson's own view that the theory in the best position to assimilate all the facts he wants to bring out is utilitarianism. But it none the less seems like the obvious place to start.

We can, however, accept that the evaluative properties are in a weak sense not action-guiding without accepting either (1) or (2) above. H. A. Prichard argued that an action can be good without there being anyone who ought to do it.[2] His reason for this was that the deontic properties require some special relation between action and agent. Another way of putting the point is that while actions can have evaluative properties in themselves, the deontic properties consist in a relation between action and agent. There are no events (even actions) that ought to happen. We cannot reasonably say 'Her being helped by me ought to happen'; the clearest expression is simply 'I ought to help her', which expresses my recognition that the shape of the situation, together with some special relation in which I stand, constitutes sufficient reason for me to help her.

For all this to be true, the special relation need not be anything very extraordinary. It could be simply that of opportunity. If it were, we would have the plausible result that if a change would have high value, anyone with the opportunity should bring it about. But if this is the sort of picture we end up with, we have not established anything like the radical independence of the deontic from the evaluative that Urmson thought he was moving towards. We have it that the evaluative properties are distinct in their role (their logical nature) from the deontic ones, but we do not have it that (1) an action which has no value can have a deontic property, and we only accept (2) that an action can have value but no deontic property in a very weak sense (for instance, where there is nobody with the opportunity to do it).

On this restricted picture we have not moved very far from Urmson's position, but we already find ourselves denying the possibility of supererogation. If supererogation requires the truth of (1) and (2), we have no room for it. Though the evaluative properties are distinct from the deontic ones, there is still a general structural relation between them. The deontic ones result from the combination of value and special relation.

As I have presented the matter so far, we have been forced to choose between two implausibilities. The first is that deontic and evaluative properties are entirely independent of each other; the second is that there are no supererogatory actions. One way to escape would be to argue that Urmson has exaggerated the extent to which the deontic and the evaluative must be able to vary independently if there is to be room for the supererogatory. But for the moment it looks as if the account we have given of the very separateness of the deontic and the evaluative leads directly to denying the possibility of supererogation.

Is it so obvious that we should make room for supererogation? The main argument that we need to do this, other than general thoughts about the difference between the evaluative and the deontic, consists in appeal to examples like that of the recruit who throws himself on the grenade. We do want to say that though the action is supremely good, he had no duty to do it and would not have been wrong to have held back, even though all would have died. Should we admit that his action was right? I think Urmson would say we should accept this if it means no more than that it was the action with the highest value, but not if it means that it was one he could be called on to do. This retains the insistence that there is no deontic property at play here.

A common move at this point is to say that the action (*qua* supererogatory) is optional and viewed as such by the agent, and that this fact serves to increase its value but could never make it wrong of the agent not to do the action. Unfortunately, this will not work. First, a supererogatory action must have high value *apart* from that derived from its optionality. Second, a supererogatory act which its agent takes to be duty still has the same high value, and on some accounts is even more valuable. Third, non-supererogatory actions that are duties gain value if their agents see them (wrongly) as optional, i.e. as not being duties but still worth doing for all that.[3]

Failing this we might be driven to deny room for supererogation because we simply cannot see how very great value can fail to create a requirement to act where there is opportunity. This is the so-called 'good-ought tie-up'; it is a philosophical boggle. If we are gripped by this boggle, we are taking it that the only way to deny (2) is to abandon the supererogatory altogether. If we deny (2), our only account of super-erogation seems to be one under which less than perfect actions are wrong but not reprehensible; failure to perform the supererogatory act is a 'wrong excused'. I call this position 'weak supererogationism'. It is distinctly unsatisfactory as a position, since it is naturally implausible. I think it one of the positions of which Aristotle would say that nobody would hold it except as the result of a theory.[4] But it has appeared that we have no intermediate space to occupy. So far as we have yet seen, the choice is between Urmson's too extreme claim that there are no relations at all between the deontic and the evaluative, and the implaus-ibilities of weak supererogationism. The only way we have found of giving a general account of the relation between deontic and evaluative properties has led to the denial of supererogation.[5]

3   THREE ACCOUNTS OF SUPEREROGATION

This is an unsatisfying result. So I now turn to consider three recent accounts of supererogation to see if we can derive any help from them. The first of these is found in Thomas Nagel's *The View from Nowhere* (1986).

Nagel

Nagel's view here is that the matrix of objective reasons would indeed create unreasonable demands on beings with human motivations. He suggests therefore that the impartial standpoint, from which all moral matters are best perceived, permits in each of us a degree of partiality. There is, as it were, a dispensation in recognition of human frailty. We should not think of this as subjective reasons disputing with objective ones. If it were that, and the subjective ones were allowed to predominate, this would make the supererogatory action *wrong*. In fact it is merely not required of us, and this leaves us room to praise the saint or hero for acting according to the strength of the reasons, without ourselves being blamed when we fail to do so. Nagel writes:

> those who undertake [the supererogatory action] nonetheless are praiseworthy for submitting themselves to the true strength of the reasons which they could not be required to follow strictly, given the mixed character of human motives.[6]

Moral demands then are reasons or values which would generate requirements but for the fact that the requirements are relaxed through what Nagel calls 'objective tolerance'. (This is by no means the only place for the notion of tolerance in this area.) And yet the reasons are as strong as they ever were. If we wanted to be unkind, we could say that they are requirements which we are not required to perform.

I see no way of escaping the conclusion that this is weak supererogationism trying to disguise itself: a sheep in wolf's clothing. It amounts, in my view, to an indirect admission that the failure to sacrifice oneself is a wrong (since it is forbidden by the available reasons, properly conceived), but a wrong that is venial.

This becomes clearer when we consider the very different answer Nagel gives to the question whether one can be justified in actions derived from reasons of autonomy which do not serve to maximize the objective good. Reasons of autonomy are those which give us the right to adopt or pursue expensive hobbies, or to spend our time, energy and money on family and friends which could be 'better' spent on famine relief. Here Nagel wants to say that there is a genuine battle of reasons taking place; the players are reasons of autonomy on one side (these are 'agent-relative')[7] and the 'agent-neutral' reasons of beneficence on the other. In this battle, the agent-relative reasons, which are still in some sense objective, since they can be recognized by the objective will, can be the stronger and so justify pursuit of one's own project at the expense of the general good.

This time Nagel's answer is in a quite different sort of trouble, that of saying why we should still approve of people who put aside their own projects in recognition of the demands of the objective good. For the justification for pursuing one's own projects was that the reasons predominate on that side. How then can it be allowable to put aside those projects and ignore the agent-relative reasons that defeat the agent-neutral ones on the other side? We cannot say that putting aside one's projects is itself one of one's projects, or that we all, as moral agents, have the project of maximizing the objective good. For these moves involve seeing as agent-relative a value which is surely agent-neutral: the value of self-denial. And nothing in what Nagel says serves to persuade us that agent-relative reasons are somehow optional, so that we can respect them or ignore them as we choose. Initially we feel that if the reasons are there, they need to be respected. No sense has yet been given to the thought that there are some reasons which we have a right to ignore – reasons which in Kagan's pleasing term, are 'non-insistent'.[8]

Raz

So I turn to the views of a strong supererogationist, Joseph Raz.[9] Raz wants to accept the existence of a structural relation between the deontic and the evaluative. He agrees that deontic properties result from evaluative ones, so that if the heroic action is genuinely the one best supported by the reasons, it will be the one which you ought to do. He tries to tell the whole story within the confines of this approach, that is, within the space of reasons. Note the contrast here with Nagel, who appeals to objective tolerance to justify departing from the action recommended by the balance of reasons.

Raz's position has an interesting structure. He suggests that there are what he calls 'exclusionary' reasons. These are higher-level reasons which justify one's failing to act on the balance of the lower-level reasons. The lower-level reasons are not silenced by this. They continue to exist as reasons in full force, which is why it is very good to act in accordance with them. But the existence of suitable exclusionary reasons permits one not to act in this self-sacrificing way.

One needs an example to see the full force of this idea. Raz suggests that an exclusionary reason can be created when someone permits you to act in a way that will damage her interests. In such a case, you still have a reason to respect her interests – the normal reason – but you are entitled to ignore it. In a similar way, the sacrifice of oneself may be an exclusionary reason which justifies you in ignoring the benefit to others which the sacrifice would achieve. So Raz is here attempting to provide exactly what Nagel's account of reasons of autonomy lacked; but he is discussing supererogation, not reasons of autonomy.

Something like Raz's picture is the only possibility if we accept that the best action (i.e. the one which leaves the world best off) is the one with the strongest claim on us, and continue (unlike Nagel) to look within the space of reasons for an account of supererogation. It is the idea of levels that is doing the work, with reasons of one sort not

silencing but allowing us to ignore reasons of another sort. But is it
coherent as an answer to the problem of supererogation? It seems to me
that it simply fails to address that problem directly. At best, Raz has
shown that there is formal room for something with some of the features of strong supererogation. To drive the analysis home, we should
ask what the reason could be that permits me to ignore the claims of
the action for which the lower-level reasons are strongest? It must be
something like 'This is very demanding.' This reason is seen as a general
exclusionary reason, so that when lower-level reasons reach the level of
being very demanding one is permitted to ignore them, though reasons
that are just below that level are ones which one is required to obey.
This seems to mean that one must disturb one's life in the interests of
others except in extreme cases, where one is justified in sitting comfortably
by the fireside. This is perhaps something of a caricature, but I think it
shows that the notion of exclusionary reasons introduces too much of
a step in what should somehow be seen as a matter of degree. The weak
supererogationist has no trouble in capturing the idea that supererogation
is a matter of degree, but Raz's version of strong supererogationism
makes it all or nothing.

Wolf

The third account of supererogation that I want to consider is that
of Susan Wolf.[10] Her position is derived from an interesting attack on
the desirability of either being or just living with morally ideal persons
– moral saints. She suggests that such persons, conceived either pre-
theoretically or within the terms of Kantian or utilitarian theory, would
be unpleasingly narrow persons who would be prevented by their moral
perfection from taking a direct interest in anything other than keeping
moral rules (Kant) or the welfare of others (utilitarianism). So moral
saints could not have a normal interest in Mozart, in improving their
backhand or in their family and friends. Wolf argues that we have
reason, therefore, not to want to become moral saints, and to be grateful if our children are not saints either.

The twist lies in the conclusion she draws from these thoughts. Instead of arguing that moral theory, or these moral theories, are mistaken,
she suggests that we have been asking them to do a task for which they
are not equipped, namely to specify what she calls a personal ideal for
an individual life. Moral theories should not be expected to tell us what
a perfect person would be like. All they are in the business of doing is
to describe the nature of a person who is perfect from a moral point of
view. There are two points of view, the moral one and the point of view

of individual perfection. Each has something to say about the other, admittedly. The moral point of view will see the perfection of an individual life as having some, though limited, value, while the point of view of individual perfection will ascribe some value to the relation between the moral individual and his world. But the two points of view are essentially asking and answering different questions.

We can see what Wolf will say about the conflict between reasons of autonomy and reasons of beneficence. The former take their place within the perfectionist point of view, and the latter reign within the moral perspective. This is why she thinks it wrong to criticize a moral theory for failing to give sufficient room to reasons of autonomy.[11] Moral theories are talking about something else. This is why we should not think of ourselves as permitted to live a non-saintly life. We do not need to apply for permission to give full scope to the very strong reasons there are for living our own lives to the full. For 'a person may be perfectly wonderful without being perfectly moral.'

For present purposes, however, we are thinking not about reasons of autonomy but about supererogation. Here Wolf's position, whatever its general merits, becomes less secure. She argues that the moral point of view requires actions of us which go far beyond anything recommended by the point of view of individual perfection. So, she says, 'since we have reason to want people to live lives that are not morally perfect, then any plausible moral theory must make use of some conception of supererogation.' The idea is that a moral theory which recognizes its own limitations will see that it should allow that the actions which we are morally required to do are actions which a perfectly admirable person may choose not to do.

This is, however, not supererogation as we originally intended it to be. It is not that there can be actions which have the highest moral value but which we are morally permitted not to perform. Wolf is not a strong supererogationist. There is nothing here like the struggle between the evaluative and the deontic; there are only evaluations from two distinct perspectives. For her, the supererogatory action is one we are morally required to perform, but this requirement is not visible from the point of view of individual perfection. That point of view, notice, does not generate reasons which *outweigh* the moral ones. Otherwise we would presumably think the better of the person who fails to be saintly. There is nothing here which is both seen as a requirement and as something an admirable person might choose not to do.

The problem, then, is that for Wolf there is no single point of view which both accepts that a perfect person would choose the saintly action and allows that an admirable person might hold back. I take this to be a crucial weakness in her account. It means that she cannot tell us why we don't think of the less than saintly person as to that extent morally defective. On her account, such a person is failing by the standards of the morally ideal, and within the moral perspective is therefore open to criticism (though of course from the point of view of individual perfection there may be no criticism to be made at all). But this is not how we think of the supererogatory. We take there to be a *moral* permission to hold back.

A further problem for Wolf's account appears when we ask about what we have *overall* reason to think or do. Do we have overall reason to prefer the action recommended by the moral point of view, despite the unattractive personal nature of the moral saint, or that recommended by the point of view of individual perfection, when we know that moral demands we accept require more of us? The fact is, I think, that these questions don't make good sense for Wolf. There is no overall perspective, for her, because 'each point of view takes account of, and, in a sense, subsumes the other.' The relation between the two is not asymmetric in a way that would enable us to prefer one to the other in general, presumably adopting some third, more synoptic point of view in order to do so. All we can do is to switch from one to the other and back again. The difficulty that I have with this is that it seems to me too much like a counsel of despair. In taking the stance she does, Wolf appeals to Nagel's paper on incommensurability, which I criticize in Appendix III; I suggest that Nagel adopts a quite unnecessarily extreme version of the claim that reasons of different sorts cannot be put up against each other. Until we see clearly that it is impossible, we should be looking for an account under which the reasons with which Wolf's two perspectives are concerned can be somehow seen for what they are and assessed for comparative strength from one and the same point of view.

I end my discussion of Wolf with a more general criticism. She suggests that even if a utilitarian may see some value in activities such as playing the oboe, this value must be indirect, and hence one's interest will not be in the oboe itself, but in the good which playing the oboe will do, or which one will be enabled to do if one relaxes with one's oboe occasionally. As a criticism of utilitarianism, or of consequentialism in general, this seems to me to be at best incomplete. In considering the claims of some theory T, it is common for consequentialist thinkers[12] to distinguish between the aims which T gives us (our T-given aims) and the motives of which T may approve (T-approved motives) and to argue that it is a mistake to read T-approved motives straight off from the T-given aims. Even if T specifies a single aim, it may allow any of a variety of sets of motives. For despite its specification of goods as values, it can allow that aiming at these goods may not be the best way to promote them. For instance, a society of perfect altruists will not necessarily be the society which realizes the most value. Instead, it may be that these goods are best achieved if people aim at other things, most particularly if they have a wide variety of non-competing personal projects with a high chance of success. In such a situation, T will approve persons motivated by a love of music, say. And it is important to note that though its approval of this motivation is indirect (since the reason for the approval is that the existence of such motivation will serve to maximize value in the long term) it still approves a direct interest in the oboe *for its own sake*.

Wolf's view is that moral ideals do not make the best personal ideals. Since we can see that moral ideals are not overall ideals, there must be a perspective from which moral value is only part of value, and not a dominant part at that. This is the point of view of individual perfection. But we could say more simply that moral theories, as theories of *value* (or of *aims*), do not as such purport to specify moral ideals or morally ideal lives (since they are officially silent on matters of permissible motivation). We do not need a perspective *other than that of morality* to recognize this fact. Hence there is no pressure on us to admit the existence of an independent point of view to recognize it from. And if this is right, it means that Wolf has not shown there to be any need for the sort of concept of supererogation which she claims any account of moral perfection must use; indeed, so far as that goes, she has not shown the need for any concept of supererogation at all.

4   The cost to the agent

What have we learnt from this examination of three attempts to understand supererogation? Nagel suggested that the facts of human motivation may be relevant, but emerged as a weak supererogationist. This was largely because he tried to set facts of human motivation against the reasons, which were all on the side of self-sacrifice. Raz did better in that respect, working entirely within the realm of reasons, but failed to capture the sense in which supererogation must be a matter of degree. Wolf failed to show that the tensions within supererogation are moral tensions, existing between considerations which should all be visible from one and the same point of view. Like Nagel, but in a different way, she took the tension to be between the moral (thoughts of duty and value) and something else.

So what I am looking to provide is an account of supererogation which places the whole story squarely within the moral realm, working within the realm of reasons, allowing supererogation to be a matter of degree and using the idea that the facts of human motivation are relevant to the problem rather than a distraction. Instead of saying that someone who fails to do the heroic act commits an excusable wrong (wrong because it was against the balance of reasons, excusable because it was so much to ask), what one wants to say here is that there is nothing wrong and nothing to excuse. I take this to be the position of common moral intuition; it is theory that is our problem here, specifically theory that is too simple. If heroic actions are supererogatory, then a failure to be a hero will cause value to be missed, but there will be no deontic property here; the deontic properties give out, or better fade away, at a certain level. Excuse is required when an action ought to be done but was not. So we must somehow see the value of the supererogatory act as failing to generate an *ought*, and the reason why it fails to generate an *ought* must be somehow related to facts of human motivation.

The way to do all this is to complicate the picture we were dealing with earlier in this chapter. There I suggested that if there is a systematic relation between the deontic and the evaluative, it is that deontic properties result not just from value, but from the combination of value and special relationship between action and agent. Now I want to say that the deontic results from the combination of three elements, value, special relationship and sacrifice involved for the agent. These three contribute in their different ways to the creation of reasons. The value that the act would create probably generates strong reasons in favour of doing it, for any person who stands in the requisite special relationship. But the cost that person will have to pay, which is already counted once during the calculation of value, counts in a different way when the prospective agent comes to consider what to do. So there is on one side the value derived from the difference it will make to the world that this action was done, which we can now call *neutral* value. But there is something else to be considered on the other side, and since it seems best to consider this something else as centred on something of value to the agent, we should think of this something else as value too, but as *agent-relative* value. What this would mean, if we could get the story to run, is that increase in neutral value need not necessarily lead to increased reason to act or make it more wrong to fail to act. For increased neutral value can be counterbalanced by increased cost to the agent, i.e. by a decrease in agent-relative value.[13]

How can the cost to the agent appear twice in the story? It is not exactly counted twice, if by that we mean that we count it once and then count it again in the same sort of way so as to cook the books.

But it appears twice, first in the construction of neutral value and then again as agent-relative value in the resultant construction of reasons. How can this be? The idea must be that in the construction of neutral value, the question who the agent is to be plays no role. The question which agent shall do the act may play a role, of course, since one may be able to do it with less sacrifice than another. But the question who that agent is – whether it is me, or you, or someone else – has so far not appeared at all. Now this question matters enormously to the prospective agent, not by way of special pleading in recognition of human motivational frailty, but straightforwardly in the consideration of whether this agent has sufficient reason to act. If the cost is enormous and it is me that is going to have to pay it, that fact matters to me in a way that was simply not addressed when its surrogate (that the agent, whoever that may be, would have to pay a high price) was entered in to the calculation of neutral value.

So I want to say that the cost to the agent creates reasons for the agent that are distinct from its contribution (presumably negative) to the sum of neutral value. And these reasons are ones that we can all recognize and appreciate. This is what enables us to recognize that it is morally acceptable for the agent not to go by the balance of neutral value alone. We should not confuse this with some sort of special pleading on the part of the agent. On behalf of that agent, we can see that the reasons (values) he appeals to are a genuine part of the reasons that are there for him. The facts of human motivation are in the story here, but not in the way Nagel used them.

Does this story work entirely within the scope of morality, or have I copied the mistakes of Nagel and Wolf? The thought that I have slipped on this point derived from taking all moral value to be neutral value, so that any reasons for action that don't stem from neutral value must be non-moral; and this will only be encouraged by the idea that the person who sees the cost to self as too high a price to pay is suffering from the standard bias in one's own favour, which is clearly not a reason which lives normally in the moral realm. But this is all a mistake. The cost to self is shown to be a moral reason by the fact that we, as outsiders, take it that the shrinking hero is within his moral rights to hold back. The contrast is not between the moral reasons for action, which all derive from considerations of value, and what we can get the weak-minded to do. It is between one sort of reason deriving from what we might call objective or agent-neutral value, and another which focuses on the agent-relative, but which still concerns value, and *moral* value, for all that. That the cost to the agent can play a role in both these contexts should not be so surprising from this perspective.

The way in which I am trying to run this story can be seen in sharper perspective if contrasted with an alternative approach. I could have maintained that there is only one sort of moral value, neutral value, but that this value generates two distinct types of reasons, agent-relative and agent-neutral. Instead, I took the view that there is a distinction between types of value which is mirrored by one between types of reasons. The difference between these two approaches, then, is on the question whether there are agent-relative values as well as agent-relative reasons. Now I confess to a certain sense that this question has no very hard edge, since it is not at all clear what might hang on our answer to it. And I am also tempted by the idea that the right way to approach the matter is not via some little argument or other, but simply to see which alternative fits best into one's big picture, which in my case is the story about shapes and saliences. However, it is worth mentioning some considerations which are at least relevant. First, surely the cost to the agent is a disvalue. Considered neutrally, it is a disvalue, and why should it cease to be a disvalue once we begin to consider it in the agent-relative way? Second, what does it mean to say that there are values in the world at all? It means that there are features which people are right to mind about. Now the suggestion that there are two sorts of values is just the suggestion that there are two ways of minding about things. And I do mind about the cost to me in two ways: first, as a cost which someone has to pay, and, second, as a cost to me. So that cost seems to be counting here as a value, and not an agent-neutral one. Finally, might the cost to the agent count as value but not as moral value? No. For we take the agent to be (on some occasions) within his moral right to hold back from sacrifice, and to say that the value is a moral value is just to say that it is one recognized by morality.

What about the other side of the coin, which is the agent's right to ignore the cost to self and make the sacrifice? The standard problem here is that if we succeed in justifying the agent's failure to do the heroic act, we can no longer approve his choosing to be a hero. (Remember how this problem arose for Nagel's account of reasons of autonomy.) I do not underestimate the difficulty of giving an account of non-insistent reasons of this sort. But I intend to postpone this question until chapter 12, so as to be able to treat it with others of the same sort.

5 DEONTIC AND EVALUATIVE PROPERTIES AGAIN

It is time to return to the problems with which I started this chapter. I had two worries there. The first was how to capture the distinction between deontic and evaluative without introducing two competing sorts of shape. I initially tried to achieve this by the idea that the deontic derives from the combination of value and special relation, and all we have now seen is that this story can with advantage be made more complex. My second worry was how to cope with the intuition that increased value generates increased reason to act. The simpler picture validated this intuition, despite the need for the special relation between agent and action if duty is to result from value. But the more complex picture seems to me to undermine the intuition completely (and with it the so-called good-ought tie-up).

The story I have been trying to tell so far is, as intended, a form of strong supererogationism, and it will give Urmson most of what he wants to claim. There has been no general dispute of the distinction between evaluative and deontic properties, which has now emerged as the distinction between value and reasons, and we have ended up accepting that there can be an increase in neutral value without there being a corresponding change on the deontic side, i.e. in the reasons. So there is at least some room for independent variation here. However, there is also a systematic relation between the deontic and the evaluative, which we expressed by saying that deontic properties are resultant properties, and they result from the combination of:

(1) neutral value

(2) special relation

(3) sacrifice involved, generating agent-relative value.

It remains to show that supererogation is, on this account, a matter of degree. But this is easy. All three elements in the story are matters of degree, and so there is every reason to expect the resultant deontic property to vary in a similar way. There is no danger here of a sudden step in the analysis. The *ought* fades as the balance between sacrifice and neutral value becomes more even, until it vanishes entirely. The person who is weighing up the cost to self may of course express one side of his dilemma by saying 'I ought to do it.' But we need not take this too seriously as a reintroduction of the deontic just when we have begun to think that *oughts* have no real place on the scene. Our hesitant hero here may be taken to be expressing merely the neutral value he sees there to be in the action. In this sense, what he says can be true as he intends it, without his failure to perform the action needing to count as a wrong excused.

Does this mean that there are no such things as moral requirements, i.e. sacrifices we are required to make despite the cost to self? No. The flexibility introduced into the system by the recognition of agent-relative value only shows that it is possible for an increase in neutral value to be attended by a decrease in agent-relative value, in a way that will change the balance of reasons. It does not show that any amount of agent-relative disvalue, no matter how small, is sufficient to overthrow large amounts of neutral value. Note, however, that where we are required to make a sacrifice, the status of this requirement is constructed on the triad of neutral value, agent-relative value and special relationship (opportunity etc.). There are no requirements that we are not required to perform. Sometimes, then, the situation will be one which calls for the sacrifice. This need not be the highest sacrifice (virtue, honour, life, whatever). It could be just taking advantage of the opportunity to add one dollar to one's gas bill as a contribution towards the fuel costs of the least well-off. Perhaps, even, on occasion the neutral value silences the reasons against, which derive from the agent-relative disvalue. Sometimes, however, what would otherwise be a requirement is not one because of the presence of agent-relative disvalue. In general, the role of theory is to show that there is room (*logical* room, as it were) for something – in this case, for moral heroism and the occasional moral right not to be a hero – not to show where the line is to be drawn.

The first part of this book is now complete. It has contained an attempt to outline and defend a genuinely cognitive theory of motivation, and has urged the merits of particularism. Chapters 7 and 8 have been part of that process. Chapter 9 takes a new start; it concerns the extent to which the sorts of reasons I have been talking about can be thought of as objective. If they are both objective and cognitive, we have done enough to establish the central tenets of moral realism.

The topics discussed in the present chapter will recur in the new context, when we ask whether the agent-relative reasons which ground the logical room for supererogation are as objective as the neutral ones which, considered alone, appear to have no real place for heroes.

NOTES

1 See Urmson (1958).
2 Prichard (1968), p. 153.
3 If this is possible, it seems to me to show that the motive of duty need not be the highest motive.
4 εἰ μὴ θέσιν διαφυλάττων.
5 This was the position I reached in Dancy (1988b); but I no longer think

that I was on quite the right track there.

6 Nagel (1986), p. 204.

7 This term, without which I cannot make the present points, is not going to be defined until chapter 10. Those to whom it, and its opposite, 'agent-relative', are unfamiliar may have to wait until they have read the discussion there before they see what is really at issue here.

8 See Kagan (1989), pp. 378ff.

9 See Raz (1975).

10 See Wolf (1982).

11 As Williams does in Williams (1976a) and (1976b).

12 See Parfit (1984) and Railton (1984). I mention the views of these writers here, but argue in chapter 13 that they are untenable.

13 I owe the main idea of how to do this to the promptings of Alec Walen and John McDowell.

9
Objectivity

1 NAGEL'S TWO VIEWPOINTS

I begin the second part of this book with a discussion of the sort of objectivity properly attributable to moral values and reasons. In a sense this is a new start, but the themes I pursue will be informed by what has gone before, and the results I reach will affect what comes after. So this chapter is the hinge or spine of the book.

My starting point is the conception of objectivity elaborated in Thomas Nagel's *The View from Nowhere*.[1] Nagel claims that his book is 'about a single problem: how to combine the perspective of a particular person inside the world with an objective view of that same world, the person and his viewpoint included'.[2] This is a problem because Nagel sees the objective and subjective viewpoints as in essential tension: a tension which both demands and resists resolution. Objectivity is a matter of degree; there are more and less objective viewpoints.

> A view or form of thought is more objective than another if it relies less on the specifics of the individual's makeup and position in the world, or on the character of the particular type of creature he is. The wider the range of subjective types to which a form of understanding is accessible – the less it depends on specific subjective capacities – the more objective it is. A standpoint that is objective by comparison with the personal view of one individual may be subjective by comparison with a theoretical standpoint still further out. The standpoint of morality is more objective than that of private life, but less objective than the standpoint of physics. We may think of reality as a set of concentric spheres, progressively revealed as we detach gradually from the contingencies of the self.[3]

A page earlier, we read:

> Objectivity is a method of understanding ... To acquire a more objective understanding of some aspect of life or the world, we step back from our

initial view of it and form a new conception which has that view and
its relation to the world as its object. In other words, we place ourselves
in the world that is to be understood. The old view then comes to be
regarded as an appearance, more subjective than the new view, and correctable or confirmable by reference to it. The process can be repeated. . . .

This then is the difference between objective and subjective viewpoints.
As I said, Nagel wants to argue that we need to adopt both viewpoints
though we can never succeed in rendering them compatible. Though the
tension between them is ineradicable, we must strive to surmount it. He
seeks to persuade us of this by various examples – cases where we both
crave objectivity and know that we cannot get it. I shall discuss three
of these, the last of which is that of moral reasons.

The first example is the search for knowledge and the attempt to
ward off the sceptic. The problem, as Nagel sees it, is that we start our
rise towards the objective view from an initial position in which we
are restricted to subjective appearances. But 'if initial appearances are
not in themselves reliable guides to reality, why should the products of
detached reflection be different?'[4]

> However often we may try to step outside of ourselves, something will
> have to stay behind the lens, something in us will determine the resulting
> picture, and this will give grounds for doubt that we are really getting
> closer to reality.[5]

So the idea here is that in the search for knowledge, which we could
hardly forgo, we want to have an objective view no part of which is
the product of some peculiarity of ourselves or of our perspective. But
there could be no such view, because at every stage something will stay
behind the lens and affect the resulting picture.

The next example is the search for autonomy. Nagel's discussion here
focuses on practical autonomy, which is the desire to form one's practical
projects and so choose actions on the basis of principles which one can
understand and judge to be correct, rather than on the basis of influ-
ences that one cannot know, understand, assess or endorse. I will however
concentrate more on cognitive autonomy, which concerns the desire to
understand and approve the principles by which we form and assess
beliefs. I think that the points to be made are the same on both sides,
but that what I want to say comes over more clearly this way.

The problem this time, in Nagel's view, is that our desire is only to
use principles judged valid from the objective view, for we want principles
which are objectively valid, i.e. which objectively fit the contingencies of

the world. Such principles would be ones adjudged valid from a point of view with no peculiarities. But there could be no such certification of all our principles at once, for with no principles to judge with the objective mind could not judge at all.[6] (This is the analogue of the remark that something must stay behind the lens.) And this matters because this is the only way of getting what is needed, for otherwise we would merely be using some of our principles to judge others.

In this case Nagel offers an unstable solution to a difficulty of principle, which he calls 'objective tolerance'. This is that we should seek principles which *would not be rejected* by the objective mind rather than those which it would endorse. This is clearly a second best, when what we really crave here is endorsement. And it is a peculiar sop, since if the objective mind is here conceived of as somehow deprived of all its principles of judgement, it is not clear how the fact that it would not reject some principle offers much solace; for it is in no position either to endorse or to reject.

The third example, which is the one that really concerns us here, is that of ethics. Here we have no hope of principles that would be endorsed by a creature with no peculiarities, and it would be a mistake to suggest that we crave any such thing. Instead, we are reasonably happy with objective tolerance, with reasons which a position that lacks all peculiarities would not reject.

Nagel holds that there are three sorts of reasons for action. The first are stubbornly subjective reasons, such as those which are in play when we are choosing from a menu in a restaurant. Here we have no desire that our reasons should somehow receive objective validation, and those reasons, depending as they do on our own peculiarities (our taste), cannot be recognized from a viewpoint at any great distance from our own. But there are two classes of objective reasons. The first are agent-relative reasons, of which we will be hearing a great deal; the second are agent-neutral reasons. Both of these are recognizable at some distance from here, as we shave peculiarities from our perspective in the move towards objectivity. The agent-relative ones are less objective, of course, though they can be recognized, and in some sense endorsed, from more objective points of view. However, what is recognized and endorsed is not the importance which the agent finds in (e.g.) his own life-time projects; this itself cannot be recognized from much further out. As we move away from the agent's own perspective, all that can be recognized is that he finds importance in them, which is quite a different matter.

There is a parallel here to the objectivizing attitude Nagel takes to subjective appearance.[7] What remains after objectification is not the appearances themselves but the fact that there are appearances. Just as the business of the objective mind is to transcend and correct appearances, so the business of the objective will is to transcend and correct inclinations in favour of the real (i.e. most objectively recognizable) reasons of ethics.

2 TWO CONCEPTIONS OF OBJECTIVITY

This then is the picture which Nagel offers us. I now want to argue that the picture involves a general distortion, in a way that undermines his attempt to establish a sophisticated form of anti-consequentialist realism in ethics.[8] In my view the tension Nagel finds endemic between two points of view is in fact a tension between two distinct conceptions of the process of objectification, both of which he is trying to run simultaneously.

The passages which I quoted early in this chapter contain the seeds of these two conceptions. The first appears in the remark that in objectification 'we step back from our initial view of [the world] and form a new conception which has that view and its relation to the world as its object.' I call this the Hegelian model of objectification. Its main features include:

1   It is linear and apparently infinite. There is no prospect of reaching a view of the world which we cannot move beyond, by a further step of the same sort.
2   In this process of objectification, nothing is left behind. Every aspect of each succeeding view is retained, though maybe somewhat altered, in each of its successors. There is therefore some reason to say that when we move away from our initial, most subjective, view of the world we change our view of the world.
3   Though it is not part of the nature of the objectification process *as such* to leave anything behind, the purpose of entering the process may only be served if we do change our view of the world as a result. This purpose is to see if the world matches the view we take of it. Should we conclude that it doesn't, we have already changed our view, and are now in a position to ask of the new view whether it matches better than its predecessor did. With any such change in view, the first stage of objectification will have to be re-run.
4   Despite the Hegelian overtones of this sort of objectification, we are not forced into the rise towards objectivity by any sort of contradiction, but none the less we cannot avoid the desire for an objective view. That desire is a feature of our humanity; we *crave* objectification. So objectification is not a luxury but a necessity for us.

5 There are good reasons for seeking a more objective view, namely
   the increase in *understanding* which such a view can offer.

The second sort of objectification emerges in the passage already
quoted from Nagel's next page. The suggestion this time is that the
move towards a more objective view involves abstracting from one's
view of the world any element which can be seen as the product of
one's own perspective. The hope presumably is to arrive eventually at
a view which has no element of that sort. This makes it appropriate, in
the light of the popularity of the notion of the absolute conception of
the world,[9] to call this the model of absolute objectification. Its prominent aspects are:

1 It is linear, but not infinite if there really is a most objective view no
   element of which can be attributed to the perspective from which
   that view is to be had.
2 A great deal is left behind in the process, since at every stage we
   separate off into a category called 'appearance' something which
   earlier was conceived as part of 'reality'.
3 Since the whole aim of the process is to achieve a view of the world
   as it is in itself, uncoloured by the contributions of the perspective
   from which we view it, the nature of the world changes – in fact,
   reduces – as our view becomes more objective. At each stage, further
   qualities are eliminated as mere appearance. (Of course, a few may
   be added as well.)
4 We are not forced into this form of objectification by our humanity
   or by some contradiction, but we can expect a more objective view
   to be nearer the truth about the world as it is in itself, so that we
   can correct earlier views from the perspective of later ones. The
   truth about the world as it is in itself is contained in what can be
   discerned by a form of understanding which does not depend at all
   on any subjective capacities in respect of which another view might
   be different.
5 So the purpose of this sort of objectification is a gain not so much
   in understanding as in knowledge of 'objective' (i.e. independent)
   reality.

It is worth pointing out the main differences between the two forms
of objectification. First, Nagel says that 'the standpoint of morality is
more objective than that of private life, but less objective than the
standpoint of physics.' This is true for absolute objectification, false for
Hegelian objectification. Nobody would say that physics is the attempt

to form a conception of the world which has the relation between our moral view and the world so viewed as its object, nor that physics is likely to occur as a later stage in the process of Hegelian objectification. In fact, physics is not concerned with the relation between our view of the world and the world so viewed at all. It is odd that Nagel doesn't see this point, since he continues 'We may think of reality as a set of concentric spheres, progressively revealed. . . .' For this notion of concentric spheres fits only Hegelian objectification. Absolute objectification, by its very nature, does not tend to build a broader conception of reality around a narrower one, but rather to banish to the realm of appearance parts of what were previously taken to be reality.

Second, Nagel is prone to talk about detachment, as when he says that physics is the science in which we have achieved our greatest detachment from a specifically human perspective on the world. But the notion of detachment varies according to which sense of objectification is at issue. If it is Hegelian, the sense in which we leave anything behind is dubious. There is certainly no antecedent guarantee that the results of the process will be our abandoning as unreal many aspects of the world as we originally conceived it. We may, of course, change our minds about something; but this is to take something to be false which we previously took to be true, not to take something to be mere appearance which previously we took to be reality. Detachment for the Hegelian amounts to this, that we stand back from our ordinary engagement with the world and view that engagement as an object. The difficulty in taking simultaneously a more and a less objective view, if any, derives from the need to be more and less engaged at the same time. This is certainly difficult, but there is no reason to suppose it to be impossible. Hegel, of course, had special reasons for saying that it is impossible to be at two levels of consciousness at the same time. This is because for him the higher level 'sublates' the lower, since we have only risen to the higher because of a contradiction below it. There is something of this in Nagel. Having achieved a more objective view, we cannot hope to return to our earlier subjective view with pristine innocence. In this sense we cannot combine an earlier with a later view, but there is no reason why we should wish to do so. Having achieved the greater understanding of the objective point of view, we should not wish to abandon that advantage. But this should not mean that we cannot return to the subjective view at all, only that on our return we will find it altered. With absolute objectification, by contrast, the whole purpose of the enterprise is to hive off certain aspects of the world as we originally took it to be in the attempt to improve our conception of independent reality. The difficulty of taking simultaneously a more and a less objective view will now be that we are committed to thinking of some aspect of the world both as real and as mere appearance. This is surely impossible on any account. But I would say that the need to achieve this impossibility is less pressing than the need to stand back from our engagement with the world for the sake of a gain in understanding. It is the latter which is required of us by our humanity; the former seems to offer much more technical advantages.

Third, Nagel takes objective reality (that part of reality which can be understood from a perspective with no peculiarities) to be incomplete in two ways. First, there may be aspects of the world which we can never understand at all. This is an expression of extreme metaphysical realism; he does not take this position for ethical truth. Second, there are aspects of reality which an objective view leaves behind. The nature of any sensory state, even one of ours, is something of which our objective understanding is at best partial. But this sort of thought seems to fit the absolute process much better than it does the Hegelian. There seems to be no reason why our own objective understanding of our sensory states need be incomplete, for Hegelian objectification is not the attempt to conceive of those states from a perspective with no distinguishing features at all, and hence the result is not likely to be a perspective from which our sensory states are likely to be incomprehensible. Hegelian objectification would be a failure if that were the result, while absolute objectification would not.

Fourth, Nagel suggests that a more subjective view is 'correctable or confirmable' by reference to a more objective view. This is true in different ways and for different reasons on the two accounts. With Hegelian objectification, our examination of the relation between our view of the world and the world itself may lead us to make a change in that view. (An example of this might be our response to Hume's doubts about induction.) But there is no sense in which the results of this objectification are to be intrinsically more real than the contents of a more subjective view. But with absolute objectification there is a definite feeling that we are moving towards the truth. 'The fundamental idea behind the objective conception is that the world is not our world'.[10] In this objective view what we reach is the result of separating out as much as possible as a facet of our response to *the* world, and what has been separated out cannot be put back again. For the sense of reality at issue is one generated by the process of separation, and the continuing contrast between the real (the independent) and our response to it.

The fifth difference between absolute and Hegelian objectification concerns the notion of generalization. Physics requires generalization of two sorts. The first is that 'it takes the particular case as an example, and forms hypotheses about what general truth it is an example of.'[11] The second is that in physics we are expected to abstract from our own perspective on the world and reduce our account of the world to those truths which can be reached and affirmed no matter what the perspective from which we start. Absolute objectification requires generalization of the second[12] but not of the first sort.[13] But there is no reason to suppose that the products of Hegelian objectification, my attempts to understand the relation between my subjective view of the world and the world I so view, either will or should meet the demand that creatures relevantly different from myself should (be able to) understand them.

Is there a most objective view? For Hegelian objectification, probably not. The process will continue indefinitely, unless we reach a stage where there is (as Hegel would put it) no distinction between our consciousness and its object. But for absolute objectification, the answer must be yes. There *must* be such a thing as independent reality, even if there could be no view of it.

Does this mean that the drive towards objectivity is a drive towards truth and away from error? No; there is no stage at which error is impossible; the distinction between truth and error is not really related to the objective/subjective distinction at all. Absolute objectification is concerned with the distinction between appearance and reality, on Nagel's view. But there is no suggestion that appearance and error are somehow connected. Or rather there *should* be no such suggestion. But sometimes there is a distinct hint that what merely appears and what is false are connected, so that the move from a more subjective view to a more objective one is a move towards truth. Nagel has a tendency to downgrade appearance.[14] This tendency is dangerous, for if we are not careful we will find ourselves saying that an objective view is one from which all (mere) appearances have been expunged, so that the objective world does not *appear* at all.

With all these differences between the two sorts of objectification, it is surely improbable that any one view can serve the purposes of both. We can, of course, engage in each, or in both together. But we should not confuse the two searches. Nagel does confuse them. The tensions he discerns between subjective and objective are in fact tensions which derive from trying to run both conceptions of objectification at once, without seeing the differences between them.

We can see this clearly in the first two examples, those of knowledge and autonomy. What drives the scepticism which Nagel expresses? It should not be the view that appearances are intrinsically unreliable or dubious, so that the starting point for objectification is flawed in a way that vitiates the whole enterprise. For even if appearances are not part of objective reality, as absolute objectification supposes, they may still be a reliable guide to reality, as colour may be when properly understood. And there is no independent reason for supposing appearances to be intrinsically misleading.

Nor should it be the idea that as absolute objectification proceeds, the later stages will merely be more 'mere appearances'. For there is no reason in advance to suppose that the attempt to abstract from the peculiarities of our own perspective cannot succeed, and so no reason here to doubt the possibility of getting nearer to the truth about the objective world.

The key to Nagel's scepticism lies in his remark that 'However often we may try to step outside ourselves, something will have to stay behind the lens, something in us will determine the resulting picture.'[15] The first half of this is true on the Hegelian conception, while the second concerns itself with the demands of absolute objectification. Crucially, one cannot argue from the first to the second. The fact that something will stay behind the lens does nothing to show that any individual feature or features of that something will determine the resulting picture. So if Nagel were to restrict himself to the demands of Hegelian objectification, the threat of scepticism would become much less endemic.

The same point can be made about our search for autonomy. We want to assess the relation between our world and our view of it. This is unproblematic and generates no paradox. The paradox comes from Nagel's remark that 'We cannot assess and revise or confirm our entire system of thought and judgement from outside, for we would have nothing to do it with.'[16] But the desire to assess the whole structure of reasons is driven by concentration on the needs of absolute objectification. The desire to work from outside is a desire to have a view from nowhere, a view with no special peculiarities but which is none the less rich enough to enable us to assess our own perspective from it. It is true that this desire is incoherent, but it is no part of Hegelian objectification. So there is no reason other than a conflation of the aims of the two sorts of objectification to suppose that the aims of Hegelian objectification are incapable of fulfilment. Hegelian objectification aims at an increased understanding, derived from an investigation into the relation between our subjective viewpoint and the world so viewed. There is nothing here which leads us to expect and aim for a final understanding which is not itself susceptible to the same questions as before and which cannot therefore be superseded. That sort of desire and expectation seems to derive entirely from thoughts about absolute objectification. So here again Nagel's problem stems not from a tension between subjective and objective points of view, but from a tension between two distinct conceptions of objectification, once one fails to see the difference between them.

3   MORAL REASONS AND OBJECTIVITY

If there are these two conceptions of objectivity at issue, which should we engage with in asking whether moral reasons are objective? The choice my examination of Nagel's work presents me with is between two options. The first is the knowledge-oriented approach, which requires a putatively objective moral reason to seek validation, or at least objective tolerance, from a perspective with fewer peculiarities than our own or preferably none that in any way affects the way it views the world. The second is the understanding-oriented approach, which requires a putatively objective moral reason to survive reflection on the relation between our world and ourselves, but does not demand either validation or even merely tolerance from creatures relevantly different from ourselves.

It seems obvious to me that the second of these is not only a more sensible aim but one more suited to the moral reasons we are really concerned with. What it tells us is that there is a sense of objectivity in which our reasons are not shown to be subjective by the fact that creatures who fail to share in characteristic human concerns would not be able to see those reasons for what they are. It removes from us the idea that our values crave an acceptance from the objective will which we know in advance they cannot get. If we conceive of objective validation on the model of Hegelian objectification, there is so far no reason to suppose that moral reasons cannot get any validation they may fairly demand.

The importance of this result is that it changes our picture of what is required of an objective reason. Objectivity may be a matter of degree, but if we have a distorted picture of the scale on which those degrees occur we make it harder for ourselves to understand the place of certain moral reasons which claim objective validity but are clearly invisible from further out. These are the agent-relative reasons. Nagel, whose dominant conception is that of absolute objectification, is unable to ascribe to these reasons the same degree of objectivity he ascribes to agent-neutral reasons. They cannot be recognized for what they really are from places much further out. Reasons that derive from personal commitments vanish, and all that can be seen is that there are these commitments; the values deriving from them are now playing a role analogous to that of an appearance. This seems to me merely to encourage the mistaken idea that agent-relative values are to be seen as distortions – justified distortions, perhaps, but still distortions – of the true values, the more objective agent-neutral ones. And once we have allowed this picture to develop we have immeasurably increased the difficulty of establishing the distinction between agent-neutral and agent-relative value as anything much more than part of the distinction between real and apparent value. I want to resist this picture. Agent-neutral reasons may be more objective in some sense, though there is nothing in the notion of Hegelian objectification which requires this to be so; but if true, it should not be taken to mean that they are recognizable by creatures that share fewer of our peculiarities. There need be no difference between the agent-relative and the agent-neutral on that score, nor need we see the validity of a reason as in any way impugned by its inability to survive that sort of scrutiny. To do so would be to face our reasons with the wrong sort of challenge.

Nagel does not see the difference between the two forms of objectification; but to the extent to which he prefers one to the other, his dominant conception is clearly that of absolute objectification. But this very conception makes it harder rather than easier to achieve one of his main aims, namely to support the idea that as well as the consequentialist's agent-neutral reasons, there are other, agent-relative ones which can compete with and sometimes defeat them. If there is no point of view from which both agent-neutral and agent-relative reasons can be seen fully for what they are, the latter being thought of as defective in point of objectivity, the agent-relative reasons have been presented as suspect on their first appearance, in a way that surely makes the agent-relativist's task much harder. This is one of my two main reasons for thinking that Nagel's form of moral realism is constructed in such a way as to diminish its own chances of success.[17]

By way of comment on the above, it is worth saying that I conceive of the project of this book as an exercise in Hegelian objectification (as indeed will be any such exercise in moral theory). It asks whether we can sustain the view we naturally take about the moral reasons we find for and against action. The world can do any of three things to the reasons we accept. It can invalidate them, permit them and validate them. Bad reasons will be invalidated. An example of this might be my original temptation to think that Gauguin's treatment of his family is rendered less morally atrocious by his fortuitous mastery of painting; reflection reveals that this is an illusion, and I readjust my outlook accordingly. Ordinary subjective reasons are likely to be permitted but not validated by the objectification process, for instance those which stem from individual preferences where there is no tendency to claim that we are right to prefer what we do. A putative moral reason which is shown on reflection to be a mere preference is one which has survived the process of objectification in a weak sense, but not passed unscathed. A reason is only validated (i.e. only survives the process in the more honorific sense that we are really concerned with) if we conclude that this reason derives from the nature of the case rather than from our nature. Genuine moral reasons, in my view, will be like this. To have a moral reason is to be faced with facts that *are* reasons. The aim of my enquiry is to show that moral reasons are the reasons we take them to be, and hence it is an exercise in Hegelian objectification.

4   DEGREES OF OBJECTIVITY

The question we should ask, then, is whether our moral reasons, or the values that generate them, can survive the process of Hegelian objectification. If they can, they have all the objectivity I think they need.

A value will best survive this sort of scrutiny if we can show that it is part of the world rather than imposed on a valueless world by human choices. In seeing human valuings as recognitions of values that exist independently, we best achieve the sort of match between the world and our view of it which makes it possible for our view to survive Hegelian objectification. Not all the things we value are of this sort, of course. But our first question must be whether any are.

I take there to be one major difficulty in giving a positive answer to this question, and this lies in the relation between value and the will. The position I have been favouring is an internalist one, which takes moral values to be intrinsically related to the will. But how can there be any such, if those values are to be objective? How can it be that the world is motivationally 'ert'? In seeing our valuings as responses to values that exist in the world, haven't we simply admitted that they are not intrinsically related to the mind, so that they can be present without our noticing them and we can notice them without minding about them? Both these admissions would be very damaging, the first because it grants values too great an independence of our recognition of them, and the second because it is an admission of externalism in the theory of motivation.

John McDowell's response to these questions[18] consists in an attempt to show that they only appear difficult because of a picture from which they spring, a picture which is at best optional. It is a contentious metaphysical picture of which aspects of the world are the real ones: a picture of objectivity, in fact. The sort of objectivity at issue, which we can call primary objectivity, can be expressed in any of a family of ways. A property has primary objectivity if:

1 It is instantiable in a world devoid of perceivers – or
2 It is adequately conceivable otherwise than in terms of certain subjective states – or
3 It is there anyway, independent of the possibility of experience.

McDowell admits that values lack primary objectivity, since no such value could be intrinsically related to the will. But he claims that there is a weaker sort of objectivity, which we can call secondary objectivity. This too can be expressed in a family of ways. A property has secondary objectivity if:

1 It is there anyway, independent of any particular experience – or
2 It is there anyway, waiting to be experienced: there *for* experience – or
3 It is not a figment of a subjective state that purports to be an experience of it.

The point now is that we can find much less difficulty in supposing that our values have this secondary sort of objectivity, and thereby show how it can be that value is both objective and intrinsically related to the will. McDowell offers us a model, which is supposed to be comparatively uncontentious. Secondary properties such as those of colour and sound do not have primary objectivity, but they do have secondary objectivity. Properties like these are 'essentially phenomenal' – essentially to do with the ways in which things look – and so they could not be instantiated in a world devoid of minds for them to appear to. But this does not prevent them from having secondary objectivity. In this sense, an object can be objectively red even though nobody is actually looking at it, in a way that does nothing to show that there could be colours of which there could be no experience.

5 THE ANALOGY WITH COLOUR

Redness is an objective property, but essentially phenomenal. The statement that an object is red is, in McDowell's phrase, only able to be understood as true, if true, in virtue of a disposition it has to cause a certain response in a perceiver. The response concerned here is, of course, an experience. But we can use this case as a model for the case of value, where the relevant response is not an experience but approval (an inclination of the will).[19] First, because of this difference, we need to generalize the notion of secondary objectivity (and presumably that of primary objectivity, though I won't bother to do that), thus:

1 It is there anyway, independent of any particular relation to the mind – or
2 It is there anyway, waiting for recognition: there to be recognized – or
3 It is not a figment of a subjective state that purports to be a response to it.

With this in hand, we can say that, like the secondary properties, values have secondary objectivity. The value is there to be recognized, and not a mere figment of a state which purports to be a response to it. But the ascription of value is only able to be understood as true, if true, in virtue of a disposition in the object to elicit a certain response in us. 'Evaluative "attitudes" or states of will are like (say) colour experience in being unintelligible except as modifications of a sensibility like ours.'[20] In this way the value is intrinsically related to the will, though part of the objective world to which our valuings are responses.[21]

This is the way in which McDowell tries to show that values can be both objective and intrinsically related to the will. His approach has the pleasing consequence that values could not systematically outrun our ability to discern them. If we conceive of them as dispositions to elicit a certain response (an inclination of the will) from us, we have already rejected any excessively transcendental realism about ethical truth.[22]

There is one final feature of McDowell's position that needs to be mentioned before I start evaluating it. This is that though he initially describes both colour and value as dispositions to elicit (or cause) responses, he reintroduces the normativity of value later by talking of value as a disposition to elicit a *merited* response. Here he wants to capture the normativity of value by talking about meriting, but not to abandon the idea that value plays a causal role. Value is to be both causal and normative. It is true that values do not 'pull their own weight' in the causal story (or chain, I suppose). This is what often persuades people to abandon objective value as redundant to the world,[23] and in particular to abandon the claim that value can be experienced. They are driven in this by the thought that experience is a causal relation, and values conceived normatively can have no part in such a relation. McDowell's reply to them is twofold. First, he does not conceive of values merely normatively. He wants to reconcile causation with normativity, to reject the mutual exclusiveness of the space of reasons and the space of causes. Second, a feature may be a necessary part of a causal story without pulling its own weight. The acid test for McDowell is not whether a feature pulls its own weight, but whether it is possible to deny its presence without abandoning the causal story. Take the corresponding case of colours. The colour of an object, conceived as a real property there, does not pull its own weight in the causal drive from the primary qualities of the object's surface to the occurrence of the experience which the colour of the object disposes it to cause. We don't seem to need the real colour for that story at all; in that sense, real colours are explanatorily redundant. But neither can we deny that the colour is there – at least not sensibly. For how could we continue to tell the story we do about the way in which colour experience takes place without allowing that the object whose colour we experience is such as to cause that sort of experience in us? To allow this is just to allow that the colour is present in the object as a disposition, distinct from both the primary qualities that ground it and from the experience it is a disposition to cause. And if this is right in the case of colour, it is right in the case of value as well.

6   ARE VALUES AND COLOURS BOTH DISPOSITIONS?

The main question I have about McDowell's position concerns the relation between the value and the disposition to elicit merited approval. Are these to be conceived as identical or not? It seems important to McDowell's position here that they should be identical, though he actually speaks in a slightly ambiguous way of ascriptions of value as only able to be understood as *true*, if true, *in virtue of* a disposition to elicit a certain response. There needs to be identity here because it is by conceiving of the value itself as a disposition to elicit a response that he is able to see the value as internally or intrinsically related to the will. If the value were distinct from the disposition, this move would not work.

It is the same with colour; the analogy that McDowell is relying on needs to see the colour itself as a disposition to cause a certain response (a colour experience). But in the case of colour there seems to me to be a problem. Seeing colour as a disposition falsifies our normal colour experience, which does not seem to be the experience of a disposition. Colour, at least as we experience it, is stubbornly non-dispositional.[24]

So far we have considered two possible views. The first is that colour *is* a disposition, and the second is that the colour exists in virtue of a disposition. McDowell's explicit remarks are ambiguous between these two, though his true view is the former. But surely the main competing view is that the disposition exists in virtue of the colour – that the disposition to cause a certain experience exists in virtue of the phenomenal property in the object. This leaves us with a richer conception of colour as it is in the object, in place of the thin conception of that property as a disposition.

If the appeal to an analogy between colour and value is to make any progress, then, we should presumably look for the same structure in the case of value. We should look to distinguish the value from a resulting disposition to cause merited approval in us. Quite apart from an appeal to the phenomenology of value experience (if there is any such thing) the metaphor of shapes and saliences can help us to make this point. Are we to hold that the shape of the situation is there anyway, independent of any particular experience of it, and that the shape *is* a disposition to elicit a certain response from us? A more promising view, it seems, is that the shape is not a disposition of any sort; rather, the disposition to elicit merited approval exists in virtue of the shape. The situation merits a certain response *because of* its shape.

If we accept this we are accepting a four-stage analysis of colour and of value. The four stages are:

1   The primary quality base.
2   The colour/value.
3   The disposition to elicit a (merited) response.
4   The occurrence of the response.

This is in preference to a three-stage analysis which sees stages 2 and 3 above as identical:

1   The primary quality base.
2   The disposition to elicit a (merited) response.
3   The occurrence of the response.

As we saw, identifying the colour or value with a disposition to elicit a response yields the thoughts that colour is essentially phenomenal and value essentially motivational. So if we distinguish the colour or value from the relevant disposition we are going to have to derive these crucial thoughts in some other way; we need a different reason for supposing them true. We might hope simply to award ourselves as obvious the idea that colour, though not itself a disposition, is essentially phenomenal in some other sense. But we cannot in this way award

ourselves the thought that value is essentially motivational, once we distinguish the shape of the situation from the resulting disposition. For
this thought was just the one at issue in the first place, the one we
offered to use the analogy with colour to explain.

The problem would not be that we can no longer retain our sense
that value is both objective and intrinsically motivational. This sense
can be expressed by the claim that stage 3 exists in virtue of (results
from) stage 2. We need not be deterred from saying that this makes
value intrinsically motivational. We have not lost the truth we are trying to capture. But what we have lost is our *explanation* of the matter.
And we have also lost our explanation of the fact that value cannot
in principle outstrip our ability to recognize it. That explanation was
previously offered by the identification of value with a disposition,
one which could not be conceived as present if we were in principle
unable to respond. If we abandon that identification we need a new
explanation.

So there is a clear reason for McDowell to stick to the identification
of value with a disposition to elicit a merited response. The question is
whether he can do this both for colour and for value, so as to retain
the advantages of the secondary quality analogy. He needs to establish
the tripartite analysis on both sides, if he is to use the analogy to show
that there need be no difficulty in conceiving of value as both objective
and internally or intrinsically related to the mind.

7 SHAPES AND DISPOSITIONS

We need, I think, to be clearer about the argument that enticed us to
distinguish stage 2 from stage 3 in the four-stage analysis. In the case
of colour, this 'argument' was a simple appeal to the phenomenology
of colour experience. We just do not experience colour as a disposition
in the object, and as realists we want an account of what colour is
which doesn't distort our experience.[25]

In the case of value we might try the same appeal to phenomenology,
but the appeal may not look so strong in this case. There are differences
between the cases which McDowell's notion of meriting seems to capture
well. I suggested earlier that we should say that the situation merits a
certain response *because of* its shape rather than identify the meriting
with the shape. But the account of shape which I gave in chapter 7
might serve to defeat this suggestion. Can we really be forced to separate two stages, first the experience of the relevant salient properties as
salient, and second the realization of what it is that they together stand

as reasons to do? My account of shape seemed to leave us with the idea that in our eventual view of the shape of the situation, we experience it as calling for such and such a response, and this seems to *identify* the shape with a disposition to elicit a merited response. There is, of course, an earlier stage in which we experience a feature as relevant, i.e. as making some difference or other to how we ought here to act, but without any clear understanding of quite what difference it makes. In the example I discussed there, I suggested that we might come eventually to see the presence of the intoxicated as a reason to take a less direct route to the station. This is the difference which this feature in fact makes to how we should act, and our recognition of this may occur at a relatively late stage; first we see that it matters somehow – that we must choose a course of action which accommodates this feature – and only later do we come to see exactly what contribution it makes to the action called for.

It is tempting therefore to think of the moral property of meriting a response as identical with the disposition to elicit a merited response. This fits the metaphysical nature of the situation, and it does not distort the phenomenology. The experience of value is the experience of a situation as calling for a certain response, and we can see this as a disposition in the case to extract a merited response from us. But now the question is whether similar remarks can be made about colour. McDowell needs to make such remarks if the analogy between colour and value is to do what he wants it to, and I doubt whether this can be made to work.

The basic move behind the identification of the value with a disposition is that of thinning out the disposition so that it is virtually transparent. In experiencing the salient properties together as calling for this response, we see them as being 'such as to merit' this action. This 'such as to' is a topic-neutral phrase which we should not take to introduce a substantial shift from the experience of the categorical to that of the dispositional. Any worries I originally had about the experience of value as dispositional derived, by contrast, from keeping the relevant dispositions thick, so as to be able to make metaphysical play with them. So the question now is whether the same ploy will work for colour. Can we see the experience of colour in these terms as the experience of an object as being (thinly) 'such as to' elicit a certain experience in us? My own view is that even if this manoeuvre does work for value, it doesn't work for colour. It simply isn't possible to thin out the disposition enough.

McDowell would like to press the question why we should be led to distinguish awareness of a shirt as blue from awareness of it as being such as to look blue. If we are working with a thin enough sort of disposition, what difference is there going to be here? The reply is that though I can indeed be aware of an object as being such as to look a certain way, this is not the way I am aware of the blueness in a normal situation. There is a certain 'raw' nature to experienced colour, which it strains credulity to see as any sort of disposition, no matter how thin.[26] There doesn't seem to be such a raw nature to moral experience, which is one reason why it is possible to think of the experience of value as the experience of a suitably thinned out disposition. Indeed, it is plausible in the moral case to see the so-called 'experience' more as a form of judgement, which is not at all so tempting in the case of colour.

If this is right, we have two options. The first is to abandon the analogy and use our account of value as meriting directly, to show an intrinsic relation between objective value and the will, while admitting that we can no longer appeal to colour as a model. The second is to revert to the four-stage analysis of value, distinguish between value and meriting, and look for a new explanation of the existence of an internal relation between value and the will. In fact, whichever we choose (and like most people I prefer the first), we are going to need a new explanation, and I end this chapter by suggesting one which might serve either approach. It will be remembered that the dispositional account of value offered to answer two questions. First, it was to tell us how it is that value is intrinsically related to the will; second, it was to say how it is that value cannot exist without the possibility of awareness, for somehow value is value *for us*. The path that McDowell followed was to answer the second by means of an answer to the first. But it might be possible to reverse this order of approach, so as to answer the first via an answer to the second.[27]

A possible way of doing this would be to appeal to a narrative conception of shape and salience, in the way I tried to bring out in chapter 7.[28] Given the stress on narrative structures in the world, we might hope to show it impossible to say that there are stories in the world unless we allow that in a good sense the world exists *for us*. This amounts to a denial of extreme metaphysical realism about value. We could then move from that to suggest that the way in which the world exists for us when it exhibits value is a practical way. Unlike elsewhere, here the sort of response that makes value possible is an inclination of the will.

But if this move has any chance of working, why should we not rely on it directly and abandon the attempt to appeal to a supposed analogy between colour and value? The conception of shape as narrative structure is one available to those who identify value with a disposition just as much as to those who are tempted to keep the two apart. So we can admit that it is plausible to see value in the world as the disposition to elicit a merited response, and thus agree with McDowell here, while distinguishing colour from value in this respect and therefore offering a different explanation of the features he wanted the dispositional account to explain.

NOTES

1   Nagel (1986); all references to Nagel in this chapter will be to this book.
2   Ibid., p. 3.
3   Ibid., p. 5.
4   Ibid., p. 67.
5   Ibid., p. 68.
6   Ibid., p. 118.
7   Ibid., p. 18.
8   I first presented this argument in Dancy (1988a).
9   For the idea of the absolute conception, see Williams (1978), pp. 64–7 and 244–9.
10 Nagel (1986), p. 18.
11 Ibid., p. 152.
12 Ibid., p. 183.
13 Despite what Nagel is tempted to suppose, but see my earlier comments on his excessive generalism in 6.4.
14 See, for example, his phrase 'clouded subjective appearance' on p. 114.
15 Ibid., p. 68.
16 Ibid., p. 118.
17 The other is Nagel's generalism.
18 See McDowell (1985).
19 In my first attempt at this topic, I mistakenly took it that the analogy rested partly on the idea that the response in both cases was an experience; see Dancy (1986). I was not alone in this. See, for instance, Wright (1988), where the concentration on the idea that a value is a disposition in the object to cause a distinctive sort of experience in a suitable perceiver (rather than an inclination of the will) leads Wright to some well-grounded but not centrally relevant remarks to the effect that no such experience occurs.
20 McDowell (1985), p. 118.
21 Our earlier discussion of Nagel brings to mind another family of ideas related to objectivity. We can call a property objective if: (1) the concept of that property can be grasped by beings with radically different perspectives; or (2) our ability to conceive of the world as exemplifying it is not to be explained as a product of any peculiarities of our perspective (at the limit, if it could be grasped from a perspective with no peculiarities, the

view from nowhere; but we don't have to allow this as a possibility). I am inclined to see this sort of objectivity as distinct in principle from both primary and secondary objectivity, and so to think of it not so much as a third form of objectivity for properties, rather hard to map onto the first two, but as a distinction between objective and subjective *concepts*. In this sense, the concepts of some properties with secondary objectivity may be subjective. Must the concepts of all properties with primary objectivity be objective? I do not see why. To say that a property is adequately conceivable otherwise than in terms of certain subjective states is not to say that creatures who lack those states will necessarily be able to conceive of the property. For one might require an acquaintance with certain subjective states in order to see the point of the concept, without this meaning that the concept is to be understood *in terms of* those subjective states. A possible example here is the concept of danger. One might not be able to see the point of this concept if one had no experience of suffering, even though the property of dangerousness is adequately conceivable in terms of physical damage, loss of life and limb and so on rather than in terms of the attendant suffering.

22 Note the way in which Nagel also rejects this sort of extreme realism, by holding that the view from nowhere would be unable to recognize value; values do not have the highest degree of objectivity.

23 See, for example, Mackie (1976), ch. 1.

24 I originally pursued this line of thought in Dancy (1986). Crispin Wright replies: 'The worry is: if redness *is* a dispositional property, should not experience as of something red – an experience which *represents* an object as red – represent it ... as possessing the relevant disposition? Well, not if the representational content of an experience is a function of the concepts which the subject is actually able to bring to bear upon it, and if it is possible to grasp the concept red without *realising* that it is a concept of a dispositional property' (1988, p. 5n). But take someone who does have the concept of a dispositional property: me, for instance. I've even come across the idea that redness is one such. But I don't believe that (Wright's 'realise' is question-begging) redness is a dispositional property. And one of my reasons is that I just don't see how to make sense of the idea, while concentrating on an instance of presented redness, that *that* property is a disposition. Though I have the relevant concepts, this in no way affects the 'raw' (see Wright, 1988, p. 12) nature of experienced colour for me. (There are, of course, plenty of cases where such changes do occur.) So since the nature of presented redness is hard to square with the dispositional analysis, I conclude that that analysis distorts the concept of colour and, in particular, makes it hard for realists to appeal to colour in support of their general programme. For part of that programme is the attempt to take seriously the idea that things are as they appear to be. Moral realism starts from the thought that there seem to us to be reasons and values in the world about which we can make dreadful mistakes, and tries to tell a story in which this

appearance comes out true. It is not promising, in the pursuit of this general aim, to take as one's model an account which announces that things are, in the relevant respect, not at all what they seem.

25 Hookway (1986) argues that this thought derives from taking colour implausibly as a single-track rather than as a multi-track disposition. I agree that if colour is a disposition, it is a multi-track disposition. But I think that our colour experience is of a quality which presents itself as not dispositional at all. What is more, I would say that we experience colour as a simple quality in a way that an analysis of it as multi-track only makes it harder to capture.

26 Wright (1988) draws attention to this 'raw' nature, but sees no problems in thinking of this as a disposition. I find this peculiar.

27 At this point we have cast off any attempt to run the analogy with secondary qualities, aiming instead to establish the essential connection between value and the will directly. In this I agree with Crispin Wright (1988), though the particular way in which I look to achieve this is different.

28 I owe to Candace Vogler the suggestion that narrativity might be the key to the problem here.

10
Towards agent-relativity

1 Non-consequentialist reasons

It is one thing to decide what an objective reason would be like if there were any, and another to decide what objective reasons there are. The remainder of this book will be concerned to dispute the consequentialist claim that all objective moral reasons are consequentialist reasons. The focus of the debate will be on the question whether there are any agent-relative reasons as well as the agent-neutral reasons which consequentialism is happy to allow. Consequentialism stands as a restriction on the sorts of reasons there can be, and typically it is said to allow only the agent-neutral. But we shall find some reason to doubt this last thought, on two grounds. First, consequentialism may err even in its conception of the agent-neutral reasons which it allows. If it does, we should not allow that it is right some of the time; this would not be the place for compromise. Second, even if consequentialism does not err on this first point, there may be neutral but non-consequentialist reasons. Indeed, I think that there are; and if there are, we need to do more to establish the existence of agent-relative reasons than to show that consequentialism is not the whole truth.

So consequentialism can be disputed on three grounds. We may say that there are agent-relative reasons as well as the neutral reasons it allows. We may say that there are agent-neutral reasons other than those it allows. And we can say, most trenchantly, that it misunderstands the neutral reasons which it allows, i.e. it distorts the way in which thoughts about consequences can generate reasons.[1] One interesting question is whether these three attacks are independent. Part of the general thrust of this chapter will be to suggest that they are not: that the first attack will have little hope of success unless we make the third, most trenchant one as well.

But despite these caveats we can work with the standard way of

seeing the debate as one between ordinary morality, which claims that
there are agent-relative reasons, and a sophisticated consequentialism
which denies that claim. The latter is a formal distillation of traditional
utilitarianism. Consequentialism claims that we assess the moral worth
of an action by appeal to its consequences – to the difference it makes
to the world that the action was done. Utilitarianism claims this too,
but goes beyond it by specifying which aspects of the consequences
are to count in the creation of value. Exactly which are to count will
depend on the version of utilitarianism we are considering. Classical
utilitarianism only looks at the amount of welfare generated; more complex versions may allow themselves to consider the distribution of welfare
as well. Consequentialism as such makes no claims of this sort at all;
it allows itself to adopt whatever the true theory of value will turn out
to be. And it can also be flexible about what is to count as a 'consequence'. Any considerations which surface in the difference it makes to
the world that the action was done may count towards the value of the
action, even if we would not normally call these 'consequences' of the
action. So a consequentialist need not deny the existence of value in an
action that is an expression of a deeply felt personal commitment, even
if that action is a complete failure. That the action was done makes
some difference to the world, and a consequentialist may adopt a theory
of value under which the world is a better place for having such expressions of personal commitment going on in it. Equally, consequentialists may say that there is value in agents' acting in accordance
with their own moral views, whether or not the actions they then do
are right or wrong. So contemporary consequentialism is extremely
flexible. But it still counts as a formal restriction on the sorts of moral
reasons there can be.

Ordinary morality takes there to be at least two sorts of non-neutral,
and so non-consequentialist, reasons. The first of these are options. In
chapter 8 I argued that at least sometimes agents have the option not
to sacrifice themselves for 'the greater good'. The idea that some actions
are supererogatory is just the idea that in certain circumstances agents
may choose an action other than the one that would most promote the
good – the one that would make the best difference to the way the
world goes. But there may be other sorts of options besides those derived from supererogation. One very common suggestion is that we
have an option to favour our friends and family – to prefer a lesser
good for them to a greater good for some stranger. This would be an
option to be *partial*.

The other non-consequentialist reasons are constraints on our freedom
to promote the good.[2] The suggestion here is that there are some acts

(or some types of acts) that we should not do even if doing them would promote the overall good. The classic examples are of acts which we should not do even in order to lessen the number of such acts. At the limit, there may even be acts that we should avoid whatever the consequences. But we do not need to go so far as this to make the initial point that some actions seem to be forbidden for reasons that do not depend on the idea that the world is the worse for their occurrence – on the difference their performance makes to the world. If there are any such actions, it would seem that the reasons not to do them stand outside those allowed by even the most flexible consequentialist.

So the question whether there are any non-consequentialist reasons, in the current state of the debate, is the question whether there are any such options and constraints. The question whether there are non-consequentialist neutral reasons is to be left aside for the moment; we return to it later.

2 Scheffler's liberation strategy

The picture of the debate which I have been outlining is one which we largely owe to the influential work of Samuel Scheffler.[3] In giving this picture, Scheffler argues that consequentialist reasons – those deriving from the difference an action will make to the world – are common ground. All should agree that the consequences of an action make a difference to its value, and the only question is whether there are any reasons other than those stemming from the consequences. If there are, these further reasons should be seen as justified departures from a basically consequentialist matrix. So consequentialist reasons are in place before we start. They constitute the background against which we are to ask whether there are any reasons *other than these*.

Starting from this point, Scheffler argues in his excellent little book that it is not enough just to appeal to intuition to establish the existence of non-consequentialist reasons. We need to establish a firm philosophical grounding for the reasons that have the support of our intuition, particularly when those intuitions are in conflict with an already agreed consequentialist matrix. Scheffler accordingly suggests that agent-relative options are to be grounded in the natural independence of the personal point of view, i.e. by 'the way in which concerns and commitments are *naturally* generated from a person's point of view quite independently of the weight of those concerns in an impersonal ranking of overall states of affairs'.[4] But he goes on to argue that agent-relative constraints cannot be grounded in this way or indeed in any way at all.

So the position he ends up with is what he calls a 'distributive hybrid'. This is a form of consequentialism which requires us to act so as to maximize the good in a way that is weighted in favour of the claims of those who have the least, except in cases where we have the option to do something else. In some situations we are permitted not to maximize the good, but we are never forbidden to do so. He thinks of this position as hybrid because it holds neither that all reasons are agent-neutral nor that all are agent-relative, but that some are agent-neutral and others are agent-relative.

Scheffler calls his suggested rationale for agent-relative options the 'liberation strategy'. A peculiar feature of his position, however, is that he admits that there is another strategy, the 'maximization strategy' which achieves as much as the liberation strategy and which is available to the consequentialist. The options with which Scheffler is concerned are those derived from personal concerns and commitments. The leading idea here is that if I have devoted myself to a project whose successful completion is essential to the integrity of my life, I have the option to commit resources to this project which would have a better effect if employed elsewhere. The liberation strategy tries to take account of the natural independence of the personal point of view by giving agents the option to devote energy to their projects out of proportion to the value from an impersonal standpoint of their so doing. But consequentialists can achieve as much from their own position, by allotting considerable value to the successful achievement of personal projects of this sort. Where one's integrity is dependent on the completion of one's project, consequentialism can see the best possible outcome as including maximum possible integrity of this sort. What it justifies in so doing is not any sort of *option*, since if integrity counts towards the values of outcomes, no thoughts about integrity will be able to justify actions that fail to promote the best outcome. In this sense the liberation strategy does give us a freedom which the maximisation strategy does not. But at least every *fact* that the friend of options wanted to appeal to has been captured within the constraints of a basically consequentialist perspective.

Seen in this light, Scheffler's book emerges paradoxically as an argument in favour of consequentialism. This is for two reasons. First, it allows that consequentialism can capture in its own terms all the relevant facts. Second, it admits that the distributive hybrid which ostensibly it aims to support is genuinely hybrid, not just in the unproblematic sense that it accepts the existence of both agent-relative and agent-neutral reasons, but in the more worrying sense that it offers no unified perspective from which reasons of those two sorts can be viewed simultaneously. We are asked to adopt the consequentialist's perspective to understand the claims of outcomes, and to adopt a different perspective if we are to see the force of reasons that stem from the natural independence of the personal point of view. In these terms consequentialism emerges as definitely superior, for it is able to see the claims of integrity, on the lines of the maximization strategy, from the same perspective as that which reveals the nature of other moral reasons. What is more, Scheffler admits that there is no chance of undermining the maximization strategy from without. So he himself seems to present the distributive hybrid as theoretically unstable in a way that I take to be damaging to the project he is pursuing.

It may be possible to see here the cause of Scheffler's failure to discern any rationale for agent-relative constraints. The liberation strategy does not manage to point to anything distinctive about the reasons that ground agent-relative options that is not equally well captured by the maximization strategy. It adduces no facts that the consequentialist cannot cope with; it merely presents what it takes to be a distinctive perspective on those facts. Now if we think that there is something distinctive about the realm of agent-relative reasons in general, something common to the options and the constraints and which is central to the rationale for both, we find ourselves in a position which Scheffler has already ruled out. By admitting that there is nothing special about the options, he has already handed over to the consequentialist the very feature that we wanted to appeal to in constructing a rationale for constraints. To accept that the maximization strategy captures every relevant fact is to abandon in the case of options the very feature we are going to need to appeal to in the case of constraints.

If this is right it serves to undermine what Scheffler calls the *independence thesis*.[5] This is the thesis that a theory can consistently accept options but deny constraints, since the rationale for options is distinct from that for constraints. Scheffler asserts this thesis because he has come up with what he takes to be the correct rationale for agent-relative options, and it is clear that it fails miserably to serve equally well as a rationale for constraints. Nothing about the natural independence of the personal point of view can serve to ground a constraint. The sort of constraint which Scheffler discusses is that which forbids me to kill one innocent being in order to prevent you from killing two (or five, or whatever). The feature that the liberation strategy appealed to was the way in which concerns and commitments are *naturally* generated from a person's point of view quite independently of the weight of those concerns in an impersonal ranking of overall states of affairs. But nothing about natural concerns and commitments could succeed in justifying me in holding back from killing one when the very concerns that might lead me to do so are better served by doing what is necessary to save the five. And Scheffler argues further that there is nothing about the status of the victims that could justify this constraint, and that nothing in the notion of agency can do so either. So the rationale (if any) for options must be independent of that for constraints (the independence thesis), and in fact there is no rationale for constraints anyway. There can be options without constraints (the independence thesis) and in fact there are (this is Scheffler's *asymmetry* thesis).

It seems to me, therefore, that to adopt Scheffler's perspective on options is to abandon the cause of agent-relativity completely, because it bids fair to prevent us from finding a rationale for constraints and is in itself already less stable than a consequentialist approach to the same facts.

If I am right about this, the problem that Scheffler ends up in is an instance of a general difficulty that faces those who want to establish the existence of agent-relative reasons (or values). This general difficulty I call the two-perspective problem. When we look around us, nearer things look larger and more distant things look smaller. Similarly, from an agent-relative point of view, some people appear to occupy more moral space than others. My family loom largest for me, then come my friends, and then my neighbours. Unknown people from distant lands are in the picture, of course, but only on the horizon; they all count for the same as each other, but none counts for as much as those nearer to me in the picture. Neutral theories, by contrast, seem to require us to adopt a neutral perspective on the world (at least when thinking morally), in which everybody, including ourselves, looms as large as anybody else. Now the point is that if we take this approach, it seems impossible to combine both perspectives. We simply cannot occupy both at the same time, because they are incompatible.

The two-perspective problem catches Scheffler because he fails to show how to knit the neutral and the agent-relative perspectives together into one coherent whole. It can catch other agent-relativists in different ways, most notably by persuading them that in order to defend the agent-relative they have to unseat the neutral. In this vein they may be moved to deny not only the existence of consequentialist reasons but also of neutral reasons in general. As we will see in chapter 11, this tendency can affect neutralists as well; it is common to find it suggested that agent-relative approaches are at best justified distortions of the neutral truth.

Before ending this section, I want to mention a rather better reason in favour of the independence thesis than the one Scheffler produces. I have spoken of two sorts of agent-relative reason, options and constraints.

But are they both agent-relative in the same sense? If they are not, we might expect to be able to find a rationale for those that are agent-relative in the first sense without necessarily finding one for those that are agent-relative in the second sense. And there is some antecedent reason to distinguish the agent-relativity of options from that of constraints. Constraints focus on agency. The general idea is that even though the world would go better if the forbidden actions were done, nobody should do them. This will be built up later, but however that is to be done it does seem that we have here a phenomenon different from the one at issue with options. My option not to sacrifice myself stems, apparently, from thoughts of the cost to me of such a sacrifice. Here ideas about agency are not the real point, one might think. So though both options and constraints are agent-relative, they are not so in the same sense.

This generates a far better argument in favour of the independence thesis than Scheffler's. His depends on his being right about the rationale for options. If he is wrong about that, he has no reason for his independence thesis. My reason does not require me to be right about anything except the prima facie difference between options and constraints. (I give my reply to this argument in 10.4 below.)

3   AGAINST THE INDEPENDENCE THESIS

I have been suggesting that we should be suspicious of the way in which the independence thesis emerges from Scheffler's discussion. But that thesis has come under direct attack from all sides. I consider here two direct arguments that the thesis is false. They may admit, as I suggested at the end of the previous section, that there is a prima facie argument in its favour. But they argue that in fact it is false (without suggesting exactly how to discount the appearances on which the prima facie argument relied).

Stephen Darwall, in a paper whose general thrust I am following in urging that Scheffler's distributive hybrid is not a promising path for a consistent agent-relativist to follow, argues that a theory that has options but no constraints must be unstable. This is not for the reason I gave above (my worries about the hybrid nature of Scheffler's overall position). Darwall argues that 'the idea of a prerogative (in my terms, an option) suggests the idea of a morally protected sphere of personal action, but without an accompanying constraint on the acts of others, the sphere will not be protected against morally sanctioned interference.'[6]

This argument seems to me quite mistaken. That I am within my moral rights to do something does nothing to show that others are not within their rights to do it instead of me or to stop me and so prevent it being done at all. Darwall is working with an optional picture of options. What is more, it had better be optional for his purposes, for his own broadly Kantian ethics, which he takes to ground both agent-relative options and agent-relative constraints, is subject to the same complaint. Darwall supposes that the agent's fundamental concern is with his own moral integrity, and that this justifies my thinking it wrong for me to kill one to prevent your killing two; in this sense there is a rationale for an agent-relative constraint on killing. But he does nothing to show that there cannot be a case where I can only preserve my integrity at the cost of yours and vice versa. In such cases, morality permits and even requires a struggle. So if Darwall is right to describe Scheffler's position as 'unstable' for this reason, he should accept that his own approach shares that weakness. Myself, I don't see it as a weakness anyway. For the idea that it is a weakness derives from an unwitting consequentialism. The picture of the moral rights, permissions and duties of every individual as all being fully exercisable together is one which consequentialism expresses. The claim that perfect agents would all rub shoulders without moral friction is in my view a consequentialist pipedream, and to see the possibility of another picture is to rid oneself of yet another consequentialist presupposition.

Representing the consequentialists, Shelly Kagan argues that there can be no options unless there are also constraints.[7] His reason is that an option to pursue a project must include an option to allow harm which one could have prevented had one's energies not been justifiably taken up with the pursuit of one's project. But if so, what will stop our having an unacceptable option to do harm where this is required for the successful completion of one's project? The most plausible justification of options is that which appeals to the cost to the agent of holding the pursuit of one's reasonable projects always secondary to the demand that one promote the good. But this appeal to cost will justify harming others as easily as it justifies allowing harm, in a quite unacceptable way. The only way to stop this is to introduce a constraint on harming.

Kagan goes on to argue that there can be no coherent rationale for such a constraint, but that is not my present concern. I am only interested here in his argument that there cannot be options without constraints. Notice too that he does not argue this in general; what options require is not some constraint or other, but the constraint against harming in particular. And when Kagan comes to argue that there can be no rationale for the constraint against harm, he does not argue that there cannot be a rationale for constraints in general, only for this one.

In the terms given above, where the option to do harm emerges really as the option to do anything required for the successful completion of one's project, we may hope to find some answer to Kagan. We might start from the idea that only certain projects are permissible, and those are ones which do not require harming others. This is a restriction on one's options, but that is not at all the same thing as a constraint. Remember that the sort of constraint we are talking about here is one which goes against the balance of consequentialist reasons, one which forbids our doing an action that is supported by that balance. The sort of restriction that is in play when I do not have an option is a different sort of limitation, one driven by the consequentialist reasons rather than standing against them.

Kagan would probably wish to press here his later question why projects that require harming should be impermissible while those which require us to allow avoidable harm are not. This is a perfectly reasonable question, and it needs an answer. But Kagan is trying to show that options require a constraint against harming before he gets into that sort of detailed debate, and in these terms and on this point I think he fails. However, I have to some extent distorted his approach to the matter by concentrating on permissible projects rather than on the option not to sacrifice oneself. What Kagan in fact argues is that an option not to sacrifice oneself will most probably be grounded on an appeal to the cost to the agent. But if I am to be justified in allowing a harm to another because of a lesser harm to myself which I would incur in preventing that harm, what is to stop me from being justified in harming another in order to escape a lesser harm to myself? After all, the cost involved in not harming may be as great, or greater, than the cost involved in preventing a harm. The only possible solution is a general constraint on harming, and so it emerges that an option not to sacrifice oneself requires a specific constraint against harming if it is to be plausible at all. Otherwise we are in danger of granting me the option to kill my uncle Albert if that is my only way of getting to inherit a million dollars.

The first thing to notice is that the sort of cost at issue here is not the sort of cost that people normally have in mind when they suggest that there are agent-relative values. There they are considering costs such as that of abandoning the projects which give one's life a meaning, or of ceasing to favour one's children. Clearly the idea that costs such as these are distorted by the consequentialist's attempt to see them in an agent-neutral light is not intended to be generalized to all costs whatever. Ordinary morality endorses regret for costs like these, whereas it is not morally permissible to regret not having a million dollars because one hasn't killed one's uncle. One possibility, then, would be to distinguish between basic and non-basic harm. The loss of a million dollars is a harm, but a non-basic one. Options are generated only by the prospect of basic harm. Basic harm is the loss of the conditions necessary for a reasonable life. If I already have a reasonable life, I have no option to kill my uncle to get a million dollars. And if I don't have a reasonable life, I still have no option to deprive him of (the conditions necessary for a reasonable) life. For this would be to deprive him of a basic good merely in order to get the same good for myself. Equally, I have a duty to give to famine relief where I have more than is necessary for a reasonable life. Where I have a surplus, and my charitable giving creates more good for others than it causes harm for me, I have a duty to share. But if I only have enough for a reasonable life, I have no duty to give, even though giving would still create more good for others than it would cause harm for me. So the consequentialist requirement to give until the cost to me is equal to the benefit for others is opposed by an option. This option only comes into play at a certain point, but it is not attended by an constraint.

4 CONSEQUENTIALISM AND CONSEQUENCES

So I do not think that Kagan manages to establish in advance that options require a specific constraint against harming. This means that neither Darwall nor Kagan manage to undermine Scheffler's independence thesis. But there are further points to be made here, which we owe to Philippa Foot. She argues that a non-hybrid understanding of the phenomena that Scheffler points to will generate constraints in a perfectly natural way. If we accept consequentialism's understanding of consequence-based reasons – the ones it is most sure about – we will not be able to substantiate either options or constraints, while if we reject it we will be able to establish both with equal ease.

Foot's perspective on this issue is distinctly Kantian. So it seems to me worth looking at the views of Kant himself before turning to contemporary post-Kantians. The first chapter of Kant's *Groundwork* is intended to motivate and express a radically anti-consequentialist position in ethics, but one which admits that the consequences of an action are not irrelevant to its moral worth. And this is just what the agent-relativist seems to be looking for – a position which accepts the relevance of consequences without putting them in centre stage as consequentialists wish to. So of the three ways of attacking consequentialism which

I distinguished at the start of this chapter, Kant adopts the most trenchant.

Kant starts from a distinction between value and moral value. Mere states of affairs can be good, but they cannot be morally good. It is good when a starving person finds food, and when a freezing person finds warmth and clothing. But these things are not morally good. If there is such a thing as moral worth, then, we must look for it else-where. As far as this goes, the consequences of an action are just so many states of affairs and cannot be thought of as having moral value. So what sort of thing can have moral worth? The obvious answer is an action – or perhaps an agent. Now an action that has moral worth cannot get it from its consequences, for the consequences have no moral worth to pass on, as it were. One cannot catch measles from someone who has not got measles, and analogously we cannot think of con-sequences as being morally infectious. Could an action acquire moral worth from its *intended* rather than its *actual* consequences? Not if the worth is to stem from the nature of the consequences intended rather than from the intending of them. For, again, no consequences, whether intended or actual, have any moral worth to pass on. If there is any such thing as moral worth, then, it stems from some features of human motivation rather than directly from what we are or might be motivated to do. (Kant's argument is an argument by remainder; like Sherlock Holmes, he eliminates possibilities until only one remains.) Ordinary human motivation is motivation by inclination – Humean motivation. But an action done out of inclination has no value of its own; it gets what value it has from that which belongs to the state of affairs one is motivated to promote, and no states of affairs have moral value, as we have already seen. So if there is to be any moral worth, there must be actions that are not done out of inclination; there must be such a thing as non-Humean motivation. Truly *moral* motivation will occur when an action is done not out of inclination but out of duty.

But what is it to do an action out of duty? What could this be, if it is to be genuinely distinct from acting out of inclination? Every action has a maxim – a description in the light of which we come to choose it. If we adopt that maxim for our own purposes, we are acting from inclination and our action has no moral worth. When we act from duty, then, we must be adopting our maxim not for our purposes but for its own sake. We must be acting not so as to serve inclination but out of respect for some feature of our maxim. But what could there be about our maxim that could demand this sort of respect? One thing that we notice is that though each action done from duty has, as it were, its own maxim, there is a good sense in which all are done for the same reason

– because they are right; all are done out of duty. So it must be the same feature of the maxims that we respect in each case. What feature do all maxims have in common? The only thing common to all maxims is that they can serve as a *law* – as a principle governing our choice. As such a law, the maxim cannot here be appealing to our desires or inclinations. It must therefore be appealing to our reason; it appeals to us not as creatures with desires but as rational beings. So maxims have this in common, that they can serve as a law for a rational being. (If they don't, then again there is no place left for moral worth.) Now there is no relevant difference between one rational being and another. All may differ in their inclinations, but as rational beings they are indistinguishable. So when we act out of respect for our maxim, we are acting out of respect for its ability to serve as a law not just for us but for all rational beings.

This is the way in which Kant reaches his Categorical Imperative.[8] Now so far he seems to hold the consequences of an action irrelevant to its moral worth. But this is an exaggeration of the true position. All he has so far established is that moral worth does not *stem* from consequences. But considerations of consequences can enter the story if relevant to the question whether it is possible for a rational being to act out of respect for some particular maxim. For instance, in considering the example of the lying promise, Kant appeals to the consequences of all acting on the maxim 'Whenever I believe myself short of money, I will borrow money and promise to pay it back, though I know that this will never be done.'[9] He suggests that if all acted on this maxim, 'this would make promising, and the very purpose of promising, impossible, since no one would believe he was being promised anything, but would laugh at utterances of this kind as empty shams.'[10] This is not the point that if we all acted on this maxim, we would be deprived of a useful social institution. If Kant argued this way, he would indeed be in conflict with his own position, as many commentators have charged. Instead, it is the point that it is incoherent to suppose that all should act on a maxim which is such that if all acted on it none could act on it. This incoherence is established by appeal to consequences. Consequences therefore do play a role in Kant's theory, but not the role envisaged by the consequentialist. There is nothing like the thought that all agree on the relevance of consequences in moral judgement. All may agree that the consequences play some role or other, perhaps. But there is no agreement on the role they play – on the sort of relevance which consequences have here.

This is why it is unpromising, in the construction of an anti-consequentialist position, to admit in advance, as Scheffler does, that consequentialists have got something right at least. This is the point that Philippa Foot is trying to establish, but without going anything like so far as Kant. She suggests that in the context of a virtue-based ethic, one which understands moral demands as those which issue from the claims on us of the moral virtues, the need to maximize welfare (to the extent that there is such a need) is to be seen as generated by the virtue of beneficence. This virtue is certainly all to do with performing actions which have certain consequences.[11] But not all virtues are like this; think of fidelity and truthfulness, for instance. And the reasons which these virtues generate are in no way secondary to those generated by bene-volence or other consequence-directed virtues. So there are naturally going to be cases where the demand that we should maximize welfare or more generally optimize consequences is defeated by a prohibition derived from a different virtue. Foot expresses this point by saying that we should do everything *permissible* to optimize consequences; but all this means is that where the demands of other virtues permit, those of benevolence are paramount.

This virtue-based approach offers an answer to the two-perspective problem; it shows us how to combine in one coherent whole the de-mands of the neutral and the flexibility of the agent-relative. Benevolence is a neutral (impartial) virtue, and care for one's family and friends is a partial virtue. These virtues are in tension, perhaps, in terms of the demands they place on action. But they are not contradictory, as the two-perspective problem wants to suggest. It is possible for the same person to have both virtues at once.

With this different placing of consequences, is Foot's position now likely to ground both options and constraints? This question is ambiguous because the notion of a non-consequentialist option is ambiguous. Foot's virtue-based approach allows that there are cases where an agent should not go by the consequentialist calculus – where some other action is required of him. But it does not so nicely capture the idea that the agent has an option to act in one way rather than another. The agent is *permitted* to pursue his own projects in certain circumstances rather than to abandon them for the sake of the optimal outcome, perhaps. In this sense there is a non-consequentialist option. But nothing is said here to make sense of the thought that in such cases there are moral reasons which the agent has the right to ignore or discount, so that he has a sort of moral *freedom*. The virtue-based approach seems to have it that where the demands of virtue do not require that be-nevolence be one's dominant motive (or, in consequentialist language, where one is permitted not to maximize outcomes), they require that it should not be one's dominant motive (i.e. that one should not maximize outcomes).[12] This was not what we were hoping for in suggesting that there are moral options. We wanted to say that on some occasions at least the agent has both the right to sacrifice himself and the right to hold back, and nothing in Foot's approach makes room for this idea.

So Foot's position, paradoxically, establishes the independence thesis in reverse: there are constraints but no real options. In this she fails in her announced aim of showing how a smooth account of options and constraints is available. I think this fact is hidden from her because she has confused the weak and the strong sense of an option. Her virtue-based approach gives us weak options but not the strong ones we really want. But I am not presenting this as a major criticism of Foot, since she does not purport to offer any direct defence of agent-relative reasons. She is trying to hit consequentialism in the place that hurts most – in its conception of consequence-based reasons. We might say charitably that she simply leaves it open whether her virtue-based approach can contribute to the rationale for agent-relativity.

The distinction between the weaker notion of an option (in which Foot's approach makes room for options) and the stronger sense (in which it doesn't) gives us our reply to the argument at the end of 10.2 that options and constraints are not agent-relative in the same sense, and that therefore there is a prima facie plausibility to the independence thesis. With the stronger sense of an option, we have the right both to sacrifice ourselves and not to sacrifice ourselves, despite the balance of neutral reasons in favour of the sacrifice. Our moral freedom is two-faced here. This notion of an option is more complex than the one which underlay the argument above. The importance of the right to choose, and so to go either way, re-focuses our attention on the concept of agency which fades from the picture if we think only in terms of the weaker sort of option.

In this section I have suggested two distinct ways of expressing the idea that even though the consequences of an action are relevant to its moral value, this fact does not need to be captured in a consequentialist way. If this idea is true, we have hit consequentialism where it should hurt most, i.e. in its picture of the reasons of which it is most certain. It is this possibility that underlies the suggestion that, by admitting that consequentialism is right about something, Scheffler prevents himself from providing a rationale for constraints as well as for options. However, it turns out that not all ways of building up a non-consequentialist account of the moral relevance of consequences will provide a rationale both for options and for constraints. Foot's fails to do so, and Kant's may well be defective in the same way.

5   THE *PRO TANTO* REASON TO PROMOTE THE GOOD

There is a consequentialist reply here which needs to be considered before we can move on. This is made by Kagan.[13] He takes the view that all agree on the existence of what he calls a '*pro tanto*' reason to promote the good. (The term '*pro tanto*' is new terminology, replacing Ross's confusing notion of a prima facie duty, which is always being wrongly taken to mean something which might at first glance look like a duty; '*pro tanto*' means roughly 'as far as that goes'.) This reason may perhaps exist alongside options and constraints, but it is permanently present and recognized both by ordinary morality and by consequentialism. Let us call this special *pro tanto* reason the PTR. Kagan obviously takes it that the PTR is in place and that the problem for the defender of ordinary morality, whom he calls 'the moderate', is to motivate options and constraints as departures from it. This is just the picture I have been complaining about.

But what is interesting about Kagan's position is that he does not just assume that moderates accept the PTR. He produces arguments. If he had not done this, it would have been easy for me to say that no particularist accepts anything like the PTR; despite the new terminology, Kagan is firmly wedded to Rossian generalism, and it is in these terms that he sets the debate.[14] So the arguments he produces must work both in favour of generalism and in favour of the existence of one generalist reason in particular, namely the PTR. The style of these arguments is that the existence of the PTR is the best explanation of judgements that moderates want to make. The PTR means that there is always *some* reason to promote the good, but not that this reason is always the strongest. Moderates accept this because they admit that, though I am not required to sacrifice my life savings to save the life of a stranger, I have *some* reason to save the stranger and so to sacrifice my savings if necessary. Again: 'Consider the case where killing one innocent person is the only way to save two others from being killed. The moderate believes that it is forbidden to kill the one; but I take it that he does not want to say that there is no reason at all to save the two – i.e. that there is no consideration at all that speaks in favour of killing the one.'[15]

One could say against this that the generalist picture is more assumed than argued for. But moderates who are not disturbed by that still have something to say. They can question the implicit principle that a desirable end generates a reason to perform the necessary means. In the killing case, the idea would be that there is strong reason to save the two, but no reason to kill the one even though this is the only way to save the two (since there is a constraint on killing the innocent, perhaps; constraints of this sort do not merely defeat but abolish or undermine or silence opposing reasons). Consider an analogy which I got from Larry Temkin: I am stranded in the desert, desperate for an ice-cool beer; the Devil offers me a beer in exchange for my child. Do I have some reason to give my child to the devil? I think not.

It might be thought that this is irrelevant, and effectively grants Kagan's point. For haven't I just admitted that there is reason to save the two? Saving the two would most promote the good. So I have granted that there is some reason to promote the good – the PTR. But this is a mistake. My moderate is saying that the action that would most promote the good is that of killing the one, and I have no reason at all to do this. And this claim is incompatible with the existence of the PTR.

If the constraint has a threshold, matters become more interesting. Now we have it that at a certain point (where I can save 1000 others by killing the one) I am not only permitted but required to kill the one. The moderate should claim that before that point my conclusive reason not to kill the one abolishes any potential reasons for killing, unless they themselves stem from constraints. But where the reasons for killing are strong enough, they escape abolition and ground a requirement to kill. There is still the conclusive reason not to kill, however. This is the stuff of a tragic dilemma. For we have a conclusive reason to kill and a conclusive reason not to kill, something that Kagan's consequentialist approach to reasoning as the weighing of reasons to see which is the stronger prevents him from admitting as a possibility. I conclude here that Kagan does not succeed in pinning his moderate (the friend of options and constraints) to the existence of a *pro tanto* reason to promote the good.

There is a certain lack of reality about the discussion above, as far as I am concerned, since it is conducted in Kagan's terms. I have accepted something close to his picture of absolute and threshold constraints, and tried to suggest that even in those terms his position is not secure. In chapter 12, however, I offer a very different account of these constraints, in terms of which the matters here discussed look quite different. So moderates who are unhappy with what has been said on their behalf so far have further resources.

It seems then that though Scheffler's approach has been very influential, it is not one which an agent-relativist is necessarily well advised to follow. It contains three questionable elements. The first and most significant is the consequentialist presumption that reasons stemming from consequences are already in place, so that all others are to be understood as departures from a basically consequentialist matrix. The second is the independence thesis, and the third is the resulting sense that constraints are going to be very much harder to justify than options are.

6   FORMS OF AGENT-RELATIVITY

There are two further criticisms that could be levelled at Scheffler. The first, which I shall only mention here in the hope of developing it later, is that in his stress on the independence of the personal *point of view* Scheffler distracts our attention from the crucial factor, namely *agency*. A central element in many attempts to provide a rationale for non-consequentialist reasons is an appeal to natural motivation – to that which we cannot be motivated by or to that which we cannot avoid being motivated by. To my mind, thoughts about points of view are not best suited to capturing this avenue of approach.

The second criticism is that there are more sorts of agent-relative reasons than the two which Scheffler's book discusses, those deriving from personal concerns and commitments and those stemming from deontological constraints. In particular, there are more sorts of options. As Michael Slote argues,[16] ordinary morality seems to recognize an option to sacrifice oneself even when doing so creates a good for others which is less than the harm one incurs for oneself. It may be that such a sacrifice is not very sensible, but in general it will not be morally forbidden and on occasions it will be even praiseworthy. A good example of the sort of view that fails to capture this point is that of Stephen Darwall, mentioned earlier. If the agent's fundamental concern is with his own moral integrity, there will be no permission for me to accept a stain on my moral character in order to save you from one. But in general ordinary morality would see nothing wrong with such a sacrifice. Slote calls this feature the self-other asymmetry. In fact, there seem to be at least four distinct classes of reasons that generate options:

1   Reasons of autonomy (these stem from *existing* personal concerns and commitments).
2   Reasons of choice (these justify us in adopting *new* concerns other than the concern to maximize the good).
3   Reasons of supererogation (discussed in chapter 8).
4   The self-other asymmetry (reasons that justify a non-maximizing sacrifice).

Some wish to collapse the distinction between reasons of types 1 and 3. But I think that they should be kept apart at this stage. The intuitive reason for this separation is that the existence of some project or other is too parochial a reason to bring up in the attempt to justify the recruit's failing to give his life for others. Even if he didn't have any project, he might still be justified in holding back – and not because of the projects he might adopt in the future, either. We can support this intuition in two ways. Both involve demonstrating that one might succeed in showing a rationale for reasons of type 1 without showing one for those of type 3.

The general problem we are dealing with here is the thought that consequentialism demands too much. It has no room for acts of supererogation, for such acts are ones which achieve more good than some available alternative would, but which we are not wrong not to do. So we can never be right to fail to sacrifice ourselves, if our sacrifice would leave the world better off. Equally, consequentialism demands that we never do any action when we could use our resources (money, time, energy etc.) to better effect, and so that we have no hobbies, no holidays, and in general no enthusiasms other than one for the Great Project. So consequentialism is *very* demanding – *too* demanding, in my view. If we act as consequentialism recommends, our lives will not be much worth living. Suppose, then, that we take this to create a philosophical difficulty for consequentialism, and that consequentialists are looking for some way of showing that their theory is not so demanding as all that. I will mention two possible ways of doing this, and both of them work far better for reasons of autonomy than for those of supererogation.

The first way is one which finds *intrinsic* value in there being personal projects and hobbies; the world is a better place if there are things like this going on in it. A consequentialist who says this, simply extending the list of things which have value, has something to put in the balance against the claims of others, which might on occasion justify one's reserving resources for it. Now I am not trying to say that this move is likely to work; in fact, I argue in chapter 13 that it doesn't. But it is a possible line, and my point here is that nothing like this is available in the defence of a failure to sacrifice oneself. Nobody could say that the world is the better for the sorts of interests that might serve to justify such failures; these interests may simply be a (reasonable, but hardly laudable) concern for one's own skin. This concern is not *in itself* something that the world is the better for. Its value, if it has any, is entirely instrumental. So this first defence of reasons of autonomy cannot be extended to cope with supererogation.

The second such move is more complex. We take a new start, by admitting that we would be wrong to see independent value in the pursuit of personal projects, in a way that could be distinguished from the sort of value promoted by beneficence. Rather there is one and only one sort of value at issue, promoted both by individuals pursuing their personal projects and by people putting themselves second in order to promote the welfare of others. It may be that if everyone were motivated to put others first, the world would be a generally poorer place, since there would be no art, music, culture and so on. But that only shows that consistent consequentialists should distinguish their theory of motivation from their theory of value, and fail to fall into the trap of reading one off from the other.[17] If we would create less value by aiming to maximize value, then we should aim for something else instead. The question what we should aim for is an empirical question, but a good possibility is that we should be the sorts of persons who are directly concerned for our own projects (not persons who allow themselves to have non-maximizing projects because they are aware of the reasons why this is not wrong – this would be a sort of indirect concern, in which one searches for something to mind about other than the welfare of all). This being so, the notion of 'acting as consequentialism recommends' turns out to be ambiguous. It can either mean 'achieving the aims that consequentialism specifies' or it can mean 'acting from motives of which consequentialism approves'. Using this distinction, consequentialism can claim that it does not demand too much, since it does not require people not to have and pursue personal projects. Motives of autonomy can be approved by the consequentialist.

The point here is that whether this reply works or not (I shall be arguing in chapter 13 that it is no more successful than the previous reply), it clearly does not even pretend to address the problem of supererogation. The sorts of motivation which would most promote the good are not likely to include a general reluctance to sacrifice oneself for the sake of others. This is further evidence that the two criticisms of consequentialism are distinct, i.e. that reasons of autonomy are not the same as reasons of supererogation.[18]

One point worth making before this chapter closes is that there may also be more than one type of constraint. We already have:

5   Deontological constraints.

But one suggestion which attracts me is that there are also:

6   Reasons of tolerance.

These will be reasons that forbid me to interfere with the moral autonomy of another, even when the cost of interference is less than the cost that the agent's misguided action will cause. There are limits to this constraint, of course; but this may be common to all constraints, and indeed to all options.

Finally, there may be reasons which stem from personal friendships and relationships; it is this sort of reason which justifies my spending money on my children which, as a consequentialist would put it, could be spent to better purpose elsewhere. These 'reasons of partiality' as I call them, seem to ground a combination of options and constraints; it is plausible to suggest that in some cases I am merely permitted to favour my children, and in others I am actually required to do so. It is hard to see reasons of partiality as pure options, if there are occasions when I am required to act in accordance with them. However these are to be classified, they constitute a last potential group of agent-relative reasons:

7 Reasons of partiality.

None of these types of supposedly agent-relative reasons is more than conjectural at the moment. It may be that after further discussion we shall abandon the claims of one or more than one of them. They stand at the moment simply as suggestions that are to be found in the agent-relativist literature, and any or all may yet turn out to be agent-neutral, when properly understood. But this proper understanding will need a more secure grasp on the very notion of an agent-relative reason, which is the topic of the next chapter.

NOTES

1 On all these matters, see Broome (1991), ch. 1.
2 The vocabulary in which these matters are discussed varies from author to author. Scheffler talks of an agent-centred prerogative and agent-centred restrictions. Kagan talks of options and constraints, and I have followed him. Options are also sometimes called permissions; Slote talks of permissions and constraints. It would be nice if usage could begin to stabilize in this area.
3 See Scheffler (1982).
4 Ibid., p. 9.
5 Ibid., pp. 81–2. In fact, as Scheffler expresses this thesis, it may mean either simply that a position which accepts options but not constraints is consistent, or that, whether such a position is consistent or not, the rationale for

options is not precisely the same as that for constraints. He writes (p. 81: note that he talks in terms of restrictions rather than constraints): 'this motivation is independent of any rationale there may be for agent-centred restrictions, in the sense that someone who is motivated in this way to accept a prerogative can at the same time consistently refuse to accept such restrictions. I will call this the *independence thesis*.' What exactly this should be taken to mean depends on the interpretation of the phrase 'motivated in this way'. But nothing that I say in the text hangs on this matter. For even if the independence thesis is simply the claim that the rationale that Scheffler himself offers for options will not ground constraints, he is still committed to the view that a consistent theory can embrace options and deny constraints; this is just what his theory (the distributive hybrid) does.

6　See Darwall (1986), p. 304.

7　See Kagan (1989), pp. 18–24.

8　One classic difficulty in the interpretation of the first chapter of Kant's *Groundwork* is how seriously we should take his apparent claim that the motive of duty only operates when it is alone; as soon as there is any natural inclination or hint of self-interest present, those motives are the only ones in play. This has always seemed quite unnecessarily harsh; and yet the remark does not seem to be a slip, since Kant repeats it more than once (and anyway one hesitates to accuse Kant of so gross a slip as this). So here is a rather fanciful suggestion, built on the interpretation I offer in the text, of how Kant might have come to this view. Humean desires, which are what is at issue in cases of inclination or self-interest, are essentially motivating states; they cannot be present without motivating. What is more, they cannot be added to by anything other than more desires of the same type. So if there is any Humean motivation present, all the motivation in the case is Humean. So the idea that one could be motivated both by self-interest/inclination and by duty is not available. And since where inclination is present it must motivate, Kant's result emerges. The motive of duty only motivates when we are shorn of all inducement.

9　Kant (1785), p. 85.

10　Ibid.

11　In this way consequences are found a natural place within a non-consequentialist ethic. This is an important point, and one which Darwall, in his related discussion (1986), does not address directly.

12　In this sense, Foot's position suffers from the defects that Kagan found in Scheffler. See Kagan (1984).

13　See Kagan (1989), pp. 47–64.

14　Interestingly, however, in Kagan (1988) he considers the possibility of abandoning generalism for some form of particularism.

15　Kagan (1989), p. 50.

16　See Slote (1985), chs 1–2.

17　For an early hint of this move, see Mill (1863), p. 290n; more recently, Parfit (1984), ch. 1, and Railton (1984).

18 Slote argues that the addition of reasons of types 2 and 4 shows that
    Scheffler's suggested rationale for options is too narrow. Instead, he offers
    a rationale in terms of autonomy, understood as the morally validated
    independence of an agent. My main criticism of this is that it seems to do
    little more than to recognize the *status quo*; there is a constant underlying
    worry that all that is offered by either Scheffler or Slote is a moral *imprimatur*
    on what is going to happen anyway, because it is going to happen anyway.

11
Agent-relativity –
the very idea

1 MOTIVATION

It is now time to look more seriously at the notion of an agent-relative reason. What exactly is being asserted by those who claim (and by those who deny) that there are such reasons?

I motivate the idea of an agent-relative reason in the following way. I have a personal project, which is to write a very good book on ethics. This is very important to me; it informs and gives sense to a central decade of my life. But I know that in some sense it does not matter much whether I succeed or fail. The world will not be much the richer for my success, nor much the poorer for my failure. It is hard to express this point uncontentiously, but there is enormous pressure to say something like 'it doesn't *really* matter' or 'it doesn't *objectively* matter' whether I succeed or fail. But it matters very much to me. We might try to say there is great value for me if I succeed, but it is not really important whether I succeed or not. Now the point here is that I know both these things. I know that it matters to me very much and that it doesn't really matter as much as it matters to me. Neither of these things is hidden from me. I have a perfectly clear idea of how much it really matters, and another perfectly clear idea of how much it matters to me. Neither idea is a distortion of the other. I am not engaged here in special pleading, or in cooking the books to suit myself. Of course, there is a tension in my position. But it is not the tension associated with contradiction. I am not making the mistake of thinking that my success matters a lot and only a little. I simply recognize that my success does not matter as much as it matters to me. (So 'matters to me' is not to be understood as 'believed by me to matter'.) In a way this is merely a consequence of the recognition that I don't matter much.[1]

I think everyone who has a personal project will feel this tension. What is more, it is a tension which remains even when I recognize that it does matter ('objectively', 'really') whether those who have projects succeed in them. Each such success is of value, but its value is as nothing compared to the value to the person whose project it is.[2] So even if I add the value of someone (me, in this case) succeeding in a central personal project to that of the publication of a good book on ethics (in this case, mine), I don't escape the tension between that limited value and the value there is to me. But this tension is one which I can live with. It doesn't undermine the wholeness or integrity of my life, in the sense that I can cope with it and not be torn apart by it. It does demand care in the juggling of demands on my time and energy and my right to ignore those demands on occasion to pursue my own project.

This sense that there can be a tension in the situation which does not derive from self-contradiction or from confusion is, I think, the leading thought in the construction of agent-relative value. We are to use the notion of agent-relative value to describe that situation as a tension between agent-relative and agent-neutral value, both of which are clearly present to the agent and to others. It is to preserve this thought that I have been trying to stress the importance of not assuming from the outset that agent-relative value is at best a distortion of agent-neutral value – a justified distortion, perhaps, but still a distortion. If we do start with that assumption we have simply begged the question against the picture that in my view drives the conception of agent-relativity. In chapter 9 I argued that Nagel makes this mistake despite his good intentions, and in chapter 10 I accused Scheffler of the same failure. That these mistakes were made by those who are sympathetic to the agent-relative is especially revealing.

I have been making this initial case in favour of agent-relativity by appeal to only one class of potential agent-relative reasons, those of autonomy. We can, however, immediately see that the point is not restricted to those. Reasons of supererogation seem likely to fit the pattern as well. I may be perfectly well aware that my sacrifice does not matter as much as it matters to me, without thinking of either of these thoughts as misconceived.

I take this as my starting point in trying to build up a philosophical account of the agent-relative. In working towards that account, I will be trying to keep three questions in mind. First, is the contrast between the agent-relative and the agent-neutral one contrast or many? (This is the same as the question whether the example I started from is one which *all* agent-relative reasons must fit; note that nothing yet has been said about *constraints*.) Second, how is the agent-relative/agent-neutral contrast related to the objective/subjective contrast? Third, what sort of *validation* or *rationale* is needed by reasons of either sort? My method will be to consider in turn the views of four writers: Kagan, Nagel, Sen and Parfit.

2   KAGAN

Kagan's intention in discussing the nature of the agent-relative is to show that there is no such thing as a genuinely agent-relative reason or value.[3]

Defenders of ordinary morality are trying to establish the existence of options and constraints – agent-relative reasons, in fact. But, in Kagan's view, they are doing this while agreeing that there is a *pro tanto* reason to promote the good (the PTR). So to establish that the PTR is not always overriding, it is necessary to discover a good or value which:

1   we are, after reflection, unwilling to deny or dismiss as morally illegitimate
2   could not be adequately appreciated from an objective point of view, because of the impartiality of that point of view
3   for the recognition of which a disproportionate concern with one's own interest is required.[4]

This is Kagan's account of the agent-relative. By way of comment on this account, I think we should quietly forget the third condition, and be wary of the second because of the notion of objectivity that it is using. After all, my enterprise at the moment is just that of asking whether all objective reasons are impartial. The first condition, however, is close to the question whether such values would survive Hegelian objectivization.

Kagan considers many putative examples of agent-relative value, as he conceives it, and rules them out in a standardly hard-nosed consequentialist way. For instance, it is nice for agents to have projects such as playing the flute or improving their backhand or attending the whole of the Ring Cycle in Bayreuth. But these projects do not go to maximize utility, and in the present state of the world there are more important things to be done. Of course, a life without projects would be dull and pointless. But there is no consequentialist ban on projects. There is one project which is not only permitted but required, namely The Great Project. Pursuit of that project may require of us many sacrifices. We must be prepared to give our goods to those in need until the loss to us is as great as the gain to them, or until our loss impairs our ability to earn more to give. But the greatness of the sacrifice is another feature of the present sorry state of the world, and of the unwillingness of others to do their share. For if all were to give, each would have to give far less. In a perfect world where all did their duty, doing one's duty would be much less onerous, partly no doubt because the burden would be shared, but more importantly because it would be a lesser burden for each.

The final example of a putative agent-relative value which Kagan considers is that of love or friendship. He is more sympathetic to the idea that the value of love is the sort of value that the agent-relativist is looking for. It is very plausible here to suggest that to love someone requires a willingness, even a keenness, to treat that person with partial favour. To want to treat all impartially is to love nobody. But love is an important, perhaps a vital, aspect of living a reasonable life. A world without love would be a world which lacks something of genuine value – something whose importance we are not, after reflection, willing to deny or dismiss as morally illegitimate. But if all values were objective and so impartial, love would be valueless. So there is at least one value which is not objective.

Kagan's reply to this is that willingness to favour is not an essential part of love, and is presumably therefore to be thought of as a form of moral weakness. For him, love can be impartial – and should be, therefore. I find this reply incredibly weak. I think that the only case where friendship and impartiality are compatible is the unusual case where one is friends with everyone in the world. There are ethics which require this of us (who is my neighbour?), but surely this is just because of the partiality of love which we circumvent by loving all equally.

There is a consequentialist response to this point, but it is one which Kagan does not want to use.[5] This is that consequentialism itself can recognize the value of love, even though love itself be necessarily partial. Love is a pattern of partial (as opposed to impartial) motivation. Those who are motivated by love are not motivated purely by impartial consideration of consequences, in the way that consequentialism seems to recommend. But it can be claimed that this creates no difficulty for consequentialism. It is highly probable that things go better in consequentialist terms if people are not motivated in a purely consequentialist way. If so, consequentialism has its own reasons for recommending that people be motivated in non-consequentialist ways.

I mentioned this move in 10.6. It will be the topic of my final chapter, where I argue that it cannot be got to work. The present point is that

Kagan explicitly eschews it; first, because he thinks he does not need it and, second, because he suspects that it is probably not better in consequentialist terms, in the current state of the world, that people should have the patterns of motivation they do. If this is right, consequentialism cannot either prescribe or permit *our* departures from it, though it might perhaps permit *some* departures. My view, however, is that it is not so easy for him to do without some move of this sort, given what I take to be the weakness of his suggestion that love does not need to be impartial. What is more, the move is surely available in the case of reasons of partiality, since it is very plausible to say that real friendship and love would be hard for those whose sole aim is to promote the objective (i.e. impartial) good, and that there are outcome reasons for preferring a world with friends and lovers in; life is *better* for the existence of people like that.

How would Kagan's approach generalize to other putative agent-relative reasons or values? In his book Kagan often suggests, with much plausibility, that the most promising rationale for agent-relative reasons (for the options, at least) will be one grounded in the cost to the agent of having no escape from the insistent demands of the PTR. This does not fit well with the suggestion that the last chance for agent-relativity lies in the claim that there is value in the existence of love despite its partiality. For this thought makes no appeal to the cost to the agent. The value of friendship is not generated by the cost to the individual of abandoning it; it is just a good which the *world* would be the poorer without. The cost to the individual of ceasing to favour those whom one loves has not come into the story.

For this reason, Kagan's favoured approach to agent-relativity fails to generalize to other cases of costs, e.g. the cost of abandoning one's projects. That cost does not come into the story either. It is not to be allowed to count. The only value there is to be found here lies in the existence of projects, and that value could be promoted best by all sharing in The One Great Project. Equally, supererogation is ruled out. There is nothing here which needs to be preserved by granting a right not to sacrifice oneself, and if there were anything of value here of the sort that Kagan's agent-relativist is being made to seek, it would mean that where the balance of value favours refraining from heroism, the heroic choice is in fact wrong, not right or very good. This sort of value is worse than useless for anti-consequentialist purposes.

For these reasons I think we should reject Kagan's picture of agent-relative value, even though in terms of that picture I think he fails to show that such values do not exist.

3 Nagel

Nagel's account is not of values but of reasons:

> If a reason can be given a general form which does not include an essential reference to the person who has it, it is an *agent-neutral* reason. For example, if it is a reason for anyone to do or want something that it would reduce the amount of wretchedness in the world, then that is an agent-neutral reason. If on the other hand the general form of a reason does include an essential reference to the person who has it, it is an *agent-relative* reason. For example, if it is a reason for anyone to do or want something that it would be in *his* interest, then that is a relative reason.

I have four comments to make on this definition of the agent-relative. First, there is a danger that on Nagel's account all Humean reasons will be agent-relative, so that the question whether there are any agent-neutral reasons will revolve around the truth or falsehood of a Humean theory of motivation. Indeed, it appears to mean that only cognitivists can engage in the debate about agent-relative v. agent-neutral reasons, all Humeans having already decided that there are no neutral ones. This would surely be a distorted perspective on the issue. One would like to think that Hume (*qua* non-cognitivist) is in as good a position as anyone to allow the existence of both sorts of reasons, though *qua* utilitarian he may side with the neutralists.

However, the thought that Nagel's account renders all Humean reasons agent-relative perhaps assumes an extreme version of Humeanism which asserts that *all* reasons are desires. A weaker version, like the one which I discussed in early chapters of this book, holds that some beliefs are reasons too; they *become* reasons when associated with a suitable desire. And if some beliefs are reasons, Humeans can perhaps accept the existence of agent-neutral reasons, namely the beliefs. Humeans can do this if they allow that the fact that I believe it to be sunny need not be among my reasons for putting on my hat when I put it on because of the sun; it is *its being sunny* (i.e. *what* I believe, not my believing it) that is my reason. A desire is an agent-relative reason because it is *my desire not to get burnt* that is (another part of my complete) reason for putting on the hat. This latter reason does contain an essential reference to me in the way that the belief-reason does not.

One might say, then, that some forms of Humeanism can find room for both agent-relative and agent-neutral reasons. Or one might (more plausibly, in my view) deny this on the grounds that to suppose a mere fact can be a reason is to move away from Humean theories altogether. But whichever view one takes on this point, it is surely very odd to find that it is the agent-relative reasons that are most securely in place, and that we are having to work hard to establish even the possibility of agent-neutral ones. It is true that Nagel's view that there are non-Humean forms of motivation as well as Humean ones (the hybrid theory of 1.3 and 2.1) puts him in a position to say there are agent-neutral reasons. But we have already moved miles away from the topic we were originally intending to discuss. The question whether some beliefs are reasons and if so whether they count as agent-neutral ones is nowhere near questions about the implicit tension between the agent-relative and the agent-neutral that Nagel is really wanting to talk about. This leads me to suspect that his official characterization of the agent-relative leaves something to be desired; it has led us off at a tangent.

Second, that characterization begs an important question, namely whether one can have an agent-relative reason for promoting a state of affairs which is not specified essentially by reference to oneself. This matters because not all personal projects are ones whose success conditions are bound up with one's own contribution. For instance, my project might be that a cure for AIDS be found, not particularly that I find it or that my efforts contribute to its being found. Of course, my having this project means that I work towards the finding of a cure, either in the lab or by raising funds or whatever. But it does not mean that I shall be disappointed (at least not with respect to my project) if someone else finds the cure in a way to which my own efforts did not in fact contribute at all. Of course, this project is in another sense impersonal, since the project is not defined with reference to myself. But it may still be a personal project in the sense we are discussing here, since it is one which is central to and gives point to much of my life.

Admittedly, I could have had the project of finding the cure or at least of being involved in the finding of the cure. But in my view that would just have been a different project, and impersonal personal projects of the sort I think possible are ones we should find room for. They are certainly more selfless than other projects. But that they are distinct is surely shown by the fact that a life which revolves around the search for a cure for AIDS may be considered well spent by the searcher, while a person whose central project in life is not that she search for a cure but that a cure be found may wonder whether her efforts were well spent if she dies when the cure is still unknown. And Nagel's account of agent-relativity rules these out by definition. This is a second defect.

Combined with the first, it leads me to wonder whether there might not be a better way of capturing the idea of an agent-relative reason.

It would be wrong to reply here that reasons that stem from personal projects are agent-relative because, even where my project is not defined by reference to myself, the reasons which it generates will be. One might think this because one feels that my basic reason for spending time and energy on seeking for a cure for AIDS is *that this is my project*, a reason which clearly contains essential reference to myself. So, although I might spend money on attending a conference on AIDS in Reykjavik which could be 'better' spent on famine relief, the reason that justifies this, if any does, will be an agent-relative one in Nagel's sense. I want to suggest, however, that this move introduces 'one thought too many', to use Bernard Williams' helpful phrase, in a way that cognitivists should try to resist. My reason for attending the conference is that this makes it more probable that I (or maybe someone else) will find the cure for AIDS. This could only be a non-consequentialist reason for me if I have a personal project of the relevant sort, but this does not mean that my having that project is here playing the role of a reason – it merely allows something else to stand as a reason.[7]

The third worry I have is that Nagel's definition is worked in terms of his generalism. The expression 'if a reason can be given a general form' raises in me unfortunate memories of his remark 'If I have a reason to take aspirin for a headache or to avoid hot stoves, it is not because of anything specific about those pains but because they are examples of pain, suffering or discomfort.'[8] The idea that every reason accepts a general form of this sort without distortion seems to me to create a very strange test of agent-relativity. As a particularist, I think that we are being asked to do something rather odd to our reasons before the test can be applied.

The last point I want to make about Nagel's approach is dependent on a later remark of his: 'Ethics is concerned not only with what should happen, but also independently with what people should or may *do*. Neutral reasons underlie the former; but relative reasons can affect the latter.'[9] First, it is odd to say that ethics is concerned with what should happen, almost as if there are events which ought to take place, it being wrong of them not to. There are no such events, as Nagel himself rightly argued elsewhere.[10] Ethics is concerned with actions and agents; these are the only objects capable of bearing moral properties. Second, it cannot be right to say that neutral reasons concern what should happen in any sense in which that can be contrasted with what people should do. We can with some strain make sense of this in some of the cases that Nagel discusses, for instance my ascribing more value to my caring for my children than to their being cared for. But elsewhere the tension between reasons that demand a sacrifice from me (the agent-neutral ones) and those which may ground an option to refrain (the agent-relative) is not usefully conceived as a tension between events that ought to happen and actions which we are or are not permitted to do. What is more, that contrast requires us to think of actions as events with peculiar sorts of causes, in a way that is food and drink for consequentialism. It effectively leaves consequentialist reasons in place, in a way that I have been trying to avoid, and then tries to add non-consequentialist reasons to them. We have already seen some of the problems this can cause if conceived of as an unbiased approach to the area.

So far, then, my general conclusion is that neither Kagan nor Nagel manage to focus our attention on the right place. Kagan takes it that the agent-relative is necessarily a distortion of the objective truth. Nagel strives earnestly to avoid saying this, but fails. I now turn to two writers who admit the existence of the agent-relative, but maintain that it can be encompassed within the general confines of consequentialism, even if those confines need to be somewhat extended to make room for it.

4   Sen

Sen's discussion, like Kagan's, is in terms of values rather than of reasons.[11] He starts by suggesting that an agent *does* things and also *views* actions and outcomes. So there is such a thing as the neutrality of a doer and the neutrality of a viewer, and then there will be the combination of the two when one views oneself as a doer. These neutralities are expressed in the following way:

Doer neutrality (DN): $\Diamond$(A permits FA) $\leftrightarrow$ $\Diamond$(A permits FB)

Viewer neutrality (VN): $\Diamond$(A permits FA) $\leftrightarrow$ $\Diamond$(B permits FA)

Self-evaluation neutrality (SEN): $\Diamond$(A permits FA) $\leftrightarrow$ $\Diamond$(B permits FB)

In these expressions, 'A permits FA' (or 'A permits himself to do F') is to be thought of as equivalent to 'A does F', and the diamond '$\Diamond$' means 'it is morally acceptable that'.

Oddly, Sen says almost nothing to defend this way of capturing what he is thinking of as neutrality, though everything in his analysis depends on these formulae and there is more than one problem with them. First, the use of the double arrow here loses the thought that if it doesn't matter who does the action (as in doer-neutrality) the value of the action should be the same whoever is the agent. All that Sen's formulation allows us to capture is the idea that if one action is morally acceptable, so is the other. I therefore think it would be better to run Sen's distinctions in terms of an identity of value, thus:

DN: V[A perm FA] = V[A perm FB]

VN: V[A perm FA] = V[B perm FA]

SEN: V[A perm FA] = V[B perm FB]

Of these three theses any two entail the third. Given this way of expressing Sen's distinctions, we have three corresponding relativity theses:

DR: V[A perm FA] ≠ V[A perm FB]

VR: V[A perm FA] ≠ V[B perm FA]

SER: V[A perm FA] ≠ V[B perm FB]

Each of these theses is equivalent to a disjunction:

DR: (V[A perm FA] < V[A perm FB]) ∨ (V[A perm FA] > V[A perm FB])

VR: (V[A perm FA] < V[B perm FA]) ∨ (V[A perm FA] > V[B perm FA])

SER: (V[A perm FA] < V[B perm FB]) ∨ (V[A perm FA] > V[B perm FB])

One hopeful thought is that one can distribute the standard examples around these three disjunctions, in the following way:

DR: (V[A perm FA] < V[A perm FB]) ∨ (V[A perm FA] > V[A perm FB])
    (deontological constraint)   (educating one's own children)

VR: (V[A perm FA] < V[B perm FA]) ∨ (V[A perm FA] > V[B perm FA])
    (tolerance)   (tolerance)

SER: (V[A perm FA] < V[B perm FB]) ∨ (V[A perm FA] > V[B perm FB])
    (reasons of autonomy)   (reasons of autonomy)

But this is ruled out for two reasons. First, it is provable that the different types of examples must involve more than one type of agent-relativity each, since any two neutralities entail the third. Second, it seems altogether too neat to hope that reasons of autonomy are somehow constructed out of reasons of tolerance and deontological constraints. (Note that if this were to work we would be constructing options out of constraints.)

There is still something wrong with the picture we are getting. The agent-relativist is represented as denying what the agent-neutralist is asserting. What is wrong with this is not that their positions are compatible; presumably they are not. Rather each is represented as holding that where there is value of one sort there cannot also be value of the other. Maybe the neutralist does hold this, but the relativist does not – at least, not if trying to capture the intuitions with which I began this chapter. Any suggestion to the contrary can only be an imposition of the consequentialist assumption that agent-relative value is a sort of distortion of agent-neutral value, so that they cannot both exist side by side. So I don't see how it can be right to start by trying to capture everything the agent-relativist wants to say using only agent-neutral value. This cannot be a fair starting point, even if we might get there in the end; and Sen's unconscious assumption that it is fair must partly explain his conclusion that a suitably modified consequentialism can capture everything that the agent-relativist wishes to say. In my view, many agent-relativists take themselves to be describing an additional sort of value, and we completely lose this thought if we insist on describing everything using the neutralist's V. So we need a symbol Va for the (agent-relative) value for A. Of course, we have so far given no interpretation for this symbol. We are still in the business of trying to find out what we are supposed to be looking for. Using this symbol we get:

DR: (Va[A perm FA] < Va[A perm FB]) ∨ (Va[A perm FA] > Va[A perm FB])

VR: (Va[A perm FA] < Va[B perm FA]) ∨ (Va[A perm FA] > Va[B perm FA])

SER: (Va[A perm FA] < Va[B perm FB]) ∨ (Va[A perm FA] > Va[B perm FB])

There remain two objectionable elements in this account, which stem from the fact that it sees all agent-relative value as concerned centrally with the contrast between different permitted actions. I would not wish to accept this as a starting point, neither the focus on actions nor the focus on permissions. With respect to action, I want to leave room for the idea that there can be agent-relative value in the completion of a project which is the agent's project but to whose completion he does not contribute. I have said a little about this above; if there are such cases their structure will be this: $Va(p) \neq V(p)$. (Or perhaps better would be $-[Va(p) \approx V(p)]$, if we feel that this assertion of lack of identity makes little sense, perhaps on the grounds that agent-relative and agent-neutral values are not fully commensurable.) The second objectionable element is the assumption that permissions are not distinctive acts with their own values. Sen is relying here on the common phrase 'I permitted myself'; this sort of permission may be morally indistinguishable from the act permitted, but most permissions are not like this. The permission may be right when the act permitted is wrong, and vice versa.

In fact, with most of the examples the importance of permissions is negligible. With the claim that I have a reason to care for my children myself and less reason for you to care for yours, the structure is $Va[FA] > Va[FB]$. One can, of course, contrast the value of my doing it with the value of my letting you do it, but the real contrast is between the value of my doing it and the value of your doing it, with both of these values being my agent-relative values. In the case of deontological constraints, where I have a reason not to twist a child's arm myself which does not convert into as strong a reason to stop you from doing so, the structure is again $Va[FA] > Va[FB]$, and the importance, if any, of permissions is a distraction. Where reasons of autonomy give me a reason that I do the action, again we have $Va[FA] > Va[FB]$. So there is some sort of pattern emerging here. Permissions only enter the field substantially when we come to consider tolerance. We might want to say that the value of my letting you do it is greater than the value of your doing it, especially if I can be right to let you do a wrong action. But I don't think we can assume so easily that the agent-neutralist cannot capture this sort of thought in his own terms. So though there may be a relation between the value of tolerance and that of permissions, I doubt that the whole story of tolerance will hinge on that.

One should also notice that the account of agent-neutral value is spoilt by Sen's focus on permissions. Surely any consequentialist will want to admit that where the action FA is heroic, we have $V[FA] = V[A$ perm $FA] > V[B$ perm $FA]$. Equally, wherever B has a strong desire to do an action that A has little interest in, we surely get $V[FA < V[FB]$, or $V[A$ perm $FA] < V[A$ perm $FB]$, in a way that I think most neutralists would wish to allow. So neutralists need not assert $V[FA] = V[FB] = V[A$ perm $FA] = V[A$ perm $FB]$. The whole concentration on permission, despite the potential link with tolerance, seems to me to be a mistake.

So it seems at the moment that the interesting cases are those where Va [FA] ≠ Va [FB]. Now normally Va [FB] = V[FB]; this will be so except in the special cases where A has a project which it would help if B were to do F. Otherwise Va[FB] is nothing special; it is just V[FB] – the neutral value of B's caring for his children. But this neutral value is equally well exemplified in A's caring for his children. So what we should be contrasting here is the agent-relative value for A of A's caring for his children with the value of those (or any other) children being cared for by their father – A for his, B for his, and so on. This is a case where Va(p) ≠ V(p).

It is possible here to confuse oneself and get stuck with the thought that the centre of the problem lies with cases where Va [FA] ≠ Va [FB]. But the fact that Va [FA] ≠ Va [FB] only serves to show that the value A ascribes to B's doing F is a value A can find equally in *his* doing F. That value is agent-neutral value. So the real underlying contrast is between Va [FA] and V[FA], or, more generally, between Va (p) and V(p). We are going to find this structure wherever p is among A's projects, and it is especially striking when it is not among A's projects that p become true as a result of A's efforts.

So it seems as if the general shape of the agent-relativist's claim is that there can be cases where Va(p) ≠ V(p). But there is no built-in temptation to suppose that in such a case A will be unable to recognize three things:

1   V(p)
2   Va(p)
3   that Va(p) ≠ V(p).

All of these things may be clear to A. And this is just what one should expect if the way in which I tried to motivate the idea of an agent-relative reason is anywhere near the mark. Putting the matter in terms now of reasons of autonomy, I can accept the existence of a gap or tension between the size or strength of my agent-relative reasons and the size or strength of any recognizable agent-neutral reason. But this gap need not disconcert me. I can live with it, and my recognizing it need not tear me apart. I can still find my own projects important, while recognizing that they are not agent-neutrally important.

The conclusions I draw from this discussion of Sen's suggestions are as follows. The right place to look for an understanding of agent-relative value is to look for discrepancies between two assessments of the one action, both made by the agent. We are not to look directly for discrepancies between evaluations made by the agent and by an onlooker, nor for discrepancies between the agent's evaluation of the action as done by him and as done by another. Each can recognize the agent-relative values of others; we are not restricted to noticing neutral values and our own agent-relative ones. So we can accept the reluctance of others to make sacrifices, since we discern the structure of values that supports this. This shows that an attempt to establish the existence of the agent-relative is not merely an exercise in special pleading on one's own behalf. Reasons like those that protect me protect all equally, without being for that reason agent-neutral.

Instead, the agent-relativist is committed to making sense of the thought that it can be important to me that this should work out right, though of course I know it doesn't really matter so much whether it does. This pattern repeats in all the standard examples. My project's being achieved may have some agent-neutral value, but it is of special importance to me. The same can be said about my children's being cared for, or about my caring for them. The success of my project may have some agent-neutral value, but it is of special importance to me. My not doing a wrong (breaching a deontological constraint) has agent-neutral value, but it is of special importance to me. And so on. The question whether value of this type can exist is not even addressed by Sen.[12]

5 PARFIT AND COMMON AIMS

Derek Parfit offers a distinction between agent-neutral and agent-relative *theories*. A theory is agent-neutral if it gives to all agents *common* aims; it is agent-relative if it gives different agents different aims.[13] (Presumably a theory may in these terms be mixed.) This definition has the merit of seeing that the event/action distinction cuts across the agent-relative/agent-neutral one, a point which Nagel missed. An agent-neutral theory may recommend as a common aim for all that children should be cared for by their parents. Even those who have no children may be enjoined here to do what they can to promote home-care of children, as it were. A childless Finance Minister might do this by increasing tax allowances for those who care for their own children. An agent-relative theory might, however, require parents to care for their own children. Here the intention seems to be to give those who are parents an aim which does not apply to those who are not. The intention is that, in the case of an agent-relative requirement, those who are parents are required to care for their own children, while those who are not parents are not required to do anything.

This notion of a common aim needs careful handling, however. The impression given by what I have written above is that a theory is neutral if it gives the same aim to everybody, and relative if it only speaks to some, as the example above only spoke to parents. This would not be an attractive account. For surely it is agreed on all hands that if there are such things as agent-relative constraints, they apply (or at least *can* apply) to all equally. Everybody has the same reason not to lie – not to be the one who tells the lie. So the relative/neutral distinction is not the same as that between theories that give aims to all and those that only give aims to some. A more interesting approach, still working with the idea of a common aim, is that neutral theories give the same aim to all (or to all the people they speak to), while relative theories give variable aims. Thus the neutral requirement above is the same for all, while the variable one gives each parent their own aim. The aim it gives me, for instance, is that I should care for Hugh, Jack and Kate.

It is easy, I think, to see the force of Parfit's distinction, but one may yet find it insecure because of the way it appeals to the notions of 'the same aim' and of 'different aims', which can be read in more than one way. (There remains a good sense in which relative theories give all parents the same aim.) McNaughton and Rawling have tried to build on Parfit's suggestion in constructing a clear formal distinction between agent-neutral and agent-relative aims.[14] They distinguish the neutral from the variable aim thus, where 'xS' reads 'x should ensure that':

neutral: (x) (xS [(y) (y is a parent → y cares for y's children)])

relative: (x) (xS [x is a parent → x cares for x's children])

The difference between the neutral and the relative aims is not that one is universally quantified and the other not, as in our first account of a common aim, but that in the account of the action that x is required to do, there is a variable x bound by a quantifier that lies outside the scope of 'xS'. This is a formal way of capturing the idea that the required action *varies relative to the agent*. We can then use this distinction to express a similar difference between *states of affairs* (or *happenings*) we are required to promote; such states of affairs may include actions by others. Suppose that there is a neutral requirement to make sure that children are cared for, and a relative one to make sure that one's own children are cared for. This comes out in the following way:

neutral: (x) (xS [(y) (y is a child → y is cared for)])

relative: (x) (xS [(y) (y is x's child → y is cared for)]).

An agent-relative requirement to promote a happening that is an action by another would be:

$$(x) \ (xS \ [(y) \ (y \ \text{is a child of} \ x \rightarrow (Ez) \ (z \ \text{cares for} \ y))]).$$

This all seems very promising. We seem to have captured in unambiguous terminology the idea of a requirement that varies with the agent, and surely this should be what we are meaning when we talk of an agent-relative requirement or aim. The worry that Parfit's original distinction appealed to a vague contrast between the same and different aims seems to have been sorted out.[15] However, there are some problems for the McNaughton/Rawling approach which do not arise for Parfit's more intuitive distinction, and this may be a sign that something has gone wrong somewhere.

I start with a fairly minor point. What is the difference between:

(a) : $(x) \ (y) \ (y \ \text{is a child of} \ x \rightarrow xS \ [y \ \text{is cared for}])$ and

(b) : $(x) \ (xS \ [(y) \ (y \ \text{is a child of} \ x \rightarrow y \ \text{is cared for})])$?

On the official criterion, (a) is neutral and (b) relative. There should therefore be a significant difference between them. But McNaughton and Rawling write:

> It is ... for formal reasons ... that we opt for (b) – we see no significant *ethical* distinction to be drawn between (a) and (b). Of course there is a distinction: (b) is vacuously obeyed by any agent who does not become a parent; whereas (a) simply does not apply to such an agent. But whilst (a parallel to) this distinction might be important in, for instance, conditional betting situations, it is not pertinent for present purposes.[16]

However, they are wrong here – and they had better be wrong, for otherwise the relative/neutral distinction will be purely formal, with no significant ethical content. Someone who at some cost to himself refrains from having children because he feels that he could not care for them properly would be rightly aggrieved at being told that he only obeyed (b) 'vacuously'. Of course, in remaining childless he ensures that (a) does not apply to him, and he might do that because he felt that if it did apply to him, he could not obey it. If so, he would perhaps be *respecting* both (a) and (b), since he makes his choice so as not to violate either. But there is still the fact that he is obeying (b) and not yet (a). He is, of course, also obeying a further and different rule, namely one which forbids us to act in such a way that we acquire duties that we have reason to believe we will not be able to fulfil. But even if he is obeying this rule so as not to break (a), he is neither obeying nor breaking (a) since he is neither doing nor failing to do that which it enjoins.

There is also another difference between (a) and (b) worth mentioning. In formal terms, as interpreted in a modal deontic logic of the sort developed by Hintikka, they make very different claims: (a) says that in perfect worlds, all those who here have children there make sure they are cared for; (b) says that in perfect worlds, all who there have children make sure they are cared for. So (a) runs the risk of leaving some children uncared for even in a perfect world. My conclusion here is that the relative, conditionalized requirement captures better what we are after when we say that parents should see that their children are cared for.

That there should be a significant difference between (a) and (b) is important. For otherwise we can trivially convert any conditionalized relative requirement into a neutral one (its 'neutral transform'). We can also, as McNaughton and Rawling recognize, trivially create a relative transform of any neutral requirement by inserting a further and quite redundant 'xS', as in the move from:

(x) (xS [(y) (y is a child → y is cared for]) to

(x) (xS [xS [(y) (y is a child → y is cared for)]]]).

So there is a danger that transforms can be created trivially in both directions, which puts pressure on the idea that the distinction is morally significant. We have seen how to block this move in one direction, by finding a significant distinction between (a) and (b). For the other direction, McNaughton and Rawling suggest that 'the fact that a rule *can* be put into agent-relative form is not enough to show that it is an agent-relative rule. It is agent-relative only if it cannot be transformed into agent-neutral form without a change in content.'[17] However, there is a crucial case which shows this criterion to be insufficient.

For there is a danger that on the official definition a central claim of utilitarianism comes out as agent-relative. If so, this would be awkward because utilitarianism is normally taken as the paradigm of a neutral theory. Utilitarianism (indeed, any form of consequentialism) claims that the right act for an agent is the one which, of all the options available to him, has the best consequences. Formally, this reads:

(c) : (x) (xS [(y) (y is the best option available to x → x does y)]).

This is a relative requirement. There is a neutral transform for it:

(d) : (x) (xS [(y)(z) (y is the best option available to z → z does y)]).

How are we to decide between these two? We *want* to be able to prefer the neutral version, since we think of utilitarianism as a neutral theory. But nothing that McNaughton and Rawling tell us enables us to do so. Let us admit that (c) and (d) have the same content. This will not permit us to assert a preference for one or the other. We need an asymmetrical criterion. I suggest that we consider whether there is any good sense in which one or the other *leads*. If we could say that one requirement holds *because* the other does, and that the latter is the neutral one, we could announce that utilitarianism is a neutral theory, on our criterion. But unfortunately it seems to me that (d) holds because (c) does. As a theory that is directed at agents, its main claim is that you should choose the action with the 'best' outcome of those available to you. Because of this, where others can do better than you, you should let them go ahead; or if you can arbitrate between two further agents, you should prefer the one whose action will be 'better'. But you should be operating in this way in the neutral arena because this is required of you by (c). This means that utilitarianism is, at least to this extent, an agent-relative theory.

Would this be a disaster for the McNaughton/Rawling account? They take themselves to be elaborating and improving on Parfit's suggestions, and Parfit, who takes it to be *theories* that are properly to be called agent-relative or agent-neutral, also maintains that consequentialism is probably a significantly agent-relative theory, since in its best form it prescribes different agents different aims. But this is not for the reason discussed above, that our prescribed aim is to choose the best option available *to us*; it is because consequentialism (probably) recommends partial motives such as friendship and parental affection. It does this because it takes the fostering of these motives to be the best method of promoting *ultimate* aims, which are common, not relative; the relative aims involved in friendship and parental affection are *derived* aims. This fairly mainstream position of Parfit's seems to have a different structure from the McNaughton/Rawling elaboration. For him, consequentialism remains centrally neutral, since ultimate aims are neutral. For them, it is in danger of being centrally relative.

However, we should not forget that most forms of consequentialism tend to distinguish their agent-theory from their act theory.[18] Of *these* two, it is the act theory that leads, and the act theory is neutral. So we could say that, even as formulated by McNaughton and Rawling, the theory is neutral at the centre, with a secondary agent-relative element (its agent-theory). Consequentialism is neutral, then, but not really agent-neutral, since in so far as it speaks to agents at all (in the aims it gives them) it is agent-relative.[19] That it is neutral at the centre is the *real* explanation of our tendency to see the neutral agent-theory (d) as the right expression of utilitarian requirements.

But even if we allow this, there is something it should alert us to. What we have seen is that agent-relativity can be found in a situation in which it lacks one of its central features, namely the idea that there is morally justifiable competition. In more normal cases, where there are relative aims, there will be bound to be competition between different agents, none of whom is doing more than they ought (given the way the world goes). For instance, if I have a duty to care for my children and you have one to care for yours, I may rightly make it harder for you to do your duty by doing mine. It is noticeable that, because of special features of the case, there is no room for this sort of competition with (c). And (c) is not the only example of relativity without competition one could bring forward. One interesting suggestion is that a theory could recommend variable aims (different aims for different agents) without being *agent*-relative; the aims might vary relative to something else. If they did, their relativity would not be captured by talking of pronominal back-reference to the agent. A possible example is the requirement that any action should be better than the previous one:

$$(x) \ (xS \ [\text{action } n + 1 \text{ is better than action } n]).$$

In this case, too, there seems not to be room for competition.

So what really interests agent-relativists is the area where there is competition *as well as* agent-variability of aim (or of requirement). There are three degrees:

(1) common aims

(2) relative aims

(3) competition

and of these some theories admit the second without going so far as the third, though where this is so it will be because of special features of the case. In Parfit's hands, however, consequentialism goes all the way; it exhibits both agent-relativity and moral competition, if it can be got to work. What I will be suggesting in chapter 13 is that it cannot be got to work, because the intended contrast between act-theory and agent-theory cannot be sustained.

We can confirm the focus on competition by looking at some of the standard examples. All constraints introduce the possibility of competition. To the extent that one's duty is not to maximize/minimize the number of such actions that are done, but to do/avoid them oneself, there will be competition between individuals wherever there are scarce resources (which I want for my child and you want for yours), or between one agent and the rest, as it were, wherever the agent has a choice between doing one such action himself and letting others do more. One might suppose that this point only works for constraints, where we speak of requirements and required aims. But very similar remarks can be made for options. The easiest place to see this is with reasons of partiality, which include both constraints and options. Just as in performing my duty to care for my children I may acceptably make it harder for you to perform yours, so in exercising my option to favour my children I may rightly make it harder for you to exercise yours. With other options the same point can be made. With reasons of autonomy, I have the right to pursue my project even if in doing so I make it harder for you to pursue yours (e.g. we are competing for a scholarship). With reasons of supererogation, we each have a morally permissible reason not to be the one that makes the sacrifice, even if the sacrifice has to be made by someone. So there is more of a parallel between constraints and options than one might initially think. With constraints, where an action is forbidden, we have a morally recognized reason not to be the one that does it; with supererogation, where an action is the best one available, we have a morally recognized reason not to be the one that does it.[20]

How does this relate to the idea of a tension which I see as central to the concept of the agent-relative – at least to that aspect of the concept that is significant in ethical theory? If there were only neutral value, there would be no place for competition. For each would rightly subordinate his own concerns (a) to the general concern and (b) to those of other individuals, where the balance of neutral value so demands. There is room for competition, as I have shown above. So there must be relative as well as neutral value. With relative value, there is room for a tension between my concerns and the general concern, and since this tension stems from the fact that the relative value I rightly put against neutral value is relative to *me*, and since such a fact is true of every agent, there is bound to be moral space for competition (even when we do not forget to consider the neutral values that are created by relative ones).[20]

My final comment on this matter concerns particularism. McNaughton and Rawling express their distinction in terms of rules; indeed, at one point they lard these rules with *ceteris paribus* clauses, which is one of the standard subterfuges of the generalist. We might ask whether these rules are prima facie principles in Ross's sense, or if not what. Either way, the particularist should not be happy to take on board their distinction just as it stands. But it is not hard to rework the distinction in terms of reasons rather than rules. The leading idea will be that the nature of the action demanded by a situation varies according to the identity of the agent.

6 CONCLUSIONS

What has this discussion taught us about the agent-relative?

Of our four writers, two focus on agent-relative values, one on reasons, and one on theories. This makes it hard to relate their views to each other. But we can work backwards from theories, through reasons, to values. Theories are agent-relative if they prescribe agent-relative aims. Agent-relative aims are not common, but vary from agent to agent. If there is to be such variation, the reasons that generate the demand for the relevant actions must also vary from agent to agent. And if this is so, the best explanation of it is that the structure of the reasons mirrors the structure of the values that form the reasons.

I started this chapter with an example, but nothing has occurred to displace that example. The idea of a tension between different claims on the agent has only been confirmed. We learnt the following things about agent-relative reasons and values:

1 agent-relative reasons have variable content, and
2 they permit (options) or require (constraints) moral competition;
3 this is because the values they stem from are not all neutral,
4 and neutral values are in tension with non-neutral ones
5 in a way of which the agent may be perfectly well aware –
6 values of both sorts belonging to the agent's actions.

Of these theses, the last two emerged in the discussion of Sen's views, and the first two in the discussion of Parfit.

Where then are we to look for such reasons or values? I intend to work with Kagan's plausible suggestion that the central notion in agent-relativity is that of the *cost to the agent* of living a life according to neutral demands. What I am going to suggest, then, is that reasons of supererogation and reasons of autonomy are driven by considerations of the cost to the agent. To make the point in the case of supererogation,

I suggested in chapter 8 that a budding hero is justified in counting the cost of sacrifice twice, once as a cost to someone or other and once as a cost to himself. The question who it is to be that will pay the cost places that cost in a new light when the answer is 'me'. In the case of constraints, it is worth at least considering the possibility of a similar move, which sees the reasons that are in tension with consequentialist ones as grounded in thoughts of a *moral cost* to the agent. If anything like this can be got to run, we will have shown why it is right to think of constraints as agent-relative reasons, and that the agent-relativity of constraints is not so different from that of options.

NOTES

1 The sense that I am unimportant but that my whole world is *my* world is part of what Nagel has been trying valiantly to bring out in his contrast between more and less objective points of view. I applaud his efforts here, even though, as I argued in chapter 9, I think them ultimately confused.

2 I don't mean to suggest that there is a common scale by reference to which values of these two very different types can be compared. The suggestion is merely that a very small neutral value is not so great a value of its type as the significant relative value is of its type, and that a very large value of one type may 'matter more' than a small value of the other type. Both generate reasons which the agent can recognize and assess for comparative strength, even if the reasons generated are of different types.

3 See Kagan (1989), pp. 356–85.

4 Ibid., p. 356.

5 Ibid., p. 364n.

6 Nagel (1986), pp. 152–3.

7 Derek Parfit suggested to me that, irrespective of the official definition he offers, Nagel could perhaps be interpreted as saying that agent-relative reasons have force only for the persons whose reasons they are. Actually, I think it is dubious even whether Nagel believes this true, let alone whether he thinks of it as definitive of the agent-relative. See Nagel (1986), p. 169, where he writes that 'the achievement of a typical personal project or ambition has no value except from the perspective of its subject – at least none in any way comparable to the value reasonably placed on it by the person whose ambition it is.' Perhaps Nagel and I can agree that agent-relative reasons create weaker neutral reasons, but that intrinsically they speak only to the agent and not to others. The question then is whether the agent-relative reasons are distinctive in this respect. All reasons speak in the first instance only to those who have them, and all generate second-order reasons for those who discern the reasons of others (and maybe their own as well). A second-order reason here is of the form 'So-and so has a reason.'

8   Nagel (1986), p. 168.
9   Ibid., p. 165.
10   In his 'Moral Luck', reprinted in Nagel (1979), at p. 36.
11   Sen (1982).
12   So the question whether its existence would refute consequentialism is not resolved by Sen's showing (even assuming that he does show) that what he thinks of as agent-relative value can be captured consequentially. The way in which this emerges in Sen's account depends on his notion of evaluator-relativity; I have not considered whether this notion even makes sense, though I may say that I think it is not vulnerable to the criticisms levelled at it by Philippa Foot; see Foot (1985a).
13   See Parfit (1984), pp. 54–5.
14   See McNaughton and Rawling (1991).
15   In fact the McNaughton/Rawling account is pretty close to earlier remarks of Nagel's, apparently abandoned in Nagel (1986). See Nagel (1970), p. 91, and McNaughton and Rawling (1991), p. 184, n. 6.
16   McNaughton and Rawling (1991), pp. 174–5, with minor changes.
17   Ibid., p. 184, n. 7.
18   Though Kagan refuses to make this distinction, as we saw above (11.2).
19   This is where Parfit's position diverges. For him there is a neutral aim written off from the neutral act-theory. Acts are best if they make the world go as well as possible, and correspondingly our ultimate aim is to make things go as well as possible. I discuss the structure of Parfit's position further in chapter 13.
20   It is true that competition is between individuals, while tension exists between the reasonable concerns of the agent and those of all. But the argument above seems to me to enable us to move backwards and forwards between these two.

12
Discounting the cost

---

1 AN ANALOGY

If there are to be any agent-relative values, we must find an account of these values which captures six thoughts. The first is that these values can be present together without incoherence. The second is that they are none the less often in tension. The third is that the agent can see both clearly for what they are; neither obscures the other. The fourth is that others can see the agent's agent-relative values for what they are (and that this may generate further reasons for them). The fifth is that in some cases (where options come into play) I have a right, though never a duty, to pay no attention to my agent-relative values and concentrate entirely on the agent-neutral ones, while in others (where there are constraints) I have no such right. The sixth is that agent-relative values are moral values (and agent-relative reasons moral reasons), not mere excuses or ways of letting oneself off the moral hook.

Let us start from the thought that neutral values call, but my agent-relative values call to me. Others can hear the latter call, but since it is not for them it does not mean the same to them in practical terms as it does for me.

Here is an analogy which I find appealing, and which takes some of the mystery out of the situation. Nowadays one can, I believe, get a sort of telephone installed in one's house which will give individual rings for different members of the family. My wife has one number which she gives to her colleagues at work, I have another to give to mine, each child has one for their friends to use, and then there is a common number for family friends to use when they are not particular about which of us they speak to. So there are different numbers linked up to the same line, and the way in which the phone rings depends on which number is dialled. There is an undifferentiated ring when the phone is ringing for all equally, and then differentiated rings, one for each of us.

All can hear all rings, but rings which are not for you don't call for the same response from you as they do from the person whose ring they are. For instance, one often puts down what one is doing to answer the phone, but sometimes what one is doing is too important to interrupt. Let us suppose that something quite important will not be interrupted unless the call is for us, something fairly important will not be interrupted unless the call is either a general call or for us, while an activity has to be quite unimportant for me to interrupt it if the call is for someone else. Still, a call for another is of some practical relevance for me; it counts somehow, though other calls count for more. Rings that are for others don't call for the same response from you as they do from them, but that does not mean that they call for no response at all, or that they make no difference at all to what you should do.

Suppose that there are two phones in the house, one ringing for all and one ringing for you. You have sufficient reason not to answer the one ringing for all if you can only answer one of them, but you can still choose to do so. The fact that the call you are ignoring is for you justifies your ignoring it in favour of the one that is calling for all. Others could not require this of you, any more than you could require it of them, but if you are willing to make the choice (sacrifice) they should recognize this as morally praiseworthy in you.

What does this analogy show? Not a lot, perhaps, in itself. But I do think that it serves to take some of the mystery out of the idea of agent-relative reasons or values. The picture we are being offered here is a fairly everyday one, but it contains much of the structure that we have found in the idea of an agent-relative reason. In fact, it captures the first five of the six thoughts with which I began this chapter. The two rings can be present together, they are often in tension, I can hear each for what it is, others can hear my rings and know the sort of reasons they give me, and I have the right but not the duty to prefer to answer the call for all rather than the call for me. And as for the sixth thought, there has emerged so far no reason to challenge the status of the reasons generated by the different rings as moral reasons, since we do not conceive of them as motivated departures from some basic matrix of moral reasons (and there is after all always someone on the other end of the line). They are and are experienced as normative features of the world. Think of what it is like to hear the phone ringing. It *demands* an answer, and in the case of your special ring it demands an answer from *you*.

2 OPTIONS AND DISCOUNTS

Let us now return to the matter of options. The basic position that I want to adopt here has already been presented in chapter 8. In the case of supererogation, what is to justify the reluctant hero in hanging back is the cost to him of sacrificing himself for the greater good. Now this cost has already been counted once in the calculation of good, since a sacrifice that costs the agent more than the benefit it creates for others is in no sense a moral duty. But the cost can be counted again, in a new way. For it appears in a new light when it emerges that the person who is to pay that cost is me. Neutrally calculated, the cost is the same whoever is to pay it, and so there is a moral calculation which is blind to the question who is to pay. It is not totally blind, of course, since it considers such matters as whether the payer can afford the cost, whether he is ill or likely to fall into special need, and so on. But all such matters are inherently general, since they relate to *any such person*. The individuality of the agent has not come into the matter at all yet; which person the agent is bears no direct moral relevance to the neutral calculation. But that the cost is to be his cost makes a great difference to him, and here the identity of the payer makes a difference as well as his nature. So the cost is counted twice, though not in the same way both times; perhaps it would be better to say that it has a double relevance.

This position faces two main challenges. The first is to establish our right to ignore this cost when it is a cost to ourselves.[1] We need to do this because we need to show not only that we have the right not to pay the cost but also that we have the right to pay it (if we choose, whatever that means) and that if we do it we do something better than if we don't. The second challenge is to show that the reasons generated by this conception of a cost to self are moral reasons rather than mere excuses. There is the danger for the agent-relativist of falling between two stools here, of succeeding in showing that we have a right to ignore the cost only by showing that the cost does not generate a moral reason but an excuse for the faint-hearted.

It might be easier to make sense of our right to ignore the cost if the cost appeared as a reason rather than as a value. For if it is a value, how can we be justified in ignoring it? Surely values need to be respected. It is wrong to ignore a value, no matter what sort of value it is. So we should try to see the cost as a reason rather than as a value. Now there are stronger and weaker ways of distinguishing reasons from values in this area. The stronger form has it that there are two sorts of reasons, those deriving from values and those that come from elsewhere. The weaker form holds only that there are two sorts of reasons, both stemming from the same sort of value. The classic version of this approach is that there is only neutral value, but that this sort of value generates not only agent-neutral but also agent-relative reasons; but classic versions are not the only possible.

The attraction of the stronger view is that if the reasons that spring from the agent-relative counting of the cost are the sort that do not spring from values, then we have something to weigh in the balance against those reasons that do. But this way out does not attract me. I cannot make sense of the necessary distinction between reasons and values.[2] If the cost appears as a reason, this must be because of the value it has for me (disvalue, in fact). The weaker view, however, fails to serve our present purpose. For it does not help us to escape the initial implausibility of saying that the relevant reasons, which are after all grounded in neutral value, can be safely ignored.[3]

I think that paradoxically we can be helped here by seeing how to deal with another difficulty.[4] Do agent-relativists really claim that there are two sorts of values? Isn't it a bit odd to think of there being, as well as the sort of neutral value that we are supposed to be so familiar with, another quite different sort of value which is extremely contentious – especially when one then goes on to claim that the same thing (the cost to the agent) can have value of both sorts, but that most things that have value of one sort have none of the other at all? I think that it is odd, but that this oddity derives from treating values in too heavily metaphysical a way. Values are not things in the sort of way that this puzzle supposes. We do better to recast the matter in terms not of values but of valuings. The position I am trying to bring out holds that there are two ways of counting the cost, and this should be seen as two ways of valuing the same thing.[5] It is altogether less puzzling to suppose that the neutral way I disvalue the cost to the agent is not changed but rather supplemented by the way I disvalue it when I realize that the agent is to be me. And neutrality is much more easily seen as a way of valuing than as a sort of value.

Now why should there be a problem about my right to ignore a cost to myself? It would be wrong simply not to notice this cost, and wrong not to see it for the cost it is. But even an item neutrally valued may be discounted, if not ignored. A sacrifice that costs the agent more than the benefit it creates for others is not a duty, perhaps, but it is not morally forbidden either; it is something, in fact, towards which a mixed response might be the most suitable. This must be because the agent has the right to discount a cost to self. And this is so whether the cost is being valued agent-neutrally or agent-relatively.

Others, of course, do not have the right to discount the cost to the agent, whichever way of valuing we are talking about. They are not entitled to impose that cost on the agent (remember that we are considering a case where the cost exceeds the benefit), nor even to ask him to discount it. Discounting of this sort can only be done by the agent.

If anyone doubts this account and asks why the agent has the right to discount (not to ignore) the cost to self, it is hard to know what one could appeal to in an answer which is basic enough to offer an advance on what we have already. The only thing that I can think of to say is that the agent has this right because it is he that is going to have to pay the cost. Now there may be theories which rule this remark out of court in some way, and consequentialism looks as if it is one of them. But without begging the question in favour of consequentialist ways of looking at things, no theory should be taken to be in difficulties on this point unless it itself serves to invalidate the apparently obvious ethical truth that I am appealing to here. And so far nothing has emerged which looks at all likely to have that effect.

But have we perhaps escaped Scylla only to fall prey to Charybdis? How can we reassure ourselves that agent-relative valuing is moral valuing? One easy point is that we do not simply appeal to the cost to ourself. There is no special pleading going on here, if by this we mean that we are trying to treat ourselves more leniently than we are willing to treat others. We accept the right of others to refuse to sacrifice themselves, just as we claim it for ourselves. But this is not by itself enough, for someone might say that though the excuse we offer is one we allow others to offer, it is just an excuse for all that. The normal reason for saying something like this is a sense that those who appeal in the sort of way I am envisaging to the cost to self, conceived agent-relatively, are exhibiting a morally disproportionate concern for their own skins. The concern is one which they do not blame others for having, but this does not make it the less disproportionate. What reply might we make to this?

Kagan expects the agent-relativist to respond with an attack on agent-neutral reasons. He suggests that an appeal might be made to the principle that 'for a genuine moral requirement, it must be possible for the agent to be *motivated* to act in the required manner.'[6] The agent-relativist is then expected to argue that nobody can be motivated by neutral reasons, and therefore that neutral reasons do not ground moral requirements. But this seems hopeless to me, and anyway no part of the agent-relativists' position. They should agree that anyone who recognizes the agent-neutral reasons for what they are will be *pro tanto* motivated to do the action they are reasons to do, for (as I conceive the matter) they are in the business of saying that there are reasons of *both* sorts. Kagan does not predict this because he sees reasons of the two sorts in competition, in a way that leaves the less secure as merely a justified distortion of the more secure. But I have already argued that this is the wrong perspective on the issue.

Another way of getting it wrong is to say that since people are not motivated by the neutral calculus much, we must recognize this fact and write our moral theory to suit it. But this is just to announce that since people are going to think and behave in a certain way we might as well say that this is morally permissible. Nothing of interest can emerge from this approach.

The way to get it right is to take what one can from Scheffler's notion of the *natural* independence of the personal point of view. Scheffler seems to run this thought in terms of the peculiar perspective which the individual adopts on matters which concern her in various ways. But this merely feeds the opposition's determination to see this perspective as somehow slewed in one's own favour. It is better, in my view, to think of this individual as an *agent* rather than as a judger. We want to relate the natural independence of the agent's perspective directly to the notion of *acting* on that perspective, not particularly to that of judging from it. The idea will then be not that one cannot be motivated by neutral moral reasons, but that one cannot help being motivated by one's personal projects and by concern for one's safety, future, friends and family.

The response will now be that though one cannot help being motivated by these things, one can help being *disproportionately* motivated by them. But we should not assume that an asymmetrical pattern of care (to take just one example) is disproportionate in any other sense than that of its asymmetry. Otherwise we commit once more the mistake of placing neutral considerations at the centre and then trying to motivate certain departures from them. This won't work, perhaps, but it is not what we are trying to do. Of course, there is such a thing as a disproportionate concern for one's own welfare and that of one's friends, and so on. But that does nothing to show that *any* asymmetry of care is disproportionate: only that one can go too far in either direction.

So the idea here is that an ethics for humans must be built on patterns of concern that are possible for humans. Such patterns contain asymmetries of concern. But what is to drive us to reject all such patterns as morally unworthy? If the answer is an antecedent conviction that an agent's basic duty is to maximize the good, we can resist it. In its place we put the claim that though we can admire the selfless pattern which contains no asymmetry (if it be possible for a human to adopt

– remember that this is not the same as discounting the asymmetries that work in one's own favour) this is not our only model of a morally fine life. There is insufficient reason to permit only symmetrical patterns of concern. The importance of exhibiting a concern for unknown others does not mean that it should be placed at the centre of moral theory. We may feel that we are insufficiently motivated by thoughts about the needs of people we do not know, but this is no reason for saying that we should be only or even merely centrally motivated in ways of which this is a prime example. To work to improve ourselves is not necessarily to aim to make ourselves unrecognizable.

This is the best I can do to defend agent-relative reasons that ground options from the charge that they are not moral reasons. There were four different types of option-grounding reasons distinguished in chapter 10, and the approach I have been trying to outline seems to cope with all of them. The first three are to be understood in terms of cost to the agent, and the last in terms of the agent's right to discount a cost to himself.

3   Constraints and moral cost

The question now is whether anything like the same approach can be run for the reasons that ground agent-relative constraints. These are traditionally thought of as much harder to deal with than those that ground options, but one ought to be wary of this idea since it emerges from peculiarities of Scheffler's approach, which I have already criticized. I much prefer Philippa Foot's suggestion that our overall approach ought to be one which establishes both options and constraints with equal ease and naturalness. Of course, there may be greater difficulty in making the account stick, but that is not quite the same point.

The obvious way in which to generalize the approach we have taken to options so as to capture constraints as well is to speak of a *moral* cost to the agent involved in the breach of a deontological constraint. This move is intended to have the advantage of being broadly similar to the way we treated options, while introducing all the differences that are necessary to cope with the fact that the cost here is precisely one which the agent is not morally permitted to discount. Here we have the idea of a cost to me which I don't have the moral right to discount.

This idea is simple enough, but it faces three main difficulties. The first is whether it is really true that we have no right to discount a moral cost to self. The second is whether the account is not dangerously circular. The third is that it seems to abandon the thought that deontological constraints are rather special, since one would naturally think that any wrong action incurs a moral cost to the agent. So in what way are the deontological constraints going to be distinctive?

The first problem asks us in a way what the proper attitude is to someone who does a morally wrong act in order to minimize the number of such acts, either by others or possibly later acts by himself.[7] Now in even raising the problem in this form we come up against the thorny difficulty of how to individuate actions. Suppose that you threaten to kill two innocents unless I kill one. Would my act of killing one, supposing that I acceded to your threat, be of the same moral type as your acts of killing two if I don't accede? I think not; the difference in motive makes what is from the moral point of view a different action. We get a straighter comparison if we take a case where you can save three by killing two, and I can save you from having to kill the two (as it were) by killing one. But even this is not perfectly straight, because in this case I act not only so as to save the three, but also to save you from paying a moral cost by taking something like that cost on myself. I have here a motive which you don't have, and on some views this will mean, again, that my act is of a different moral type from yours.

What this means is that we have to be careful in the way we raise the question. We can ask what the proper moral attitude is to someone who kills one innocent to save two from being killed, but we should not see this as the question whether it would be wrong of me to do one wrong act to prevent you from doing more of the same.

Stephen Darwall has pointed out another difficulty with the way this question is raised.[8] It is open to deontologists to say that, appalling though it may be, one is morally obliged to take on oneself the guilt of the murder of one innocent if this is the only way to prevent someone else from murdering two. Such an action would not be without moral cost to the agent – the cost of being a murderer, however that is to be understood. But it would still have to be done. In this way deontologists might come to agree with consequentialists about the need to kill one to save two. But there is still a way of distinguishing the deontological view from the consequentialist view here. For consequentialists say that it can make no difference to the moral value of an action who does it. It is therefore morally permissible for me to kill one to save you from killing one, and it might even be required if consequentialism wants to ascribe some intrinsic value to the occurrence of acts of self-sacrifice such as this. (Remember that consequentialism can ascribe intrinsic value to acts done from a certain motive, holding that the world is the better for the occurrence of such acts.) Here, however, deontologists can and should disagree. For them it does matter who does the action, and there is a moral reason for me to prefer your doing it to my doing it, even in a case where my action is of exactly the same moral type as yours.

Let us return to the question whether one ought to kill one innocent to save five from being killed. What attitude should we adopt to someone who actually does this? First, consequentialism is not in the unenviable position of saying that wholehearted approval is in order. We established in chapter 7 that consequentialism can make good sense of regret (in the rather technical sense there at issue) for an element of disvalue in a right choice. So the consequentialist position should be that killing the one is required, but that one should regret doing it. Someone who killed blithely, with a clear conscience, would be someone who had simply failed to take into account all the morally relevant features of their action. Someone who did it with a proper regret would be a person towards whom our attitude should be a mixed one of approval and sympathy.

Those who accept the existence of deontological constraints should, I think, take a similar view. We may presume that if there are any constraints at all there is one against killing. And we may also take it that this is an absolute rather than a threshold constraint.[9] A threshold constraint is one which only applies up to a certain threshold, and thereafter lapses as a constraint (though not as a reason – more on this below). We might think that even if there is a constraint against lying, there still comes a point where one ought to lie (perhaps to save a life) and where, though it would be better if one did not have to lie, this lie is not one of the ones that there is supposed to be a constraint against. But the constraint against killing does not lapse in this way. There is a complete reason against killing the innocent, and if there comes a point at which one ought to kill an innocent being, this must be seen as a case of a tragic dilemma. In a case like this there is a complete reason against killing the one and a complete reason in favour of saving the million (say), and our right attitude towards someone caught in this unenviable position is one of sympathy rather than outright condemnation. But this does not mean that the act of killing the one is right (overall). It is not; as a tragic dilemma, the case here is one in which our agent cannot escape doing a wrong, whatever choice is made. There is a moral cost to be paid either way.

All this affects the question whether the agent has the right to discount the moral cost involved in killing in certain circumstances. Suppose first that I take on myself the task of killing one innocent in order to prevent you from killing five. There being a complete reason against killing the innocent, I cannot escape the moral cost involved here. Do I have the moral right to discount a cost I cannot avoid? If I have that right and exercise it, this would mean that my action of killing the one becomes an act of superlative value, as a form of moral self-sacrifice. This is not the way deontologists want to go at all, since it leaves behind completely any thought of constraints; we have returned to options. However, we do have to cope with the fact that there seems to be something admirable about this sort of moral self-sacrifice. The way to cope with this is to find a way of contrasting moral cost, which I don't have the right to discount, and non-moral cost, which I may discount. In the non-moral case, it is one thing to say that I have the right to discount the cost and another to say that I don't have to pay it; in fact the first is true and the second false. Here, even if I pay a cost greater than the benefit I create, I have the right to make that choice, discounting the effect the cost has on the balance of reasons. Equally, I have the right to be judged on what I do with the effect of that cost discounted and to be judged as a person who is willing to discount this sort of cost to self. But we cannot make the same remarks about moral cost. Here, since I do pay the moral cost, judgement cannot be expected to discount that cost. To discount the cost would be the same as saying that I don't have to pay it; it would be to allow that I am not morally the worse for my action here. This is quite different from non-moral cost, which can be both paid and discounted. But though I pay the moral cost, and though judgement cannot ignore this fact, our proper attitude to the person who chooses a moral self-sacrifice is a complex one. My very willingness to pay this cost is something which I have a right should be counted as well, and this means that no simple attitude of approval or disapproval meets the situation fully.

A specially poignant case would be where a father chooses to take on himself some shameful act, one governed by a deontological constraint, in order to prevent that shame accruing to his son. Here, as well as the agent-relative reasons deriving from the constraint, there are those of partiality to be considered (if such exist at all). The father has more reason to make this moral self-sacrifice if he does it to save his son from shame than if he does it to save a stranger. Such matters should be remembered in constructing our complex response to the father as a moral agent, but they do not abolish the moral cost which the father has to pay.

4   BEGGING THE QUESTION

The second problem for the way I am trying to use the notion of moral cost is the charge that it begs the question, because it fails to establish independently that there is any moral cost to pay.[10] We may perhaps establish that there is room for a notion of moral cost which can in principle be used to ground deontological constraints. But as soon as we try to show that there really is such a constraint – the constraint, say, against killing – we are in grave danger of moving in a circle. The basic idea of moral cost is that a wrong action can diminish my moral status; this is the moral cost which one pays when one kills, even if one was killing in order to diminish the number of killings. But an action cannot be wrong because it diminishes my moral status. It diminishes my moral status because it is wrong. So even though my being a killer does diminish my moral status, the wrongness of killing, and in particular the existence of a constraint against killing, needs to be established independently.

This problem forces me to take a step beyond anything established so far. The basic idea behind consequentialism is that of a valuable outcome, of ways in which the world can go better or worse. The basic idea behind deontology is that of the sort of person one ought to be.[11] To be the right sort of person is to have all the moral virtues. So a deontological approach to ethics should start with a list of virtues. Killing is wrong because of the attitude to others which it expresses (among other things), which is incompatible with any plausible list of virtues. So to kill is to diminish one's own moral status – an injury which can only be inflicted on one by one's own actions.

So the wrongness of killing is not established directly from the damage it does to one's moral status, but rather from the fact that killing is necessarily at odds with a virtue. How then are we to justify our list of virtues? One suggestion, dear to the hearts of consequentialists, would be to base that list on the way in which each member contributes to the furtherance of outcomes established independently as good. This has the appearance of putting personal ethics on a solid, external foundation; consequentialism can offer a list of personal virtues, but each of these will be justified from outside, as it were. By contrast, a virtue-based theory has nowhere further to look. It is reduced to the sort of justification I described in chapter 7, namely that of describing the virtuous person in such a way that the claims of virtue are convincing. But I do not find this a defect, since I see no reason for supposing that the sort of external justification that consequentialism offers need be available, so that our position is only rational if we can produce it. And though there can be no external justification for our list of virtues, that list can provide an independent justification for claims about particular constraints. There can be constraints because one has a good reason to be relieved if others take some moral shame on their shoulders which one would otherwise have to bear oneself.

This way of putting the matter makes it seem as if the moral agent's main concern should be their own moral health – the concern to keep their hands clean. But that would be a distortion of the true position. People who are primarily concerned about their own moral standing are not virtuous. To have the virtue of benevolence is to be motivated directly by thoughts about the welfare of others, and such persons act for others' sake, not to keep their own hands clean. But this admission shows that however closely related the two stories of options and of constraints, in terms of cost and of moral cost, the notion of cost is not playing quite the same role on both sides. For the reluctant hero is properly motivated by considerations of cost to self, while the person who recognizes a constraint is not, or should not be, one who is noticing and motivated by a moral cost to self. There is a moral cost to be paid if one makes the wrong choice, but that is not properly what motivates.

5   ABSOLUTE AND THRESHOLD CONSTRAINTS

These thoughts take us straight into the third problem for my approach, namely the question whether it is able to see deontological constraints as the very special beasts they are traditionally presented as being. Surely a virtue-based theory is going to see all wrong actions as ones which are in one way or another incompatible with virtue, so that each of them will diminish one's claim to virtue and so diminish one's moral status. This goes flatly against the normal view that only a very few wrong actions – those that involve harming others, say, or killing – are governed by constraints. This normal view lies behind Kagan's desperate if ill-intentioned efforts to discover something special about harming which will serve to ground a constraint. Failing to find anything special, he concludes that no constraint is in place. But if *all* wrong actions were governed by a constraint, so that I always have a reason to prefer your doing one to my doing one, the failure of Kagan's search need not worry the agent-relativist.

There remains, of course, a sense that there is something especially wrong about certain actions: perhaps that they should not be done at any price. If there are such actions, their existence lies behind the view that constraints are special, for *these* constraints *are* special. The normal view may have been misled by this into supposing that all constraints are special in this way. But that there are absolute prohibitions – non-threshold constraints – may not be the crucial point. Normal constraints may be threshold constraints.

To build this suggestion up we need to make sure that we do not distort the idea of a constraint, and so mistake both the notion of a threshold constraint and that of an absolute constraint. It is common for writers to see absolute constraints as those which we can never be required to break. This is a mistake, if only because it ignores the possibility of two such constraints conflicting with another. But anyone who accepts the possibility of serious incommensurability will accept that occasionally one will be forced into a position in which whatever one does is wrong. In such a case one is morally required to make a choice, and whatever choice one makes one will break an absolute constraint. So we must not make our picture of absolute constraints so strong as to rule out the possibility of incommensurability. Most discussions of this topic (e.g. Kagan's) make this mistake. Second, our account of threshold constraints must be sensitive to our account of the behaviour of defeated reasons. If we say that once the threshold is reached there is nothing wrong with doing the action (telling a lie to save a life, say), we have forgotten the importance of leaving defeated reasons in place – something that gave us a lot of trouble in chapter 7. We are supposing, wrongly, that the entire role of a defeated reason is to reduce the rightness of the overall right action.

It is this notion of a defeated reason that is the clue to the problem of whether constraints are special or not. In normal moral dilemmas we hope to reach a solution, by seeing which action is the right choice. We suppose that if one action is right, its alternatives are actions we would in the end be wrong to do, despite what there is to be said for them. But where there is incommensurability things are not like this. Here our choice of one action leaves us knowing that we have left undone something we ought to have done, even though we have done something we ought to have done, or that we have done something we ought not to have done, even though this was our only method of avoiding another action equally wrong. In a case of this sort, there will be an absolute constraint and there will be inescapable moral damage to the agent. Even though I am the only person who can cause moral damage to me, in these cases that is what I will be forced to do. This is what non-threshold constraints are like. Even if I am morally forced to kill one to save a thousand, I breach an absolute constraint and in doing that wrong damage my moral status.

But there are also threshold constraints. We get one of these wherever an action is ordinarily wrong. The wrongness of an action gives agents a moral reason to prefer that someone else do it instead of them. If we can construct a case where I do a bad act in order to prevent your doing one of *exactly* the same moral type, I would always be wrong to make that choice (I would pay a moral cost). This remains true all the way up the line. All constraints, threshold or absolute, are like this. But a threshold constraint gives out at a certain point, where the action concerned is not wrong but right. Once the action becomes right, then of course I no longer have any reason (other than laziness – but this is not a moral reason) to prefer that you should do it in my stead.[12]

This, however, only raises another difficulty. If the action is right, and if my primary concern is with my moral character, will there not be the same competition to do it as there was not to be the one who did the wrong act? Won't I now have a reason to pre-empt your doing it in order to get the moral credit for myself, as it were? Worse, I will have a reason to do an act of less value even if this prevents your doing one of more. This would be an uncomfortable result. But the approach I am taking does not have this consequence. It appears to have it because of the way it puts stress on one's moral character and the damage one can do to it by the breach of a constraint. The thought that agents' primary concerns are for their own moral character seems to impute to us a sort of moral selfishness, as if one's primary moral aim were to keep one's moral hands clean. Seeking the good of others is only in order if we thereby get the moral credit, which is what we are really after. All this is a distortion, as I tried to suggest at the end of the previous section. A person who does a charitable act in the search for moral credit is not a charitable person and is not acting charitably; it is only by courtesy that we described the act as charitable at all. In fact it is not charitable, but rather a peculiar form of moral self-seeking. The sense in which our primary concern is for our own moral character is not that we should be primarily interested in improving our moral status and avoiding damage to it. Such an interest would be self-defeating; to have it is already to undermine it. The point is merely that we have a direct reason not to kill, a reason other than the reason why there should be as few killings as possible.[13]

6   PARTICULARISM AND THE AGENT-RELATIVE

This completes my account and defence of agent-relative reasons, in which my aim has been throughout to defend the idea that these reasons are as objective as other moral reasons. I end this chapter with three comments on the picture I have been trying to draw. The first is short. It is to point out that on my account there is no sign of either of Scheffler's two theses, the independence thesis and the asymmetry thesis. The independence thesis holds that the motivation for options is different from that for constraints. The common role played by the notion of cost to the agent in my account of options and constraints seems to me an implicit rejection of this thesis. It is true, as Scheffler says, that constraints are not more of the same sort of things as options. But the sense in which this is true does not sustain the independence thesis. The asymmetry thesis is just the claim that there are options but no constraints; this too I reject.

The second comment is a much lengthier matter. It concerns the relation between my defence of the agent-relative and my particularism. First, are these compatible? Second, what effect does the particularism have on the sustainability of the picture I have been presenting? It would be nice to show that particularism makes life easier for me here. As we shall see, in some respects it does; but there is also a natural thought that particularism cannot countenance constraints at all. What I shall argue is that particularism improves our account of options and of threshold constraints, and that it is able to allow the existence of absolute constraints as well.

My picture of options holds that there is a non-neutral reason which may on occasions justify agents in failing to sacrifice themselves for the 'greater good'. Whether the present case is one in which the sacrifice is required or not is exactly the sort of question that particularists are happy to discuss. They do not expect to find a general principle to which one could appeal in advance, as it were. All will depend on the nature of the case. So as far as this goes, particularism merely makes our account of options more flexible. And this is what we should expect, since particularism effectively demands less of our reasons than generalism does. But there remains a question about reasons of autonomy, namely what if anything justifies a restriction on our option to adopt personal projects. All such projects will involve us in allowing harm which we could have done something to prevent. But we feel that a project which involves doing harm is not permissible. Mustn't there then be some general distinction between the morality of allowing and of doing harm, in a way that particularism cannot allow?

The beginning of a response to this is to point out that particularism takes doing harm to be only sometimes worse than allowing harm. (Remember the discussion of drowning nephews in the bath in 5.7.) Sometimes both are equally bad. Where doing harm is not worse than allowing harm, then either both are forbidden or neither is. Is it inconceivable that a project which involves harming others should be morally permissible? If we mean by this 'Could it be permissible to harm another in pursuit of a personal project?', I think that on occasions the answer is yes. If boxing is a morally permissible pursuit, any boxing match will be an example. For an example of permissible non-physical harm, suppose that you and I are the only two candidates competing for a prestigious law scholarship. If you get this scholarship you will be well on the way to a partnership with the distinguished City firm of Sue, Grabbit and Runne, and the same is true for me. There is only this difference between us, that I exist for the moment on an allowance from an uncle who has a grudge against your family, so that if you win the scholarship instead of me he will withdraw his support and my chances of pursuing a career at the bar will vanish. You, on the other hand, have a nice little legacy to tide you over the initial lean years. Suppose that you win the scholarship. In doing so you cause significant damage to my prospects; this is not physical harm, but it is still harm. But it seems to me morally permissible for you to cause me that harm in pursuit of your own admissible project. (This example assumes throughout that a career with Sue, Grabbit and Runne is a permissible project.)

It might be said that examples of competition, where all agree to compete for the sake of the gains of victory, but at the risk of the costs of defeat, are somehow special. But surely we could all accept that non-significant harm to another might be reasonable if required for the completion of a personal project that has taken thirty years of sustained effort.

There is, however, a different question which might be meant by someone who asks whether projects which involve harming others are permissible. This is whether it is permissible to have it as one's project that one should harm others; the harm here is to be part of the intentional content of one's project. For instance, could I have it as my project that all rapists should be castrated? Perhaps this is not a case of harming innocent others. For that we would need a different example. One such might be the project of successfully shoplifting from each shop in a certain street; another might be that of shooting all one's neighbours on the cheek with an airgun from one's bedroom window (for those who think that physical harm is somehow special). Could a project of this sort be permissible? This question is harder to answer than is the question whether it might be permissible to aim at the ruin of all members of a certain family, or to try to pull all the fingernails off a child in under one minute. One would only worry about these last if one thought that 'it is my project' conferred a sort of moral immunity on the agent or acted somehow as an exclusionary reason in Raz's sense. It doesn't, and on my account it doesn't. Whatever the strength of reasons of autonomy, it is not sufficient to justify adopting or acting in pursuit of projects of this sort.

Suppose that some harms are justified. Then a project to do those harms will be permissible. The bounty hunter is not an attractive figure, but his actions are not immoral, and I see no moral constraint on his choice of this way of life. So we are assuming that the projects governed by the constraint are projects to do impermissible harm. Such projects are wrong because the actions that are their intensional contents are (implicitly taken to be) wrong. Suppose again that some cases of allowing harm are justified. If there is a question whether a project whose intensional content is that of allowing harm is permissible (it is admittedly hard to think of an example of this), we can say again that there is an implicit assumption that the allowings we are talking about are not the justified ones but the wrong ones; and so the project is wrong.

In this way we can effectively agree that projects whose intensional content is that of harming others are not morally permissible, without any appeal either to a constraint against harming or to a significant distinction between harming and allowing harm of a sort which particularism might find it hard to countenance. So I take it that particularism has no problem in claiming that there are options. Indeed, the flexibility of particularism is a significant help in avoiding the question what principle underlies distinctions we want to draw between particular cases. A good example here can be found in Philippa Foot's discussions of the moral relevance of the distinctions between intended and unintended consequences (the doctrine of double effect), and between killing and allowing to die.[14] She writes, for instance, 'Nevertheless there are circumstances in which it is morally permissible to bring something about without *aiming* at it although it would not be morally permissible to aim at it; even though the balance of benefit and harm in the consequences remained the same.' The way in which she speaks here of this being so in some cases is very congenial to particularism, but (from my point of view) she spoils it by insisting that there must therefore be some principle at stake which with sufficient ingenuity we could unearth. I want to accept her view that there are circumstances in which this can happen, without supposing that this needs to be supported by a general statement of the difference between those in which it happens and those in which it doesn't. Since no such general statement is easily forthcoming, there is a sense here in which my particularism lets me off an awkward hook. I view this as an incentive for being a particularist, but not exactly a reason for particularism.

So I turn to threshold constraints. These are much easier to deal with. The core idea here is that, as long as the constraint applies and the action is wrong, I have a reason to prefer your doing it to my doing it. Here again the wrongness of the acts concerned is assumed, and that derives not from a single feature but from the shape of the situation in which we are involved. This sort of wrongness is something which particularism is very happy to discuss. There is nothing in this sort of threshold constraint that it cannot countenance. One would only miss this point if one thought that threshold constraints function rather on the lines of *pro tanto* reasons. They don't, on my account. I do not allow the existence of a general threshold constraint against lying, for instance. My conception of a constraint is not antecedent in this way, but internal to the logical structure of the present case.

Matters are quite different with absolute constraints. This is not because of the difference between absolute and threshold constraints as such. There is no greater difficulty in seeing that this action is one which we would be wrong to do, no matter how much we weight its consequences on the other side, so long as the wrongness is thought of as emerging holistically in the way that particularists suppose. The problem with absolute constraints derives rather from the nature of the examples given; the classic absolute constraint is against killing the innocent, and the suggestion is that any action which involves killing the innocent is wrong, whatever other features it may have. This is an exceptionless general truth which links the wrongness of the actions it concerns with an isolable feature with which it is invariably associated. As such it cannot avoid generating just the sort of moral principle that I attacked in chapters 5 and 6 – in chapter 5 especially, since the sort of moral principle we are being offered here is not a prima facie principle, but an absolute one related to a limited feature, in the way that Hare's doctrine of universalizability supposes. So it seems that the existence of absolute constraints is incompatible with a full particularism. How then can a particularist be an agent-relativist who accepts both options and constraints?

It is worth distinguishing this objection from the one I discussed in 4.3, which is that there are some intrinsically wrong-making features; the standard example is that of causing pain. It is common to suppose that any action which involves causing pain is to that extent wrong. To say this is to suppose that there is a genuine prima facie principle at issue - 'It is wrong to cause pain' – which may not always win the day (since some such actions are overall right) but which makes the same contribution in every instance where it occurs. The objection is different because of the fact that it offers a prima facie rather than an absolute principle.

It would be possible for a particularist to accept both these points and carry on all the same. For however it may be with these special features, one can insist that there are very many other morally relevant features which do not make anything like this regular contribution to any action that has them, and whose role is very much dependent on the context in the sort of way that a particularist is getting at. Wherever there are no such special features present, the situation is purely particularist; where there are, it is to some extent a mixture. But this is not a way of letting generalism in by the back door, since there is no general admission that what matters here must matter in the same way everywhere.

I distrust this sort of compromise position, and not just because it is not theoretically neat. One reason is that part of the attack on generalism was that it didn't make sense. No working account of a prima facie reason was in fact to be found. If we then admit that there are at least some such reasons, our case against them is correspondingly weakened. The compromise position supposes that it is to some extent a contingent matter how many generalist reasons there are, and I think that with this we are directing our attention to the wrong place. So it is worth trying to see whether it is possible to answer the present criticism directly within the limits imposed by particularism.

Let us begin by considering what the constraint we are talking about amounts to. As standardly conceived, it does not govern killing as such. It is not that we are required not to kill the guilty, so that the death penalty could never be enforced. We are talking about killing the innocent. Let us agree for present purposes that this is wrong, and that it cannot be rendered right by peculiar circumstances; no amount of reasons on the other side can make it the right choice. Now the role of innocence here is interesting. It seems to me to encapsulate the thought that only an act of one's own can justify one's being killed.[15] If one has done nothing wrong, one is innocent and there is a complete reason against one being killed. There are of course (or may be) various ways in which one can undermine one's own immunity against being killed. But to say straight out that one is innocent is to say in advance that none of those ways has been operated in this case. So to kill someone who is innocent is to kill someone of whom we know already that there is no justification for their being killed. It is not surprising that an action of this sort is always wrong; but its wrongness is, as it were, a structural feature, built into the description. The question whether any such justification is present is, of course, one which particularists are perfectly happy to discuss, and it must be discussed before we decide that the action is governed by an absolute constraint.

However, this should not be taken to mean that the relevant constraint is against killing the innocent. What is wrong with killing the innocent is the killing; that one's victim was innocent does not make it worse. Innocence is merely the absence of a justification for the killing. Such absences do not make the killing worse, even though if there were some justification present the killing would not be wrong.[16] So the constraint is on killing, and it is an absolute constraint which applies unless the victim is not innocent, i.e. unless there is a justification. So to call it absolute is not to call it exceptionless; it is merely to say that if it applies, no accumulation of considerations on the other side can justify a breach of the constraint. This is not tautologous. Since we know in advance that the constraint applies unless the victim is innocent, we have the substantial truth that there is a complete reason against killing the innocent that cannot be overwhelmed, without this creating the sort of absolute constraint that seems to raise problems for particularism.[17]

This is the way in which I think that particularism should try to cope with the fact that it is always wrong to kill the innocent, if we admit this as a fact. It amounts to admitting that there is a default position about killing: in the absence of suitable justification, it is wrong. (This might remind us of Ross's attempt to define a prima facie wrong-making feature as one which would decide the issue if it were the only morally relevant feature of the case.) But we should not conclude from this that killing has everywhere the moral relevance it would have were it the only relevant feature. For instance, euthanasia need not be wrong although here we are killing an innocent but willing victim, nor need it necessarily be wrong to kill someone who wishes to sacrifice themself for someone else. Perhaps the example of euthanasia shows that the absolute constraint, if there is one, is not against killing the innocent but against killing the innocent and unwilling. But if so this seems to me merely to be a more complex but still structural matter. Killing an innocent and unwilling being is always wrong – absolutely wrong – since there is a default position against which we already know there is nothing to put in this case. But the role which killing plays in the default position is not one which it necessarily plays in other cases where there is guilt or willingness. The wrongness of killing is not essential to it, even though an ordinary act of killing the innocent is absolutely and intrinsically wrong.[18]

7   Is AGENT-RELATIVE MORALITY DEMANDING ENOUGH?

My third comment on the story I have told is a caveat. The matters I have been discussing have often been presented as a debate between those who think that consequentialist morality is too demanding and those who don't, as if the latter party are setting out to defend something recognizably similar to the ordinary way in which people live in

England, closing their eyes to the needs of the Third World and giving enormous Christmas presents to their children while occasionally sending a small cheque to a well-publicized appeal as a sop to their 'consciences'. Viewed in these terms, the debate is between the austere and the indulgent. But it is quite possible to defend the existence of agent-relative reasons without thereby constructing the sort of morality which will validate most ordinary lives. All parties to the debate can agree that morality is very demanding, and bewail the failures of themselves (as of others) to live up to what is morally required of them. *Where* and *how far* the flexibility introduced by agent-relative reasons comes in is a matter for debate. Nothing has been said here about the extent to which my right to pursue a personal project can be set against the duty to contribute to famine relief. What has been disputed is the philosophical picture of that duty as centrally driven by thoughts about maximizing outcomes, against which other considerations appear merely as occasional blips, tolerated at best in recognition of human weakness. The structure of moral reasons is more complex than this picture allows.

I close this chapter with a summary. I have tried to give a smooth account of options and constraints in terms of cost to the agent, while recognizing the important differences between these two sorts of costs. Then I tried to defend my approach against the various objections that recent literature has thrown up – notably those made by Shelly Kagan. I do not claim that the result is particularly stable, but in the context of the present debate that would be too much to hope for. The important thing is to see that despite the barrage of difficulties that can be put up for agent-relativism, there is some chance of finding a position with sufficient structural complexity to do what needs to be done here.

NOTES

1   This challenge is pressed particularly hard by Kagan; see Kagan (1984) and (1989), ch. 9, pp. 369–85.
2   I tried, but eventually succumbed to pressure from John McDowell.
3   A more substantial motive for rejecting the weaker view, which has two sorts of reasons, both grounded in value of the same type, is that it is more susceptible to consequentialist claims that they can accommodate whatever agent-relativists have to say (see 13. 1). I don't believe these claims, but the distinction between outcome theory and theory of motivation, or between agent-theory and act-theory (discussed in chapter 13) is made more plausible, and more probably effective, by the weaker view.
4   Here I am much in debt to Marc Lange.

5   Note the difference between this approach and Nagel's view that there must therefore be two different sorts of things being valued, events valued neutrally and actions valued relatively.

6   Kagan (1988), p. 277. He calls this principle 'internalism'; but of course it bears no relation to the views discussed under that name in this book.

7   I owe to Broome (1991), ch. 1 the idea that there may be a deontological constraint against doing one wrong action now in order to prevent several similar actions of one's own later.

8   See Darwall (1986).

9   For this idea, see Kagan (1989), pp. 4–5 and 50–1.

10 I associate this charge with Nagel, but cannot give a precise reference.

11 Foot (1985b) is required reading here.

12 The picture I am trying to give of a threshold constraint is one which concentrates self-consciously on agency – on who is to do the action. The reason for this is that it enables me to think of these constraints as agent-relative. We can contrast the approach taken by Kagan. For him, a threshold constraint is one which it is permissible to breach if enough is at stake. I think that this takes our attention away from the notion of a deontological constraint (and the associated focus on agency). Kagan's picture would be satisfied by any *neutral* non-consequence-based reason. Such a reason may be put up against consequence-based reasons, and as they grow it will eventually cease to win the struggle, without our seeing here any trace of the tension between agent-relative and agent-neutral considerations. This sort of constraint is not one which it is permissible to breach, but one which ceases to be a constraint at the moment of breachability.

13 In this way I hope to do better than Stephen Darwall; see Darwall (1986). The approach I am taking is definitely 'inside-out' rather than 'outside-in', in Darwall's sense, but I am trying to avoid any suggestion that one's primary moral concern is properly with one's own moral rectitude – a matter which in Darwall's hands becomes a concern with the authenticity of one's own moral judgements.

14 See Foot (1985a); the passage quoted is on p. 25.

15 There are two possible objections to this announcement. The first is that no such thought is encapsulated in the way that innocence functions in this constraint. The second is that general remarks of this sort are not available to a particularist. On the second, it is worth pointing out that a particularist does not try to avoid all general remarks in ethics. One can, for instance, be both a particularist and a consequentialist, for there is nothing in consequentialism that militates against holism in the theory of reasons. The claim that only consequences are morally relevant is the sort of general structural remark that I am making in the text here. The only reason for doubting this is if one supposes that it is of the essence of particularism to hold that in suitable circumstances anything whatever could be a reason either for or against anything whatever. But this claim is unnecessarily strong; our holism is not so indiscriminate.

16 Here I attempt to avoid a switching argument of the sort discussed in 4.3. The crucial point here is the distinction between applying and winning. Absolute constraints are those which win iff they apply; threshold constraints may apply without winning.

17 Have I just argued that where the absolute constraint fails to apply, there is no constraint against killing? No. It is quite compatible with what I have said so far to hold that where the absolute constraint fails to apply, a threshold one comes into play. With killing, I imagine that this is what happens in many cases – though not necessarily all.

18 It is worth remembering that not all cases of causing pain are therefore wrong. It may be that it is only causing pain to the innocent that is banned. If so, the remarks I make here about killing the innocent will be relevant to the case of causing pain, discussed in 4.3.

13
Consequentialism and the agent-relative

1 Is CONSEQUENTIALISM SELF-EFFACING?

In this final chapter I consider the question whether consequentialism could survive the admission of agent-relative reasons, and argue that it cannot. I have already considered Sen's argument that agent-relativity can be captured without difficulty without breaching the constraints of a consequentialist perspective, and suggested that this hopeful result stems from a failure to take the agent-relative seriously. The sort of agent-relative reason that I want to argue for resists Sen's assimilation. But there are two other ways in which consequentialism might try to absorb the agent-relative. I shall consider the first briefly, and then spend much longer on the second.

Consequentialism presents us with an account of value. It then writes an account of moral reasons (those reasons on which it can approve our acting) which is taken directly from the account of value. The matrix of reasons mirrors the matrix of value. Agent-relative reasons do not fit the matrix of neutral value. So if we accept their existence as moral reasons, we are committed to abandoning consequentialism. Or so it seems.

But consequentialism could become cleverer. It could try to separate what it says about reasons from what it says about values. It could abandon the idea that moral motivation and morally sound reasons can be read off directly from the matrix of neutral values, in an attempt to grant and even capture the discrepancy between reasons and neutral values within a perspective which retains the consequentialist starting-point: the value of outcomes. This is the move which I shall consider second.

There is an alternative. Consequentialists can instead suppose that agent-neutral values are promoted by the recognition of agent-relative ones. For instance, they could say that love and friendship are agent-relative values; they are values because the world goes better if they are included in it, and they are not neutral because they underly patterns of concern which are asymmetrical, as where I prefer a lesser benefit for my child to a greater one for a stranger. (Kagan toyed with something like this idea before rejecting it.)

The idea is not quite that the admission of agent-relative values is a sort of noble lie. Rather it is to grant the agent-relative a sort of secondary existence; agent-relative values exist, but not in their own right. They exist as means to a neutral end. Basic values are still neutral. But this fact has to be camouflaged, for if we insist on it the value contributed to the world by love and friendship will no longer be available. For love is only possible, let alone valuable, if it takes itself seriously, i.e. if the loved ones are loved for their own sake rather than because the love contributes to some neutral good. Equally, someone who is told by their doctor to take up a hobby and therefore doggedly engages in model engineering for their health's sake is not someone who has that as a hobby in the sense the doctor intended, and is not going to reap the benefits of having an engrossing concern outside themselves. The point wasn't the physical exercise but the mental change. The ideal situation here is that the patient, when asked why she devotes time and money to model engineering, can say that originally she did it because her doctor advised her to take up some hobby, but now she does it for its own sake. But if so she has already moved away from a position which sees value in model engineering only as a means to something else.

Can similar remarks be made in ethics? My right to engage in non-optimizing personal projects stems from the way in which such projects emerge naturally from ordinary human motivations, and from the cost to me of doing without such a project or of abandoning it once formed. That right is in permanent tension with the demands of neutral considerations, but it should not be seen as dependent for its existence on its contribution to those considerations. For if we see it this way, we prevent it from being the value it is supposed to be. If the idea behind the admission of agent-relative values is to free us from the thrall of the neutral, we must either abandon or at least disguise our view that agent-relative values are only admissible as means to the agent-neutral. Since we cannot abandon it without ceasing to be consequentialists, we must disguise it. The central plank of consequentialism – its view that neutral values lie at the centre of ethics – is something to which we cannot admit. Our consequentialism has become self-effacing.

This point can be put another way, congenial to the general argument of this book. My project has been to establish that agent-relative reasons or values are no less objective than are agent-neutral reasons or values. To this end, I maintain that they survive Hegelian objectification as well as other moral reasons do. Could a consequentialist make this claim? I doubt it. There is an awkward dilemma here. The first horn is one in which the admission of the agent-relative is a mere sham or pretence, because the way in which we are allowed to find value in love and friendship is not one which fits any value that those states actually have; agent-relative values of this sort would fail blatantly to survive the first stage of Hegelian objectification. On the second horn we allow that there really is the sort of value that we find in those states of partiality, at the cost of preventing ourselves from reasserting the dependence of such value on neutral value. The second horn is the less damaging, but it is one on which consequentialism can no longer admit to its own central message.

The simplest way of making this point is to say that for our reasons to be objective, they need to survive the process of Hegelian objectification. But we seem to be expected to start from an original set of reasons which mirrors the matrix of neutral value, and then move from that to a different, wider set of reasons which doesn't fit the basic consequentialist message in that neat way. And once we have reached this new position, we will be in the peculiar position that *we* won't be able to point to the basic reason why our reasons are good reasons. So our position will fail to survive objectification. The problem is that having left our source behind, we can no longer give for ourselves the correct justification; that must remain opaque to us.[1] Consequentialism cannot escape the need to camouflage its central message.

Once this point has been established, it seems to me futile to try to argue that this need to efface itself is not highly damaging. Consequentialism offers a reasoned constraint on the sorts of reasons there can be, and if the reason for that constraint cannot be brought out, we have, it seems, no reason to accept anything that the theory says thereafter. Not only cannot we capture the role of neutral value, but we will therefore distort the sort of value that the theory is willing to allow to relative value. We will fail on both counts.

2   ENDS, AIMS AND MOTIVES

I now turn to the alternative way of surviving the admission of agent-relative value, that of claiming that though there is only one sort of value (neutral value), consequentialism has its own reasons for allowing patterns of motivation (reasons) other than those which exactly match the matrix of value. Here the idea is that consequentialism is a theory which gives us certain ends, but which is officially silent on which patterns of motivation may best promote those ends. There may be a number of such patterns that are equally good at promoting the given end, and consequentialism merely allows, or recommends, any such pattern, whether or not it bears any significant relation to the pattern of neutral values. Now the end which consequentialism gives us is the promotion of neutral good. Again, it does not specify the nature of neutral good, but merely borrows such a specification from some independent theory of the good, and holds that right actions are those which most promote the good so conceived. So it stands in between a theory of the good and a theory of motivation. This should not persuade us that it has not got a lot of content.

For the rest of this chapter I examine the question whether the theory of motivation can be divorced in this way from the theory of the good. In particular, I pursue Derek Parfit's attempt to show that this divorce cannot be turned into a refutation of consequentialism, since his is the most sophisticated presentation I know.[2] Instead of contrasting a theory of ends with a theory of motives, as I did in the last paragraph, he prefers to speak of *aims*. According to Parfit, consequentialism's central claim is that there is one ultimate moral aim: that outcomes be as good as possible.[3] (Since this notion of an aim is very important, it is worth while noticing its introduction.) Consequentialism gives us this aim, but it does not specify any recommended motives; instead it leaves it open which sets of motives would best promote the aims it specifies.

There are two distinct sorts of reason for distinguishing in this way between theory of aims and theory of motives. The first we have seen; it is the attempt to capture agent-relative reasons or values within the constraints of consequentialism. But Parfit's discussion concerns another reason, which is that consequentialism, viewed as a theory which gives us certain aims, may be what he calls 'indirectly self-defeating'. This is because if people try to achieve the aims the theory gives them, they are less likely to achieve them than if they had some other aims.[4] A theory that conceives of personal happiness as one's main or sole good would be self-defeating in this sense if it is true, as many believe, that to be exclusively or mainly concerned with one's own happiness reduces one's chances of being happy. Parfit believes that consequentialism is self-defeating in this sense. But he argues that this sort of self-defeat is not damaging because a theory can consistently specify an aim without saying anything about how we should be motivated – about what sorts of motivation we should have. So this is a second reason for distinguishing between theory of aims and theory of motivation.

3 ACTS AND AGENTS

In Parfit's hands, consequentialism (which I will follow him in calling 'C') has a certain structure. First, it makes one central claim:

> There is one ultimate moral aim: that outcomes be as good as possible.[5]

But C does not restrict itself to this one remark. Parfit says that 'applied to acts, C claims both:

> What each of us ought to do is whatever would make the outcome best, and

> If someone does what he believes will make the outcome worse, he is acting wrongly.'[6]

These remarks are about the rightness or wrongness of *acts*. As such, they can be more clearly re-expressed as follows:

> An *act* is *objectively right* if its outcome is the best possible

> An *act* is *subjectively right* if the agent believes that its outcome will be the best possible.

What about agents? The worth of agents is defined in terms of that of motives or sets of motives. A motive is a member of a set of motives which it would be right in C's terms for an agent to cause himself to have and wrong in C's terms for him to cause himself to lose if our having that set of motives would lead to outcomes at least as good as the outcomes of any alternative set of motives. We can call such a set of motives 'C-approved', and define something called 'agent-rightness' as follows:

> An *agent* acts *objectively rightly* (here) if his motive is a member of a C-approved set of motives.

> An *agent* acts *subjectively rightly* (here) if he believes his motive to be a member of a C-approved set of motives.[7]

Notice that our assessment of an individual motive depends on the question what other motives it is present with. Motives are assessed not individually but in sets which are up for C's approval as a whole. As a result there may well be more than one set of motives which is C-approved. One crucial point for Parfit is that C itself should not amount to the specification of any recommended motive or set of motives. He holds that C specifies aims but not motives; C leaves it open which motives would best realize C-given aims.

There are two things to be said about the distinction between the objective and the subjective. The first is that, as I have laid it out, there is a clear distinction between the (subjective or objective) rightness of the agent and the subjective rightness of the act. We must be careful, therefore, not to confuse the two. The second is that the objective/subjective distinction turns out, perhaps rather surprisingly, not to make any difference. For it only comes into play when the agent is either ignorant of or mistaken about some relevant fact. And none of Parfit's examples are of this form. So despite the potential complications introduced by the objective/subjective distinction, all the real work in Parfit's defence of the claim that C is undamagingly self-defeating is done by the distinction between act and agent. I now turn to consider that defence.

4 A SELF-DEFEATING THEORY?

There are two sorts of indirect self-defeat.

If we call some theory *T*, call the aims that it gives us *our T-given aims*. Call T:

> *indirectly individually self-defeating* when it is true that, if someone tries to achieve his T-given aims, these aims will be, on the whole, worse achieved.[8]

By contrast,
Call T:

> *indirectly collectively self-defeating* when it is true that, if several people try to achieve their T-given aims, these aims would be worse achieved.[9]

C is indirectly collectively self-defeating. Parfit considers various ways in which outcomes will be worse if we are 'pure do-gooders', i.e. if our only motive is that outcomes be as good as possible. For instance, we would have to abandon our normal practice of caring especially for our family and friends. Parfit suggests that there would be an enormous cost in this, since we would all be left with very strong desires to favour family and friends which will remain unfulfilled.[10] But his response to the fact that C is indirectly self-defeating in this way is that this does not matter because there are no aims which C recommends us both to have and to avoid. Instead, our C-given aims are one thing, and the motives from which we should act are another. If our motive is simply to achieve our C-given aims, we will fail to achieve them or at least achieve them less completely than if we had some other set of aims. And this shows that C itself tells us to adopt some other set of motives, a C-approved set whose adoption will further as much as any our C-given aims.

But this seems to mean that we have a theory, C, which specifies a single ultimate aim for us, an aim which we *ought* to pursue, and then tells us that we ought not to pursue it because the very pursuit of it reduces one's chances of achieving it. We have here a moral aim which in some sense it would be immoral to aim at, since there is available to us a better alternative practice. The question is whether Parfit succeeds in showing that this is better than self-contradictory. The problem arises because we have here a theory which is silent on outcomes. C does not specify a desirable outcome; it gives us an aim, that outcomes be as good as possible. It then tells us not to aim at this aim: not to adopt it as an aim. Can this be coherent?

Parfit's reply to this is effectively that the notion of a C-given aim is ambiguous. There are aims we ought to have in the sense of motives which we should adopt, and there are aims we ought to have in the sense of outcomes whose nature determines how well the world is going and how well we have acted. The appearance of contradiction in the idea that there are ultimate moral aims which it would be wrong of us to pursue derives from failing to keep apart these two senses of 'aim'. Since the worth of agents is determined by the motives from which they act, this resolution can be expressed in terms of the act/agent distinction. A case where we act from a set of motives which we ought to have, but where our action does not lead to the best outcome, is not one where what we did was both right and wrong, but one where though what we did was wrong, we were right to do it – a case, that is, of blameless wrongdoing.

5   BLAMELESS WRONGDOING

Parfit offers us two examples to persuade us that the idea of blameless wrongdoing is coherent. The first is that of Clare. Clare loves her child, and her love for her child is a member of a C-approved set of motives which Clare has. She could either give her child some benefit, or give much greater benefits to some unfortunate stranger. Because she loves her child, she benefits him rather than the stranger. This action makes the outcome worse, as Clare recognizes. But the set of motives of which Clare's love for her child is a part is a set which it would be wrong (in C's terms) for Clare to lose and right for her to get. So it would be wrong of Clare to change her motives (even if she could) unless there is some other set of motives which is more C-approved than hers and which she could without serious loss have adopted. There is no such set of motives. So Clare acts rightly in benefiting her child because of her love for it, even though her act in so doing is wrong (in C's terms) because its outcome is worse than the outcome of some available alternative act.

Though Parfit puts the case of Clare first, I think his diagnosis of Clare as a blameless wrongdoer is intended to be supported by his second example, that of 'My Moral Corruption'. In this example I am a politician who has an enemy who wants to corrupt me, i.e. to turn me into an accomplice to his crimes against my will. He threatens to kill my children unless I allow him to take a film of me engaging in obscene acts. Later he will ask me to help in his criminal activities, on pain of publication of the film and the ruination of my career. I know that I will accede to these requests, so as to avoid exposure and protect my career; my enemy has assured me that once I have made the film, there will be no further threat to my children unless I voluntarily abandon my career. So I will have a choice between being exposed and engaging in criminal acts, and I will make the wrong choice. (It would be the right choice if there was any continuing threat to my children.)

Given the choice presented to me, I ought to let my enemy make the film. But once I have done this, I shall have a motive to engage in criminal acts. So, in C's terms, there is an action which I ought to do but which will have the effect of causing me to acquire a set of motives which is not C-approved. I ought to cause it to be true that I shall later act wrongly.

In this case there are two actions and two sets of motives: the first set causes me to allow the film to be made and the second causes me to commit criminal acts to protect my good name and career. My first act is right, and I act rightly in doing it because it stems from a C-approved set of motives; but the second act is wrong and I act wrongly in doing it, since it stems from a set of motives which is not C-approved. The peculiarity of my moral corruption is that the second set of motives, with its attendant actions, is a predictable consequence of the first, right act. So the wrong act springs somehow from a C-approved set of motives. Parfit knows that my criminal acts are wrong and that I am wrong to do them. What he is using the case of my moral corruption to show is that it is possible for an acceptable moral theory to tell us to cause ourselves to do what the theory tells us is wrong. This is intended to back up the conclusion that Clare is someone who is told by C to do acts which are wrong in C's terms, without this being an objection to C. But the case of my moral corruption cannot be used in this way, for the simple reason that it offers no *one* action which (1) is wrong and (2) I am right to do. But this was the apparent paradox which it was supposed to help dissolve. The claim for Clare was that she was involved in blameless wrongdoing, and nothing in my moral corruption can help us to see how this is possible.

Let us then return directly to Clare. If my moral corruption offers no help, our only other resource in dissolving the appearance of contradiction is the act/agent distinction. Clare is to be described as being right (in C's terms) to do an act which is wrong (in C's terms). Should we accept this description? Note that Clare is not facing the choice we face every day between spending money on our family and sending it to Oxfam; she is in an unusual situation where there is a particular stranger whom she could help by giving him the money she was going to spend on taking her child to the Heritage Theme Park. Let us take it, as Parfit does, that Clare's motives are a C-approved set, and hence by the definition of agent-rightness that she is acting rightly in preferring to give her child this small benefit rather than give the stranger the much greater benefit. Should we also agree that Clare's *act* is wrong? An act is wrong if there is an available alternative which would produce a better outcome. Is there such an act available? This depends on our approach. We might say that Clare could give the money to the stranger, and if she did outcomes would be better. So that action constitutes a better available alternative. But there is a different approach. Clare defended herself at one point by saying:

> I could have acted differently. But this only means that I *would* have done so if my motives had been different. Given my actual motives, it is causally impossible that I act differently. And, if my motives had been different, this would have made the outcome, on the whole, worse. Since my actual motives are one of the best possible sets, in Consequentialist terms, the bad effects *are*, in the relevant sense, part of one of the best possible sets of effects.[11]

In saying this, she is allowing consideration of motive to affect her evaluation of acts. Her point is that an act is not a better available alternative if she would need to have some less C-approved set of motives to do it. For if she needs another set of motives to do it, and if her having that set would be worse in C's terms, her doing that action would in fact be worse in C's terms. If she did it, outcomes would be worse than if she didn't. To put the matter in possible world talk for an intuitive check on her argument:

> In the nearest group of worlds in which she does the alternative act, her motives are not her actual set Ma, but a different set M1.

> The nearest group of worlds in which her set of motives is M1 are worse in C's terms, contain worse outcomes, than the nearest group of worlds in which her set of motives is Ma.

> So the nearest group of worlds in which she does the alternative act is a group in which outcomes are worse in C's terms.

> So (unpacking the possible worlds metaphor) if she were to do the alternative act, outcomes would be worse in C's terms.

> So this alternative act, at least, is not one which would lead to an improvement in outcomes.

> So her act of benefiting her child in preference to the stranger is not shown to be wrong in C's terms by the existence of this 'available alternative'.

What this shows is that Clare's defence of herself can be turned into a defence of her act, so that instead of having an agent rightly doing a wrong act we have a right act which the agent is right to do.

6 Two criteria

So there are two approaches to Clare. The choice between them is a choice between a broader and a narrower interpretation of the consequentialist criterion for acts. C's central claim was that there is one ultimate moral aim: that outcomes be as good as possible. Parfit extracts from this the following criterion for act-rightness:

> 1 an act is right if its outcomes are better than those of any available alternative.

But there is a different criterion available:

> 2 an act is right if outcomes would be better if it was done than if any alternative were done.

With this broader criterion we do not restrict our attention to the effects of *this* action. Instead we look to see in general what the world would be like if this action were done; in possible world terms, we look to the outcome-differences between this world and the nearest world in which the action is done. Though not purely causal, (2) is still an outcome-based criterion, and it is one which enables us to include in our assessment thoughts about motives. In particular, we can now find relevant the question what other effects might flow from the motives which we would most probably have if we were to do that action.

The point now is that if we were to decide that criterion (2) is preferable to criterion (1), we would have established that there couldn't be the sort of example of blameless wrongdoing that Parfit needs to show C to be undamagingly self-defeating. For the adoption of criterion (2) will have the effect that our assessment of act and of agent must coincide. For (2) allows us to include in our assessment of the act consideration of the other implications of the motives from which the act is or would be done. If the motive is one which is C-approved, it will be one whose operation leads to the best results overall. In which case the world in which the action is done must be one which is better in C's terms – in terms of outcomes.

So, is criterion (2) preferable to criterion (1)? Parfit's use of the latter is perfectly standard, but that is no justification. We must, of course, consider this question in consequentialist terms. And in terms of outcomes, it seems undeniable that if all our acts satisfied criterion (2), things would go better in outcome terms than if we all restricted ourselves to criterion (1). So there is a direct consequentialist reason for preferring criterion (2).

I can think of two replies to this point. First we might say that whether there is a need for criterion (2) or not, we need criterion (1) as well. For I want a theory which will tell me what to do *now*, when I am, as it were, standing before the situation with all patterns of motivation fixed (for the moment). Of course, there are all sorts of interesting things to say about which patterns of motivation it would be best for me to have, either in general or in the sort of circumstances that I currently find myself in. But such remarks are of no help in my present decision, which is simply what to do here.

This reply is both natural and peculiar. The picture within which the reply makes sense is one which sees my pattern of motivation as both rigidly fixed (for present purposes, as it were) and insufficient to determine what I will do, in a way which could be remedied by the promptings of a moral theory. But there is a different picture which gives a different result. We might see a pattern of motivation as neither rigidly fixed (even for present purposes) nor as *either* able rigidly to determine what we shall do *or* failing to achieve this in a way which therefore shows the need for help from outside. Patterns of motivation do not need to suffer from either of these sorts of rigidity. A pattern may be complete but influenceable. If we conceive of a pattern as a flexible object, so that there are many actions compatible with my present pattern, and so that different strands in the pattern can be reinforced in various ways at different times, we get a picture under which my question will not be what shall I do now (with all motivation both fixed and insufficient) but what I should be motivated to do here. Here the stress of the question is retained, but its focus has changed, in a way compatible with a tighter relation between motives and acts.

The second reply will be familiar. It is that no moral theory can recommend us to act from a certain motive, since it is not up to us what motive we act from. We cannot adopt nor discard motives at will. But we can act at will. So ethical theory must focus on a notion of an action which is divorced from all considerations of motive.

There is something right about this move, but much more wrong. First, we may not be able to adopt or discard motives at will. But there are many things we can do that we cannot do at will (make money, for instance), and altering our motives may be one of them. What is more, most morally interesting actions cannot be done at will; they require cooperation from people or circumstances beyond our control. So the contrast between acting and adopting a motive is overstated. Second, it is true that we cannot first decide on an action, and then decide on the motive from which we shall do it. (This is the main element of truth in the second reply.) But there was never any suggestion that we should do that. Rather the suggestion is that each available action comes with or from an available pattern of motivation, and in choosing an act we effectively choose to be motivated in that kind of way. Here action and motivation come together; choice of action is choice of motivation. So there is a sense in which we can choose our motivation, but we cannot do this at will and we cannot do it independent of our choice of action.

There seem to me therefore to be consequentialist reasons for preferring criterion (2) in our moral assessment of acts. And with this we lose Parfit's understanding of Clare as a comprehensible case of blameless wrongdoing. The case of Clare was supposed to show us how to marry the act/agent distinction with the motive/outcome distinction in a way that made sense of the idea that we should have an aim which we should not aim to achieve. But it fails to do this; indeed nothing in Parfit's discussion gives us what we need to dissolve the threatened contradiction. So there remains a good sense in which C specifies an aim which it is both right and wrong for us to have, and is therefore damagingly self-defeating.

Can we still show that C is damagingly self-defeating? Here is a possible line of defence for Parfit: with criterion (1) C is self-defeating, but not damagingly so, while with criterion (2) C is not self-defeating at all. On neither account do we have a theory which is damagingly self-defeating.

First, we should recognize that Parfit's 'proof' that C is self-defeating was never very strong.[12] He says that if we were pure do-gooders we would have strong desires (to favour our family and friends) which we would not satisfy, and so our lives would all go worse in C's terms.[13] But this is surely a mistake. If we were pure do-gooders, we would no longer have those strong desires; for to be a pure do-gooder is to have a certain pattern of motivation, which is inconsistent with the continued existence of the strong desires to favour one's family. So *this* won't show that C is self-defeating in any way. Perhaps C isn't self-defeating at all (after all this!).

The question is whether it would be possible for people who all had C-approved sets of motives so to act that outcomes are worse in C's terms. The clue here (if there is one) has to be the collective nature of C, and that collective practice may defeat the C-approved practice of the individual. (Remember that C is collectively but not individually self-defeating.) We are not now asking whether one person (Clare, perhaps) might have a C-approved set of motives and therefore create outcomes that are worse in C's terms. Rather we are asking whether we might not each, in our attempts to create the best outcomes we can individually (so that C is not individually self-defeating), somehow so combine that our mutual efforts are unavailing: each does the best he can, but together we do less well than we might.

Parfit allows that C is not directly self-defeating. It is not that we might succeed individually but fail collectively in a way that is familiar from discussion of Prisoner's Dilemmas, but that our attempts at individual success might generate collective failure.

C is indirectly self-defeating if, were we to be pure do-gooders, we would do worse collectively in C's terms than if we had some other disposition. Now the difference between criterion (1) and criterion (2) creates two notions of a pure do-gooder. The first is the familiar one of someone motivated to do those actions which cause the best outcomes (of those available in the circumstances). With this notion of a pure do-gooder, C is almost certainly self-defeating. It is hard to give an absolutely conclusive example, but one which appeals to me is the thought that if we were all pure do-gooders in this sense there would probably be no art and culture, because in each case there would be something more pressing that could be done with the relevant resources. However, criterion (2) creates a different notion of a pure do-gooder, that of someone who is motivated to do those actions of which we can say that things go best if they are done. This notion has a much less narrow focus; instead of starting from here and looking only at the effects of one change rather than another, in a way which makes it possible that though every choice we make is fine the overall result is ghastly (all in C's terms), we are able to backtrack in order to cope with that sort of possibility. In the example given above, the pattern of motivation recommended will be somehow skewed so as to cope with the danger of our ending up artless and culture-free. So in this case, with the second notion of a pure do-gooder, C would not be self-defeating. Will there be other examples where this move will not be available? I cannot see how there can be. So my slightly tentative conclusion is that with criterion (2) C is not indirectly self-defeating.

Where does this leave us? The conclusion that C is not indirectly self-defeating is some sort of a defence of consequentialism, one might think – especially if I am right in thinking that to be indirectly self-defeating is more damaging than Parfit wants to allow. But in the present context it is far from a complete defence. The position was that consequentialism hoped to make room for agent-relative values by means of a distinction between theory of value and theory of motivation. And what we have discovered is that this distinction cannot be drawn in the radical form that is necessary for the purpose. To draw that distinction one needs to give different assessments of acts and of agents. But the strongest form of consequentialism is one which gives the same assessment of acts as it does of agents, by relating what it says of acts to what it says of motives. So we cannot run the sort of outcome/motive distinction that is necessary if consequentialism is to make room for the existence of agent-relative values. Consequentialism thus turns out to be unable to recommend the sort of partial motivation that would lead us to favour our own children. This means that the existence of agent-relative values constitutes a refutation of consequentialism.

7   THE ACT/AGENT DISTINCTION

What now has happened to the distinction between act and agent? One might think that there is no point in arguing against Parfit's attempts to dissolve the apparent contradiction by appeal to the distinction between act and agent. After all, we are going to need such a distinction anyway, and however it comes it is going to generate the sort of difference between rightness of act and rightness of agent which will give consequentialists all they need to keep going. But this would be a mistake. The act/agent distinction is in fact four distinctions, only one of which will serve consequentialist purposes; and that one is the one that can be called in question.

When I say that it is four distinctions what I mean is that there are four reasons for making an act/agent distinction but they are not reasons for making it in the same way. Each reason creates its own distinction. The first reason is the need to say something about cases of error and/or ignorance. Where the error or ignorance is not culpable though the action goes wrong in some way, we feel that there is something here to approve and something to disapprove. One way to work this is to carve things up so that the approval goes to the agent and the disapproval to the action.[14] My own view about this is that Parfit is right to cope with this sort of problem by means of the objective/subjective distinction. What we need is not so much one sort of evaluation and two different objects, but two ways of evaluating the same object. There is indeed something to approve of in an agent's acting mistakenly but for the best, but we should not take this (no doubt muted) approval away from the agent and give it all to the action. In particular, we should not be led to suppose that even where there is no error or ignorance, there is still a distinction to be drawn between the evaluation of act and that of agent. This would be an instance of the argument from illusion, which in general I reject as merely another form of 'switching' argument.

The second reason is the need to distinguish long-term evaluations from short-term ones. We may feel that an agent is in general to be approved of because she is a person of goodwill and sensitivity, though here she allowed her prejudices to run away with her. There is no problem with this. Of course, we do need to make such a distinction to cope with the vagaries of moral experience. And we could announce that the long-term evaluations are of agents, while the short-term ones are of acts, and hope to focus the long-term on motives and the short-term on outcomes. We would then end up with Parfit's marriage of the act/agent distinction with the outcome/motive one. Sadly, however, this will not wash, for two reasons. First, short-term evaluation may still be sensitive to motives – not of course to one's normal pattern of motivation but to that operative in this unusual case. Second, we want to leave room for moral evaluation of what I called above the agent-in-acting. But seeing the short-term/long-term distinction as identical with the act/agent distinction closes this option off.

The third reason is a sense that the action is effectively to be assessed as a change in the world, while the agent is to be thought of as a sort of intention in practice. Compared with the second reason, this pulls the agent back towards the particular case, but pushes the action out into the realm of mere events. This cannot give us a distinction between act and agent that is operable within the moral realm. Events as such are not susceptible of moral assessment at all; we have only managed to separate act from agent here at the cost of removing the act from the moral realm altogether. (Actually things are worse than this: by carving things up into an agent and an event, we lose any room for the notion of an action altogether. But that is another story.[15])

The fourth reason for drawing an act/agent distinction is the one Parfit has been concerned with, namely the need to show that a theory which separates what it says about motives from what it says about aims is not contradictory. This is a much more specific need, designed to save a specific theory from a specific form of refutation, and I have been arguing that the attempt to run the act/agent and the outcome/motive distinction together does not work. My suggestion has been that we should focus our *moral* evaluation on what I call the agent-in-acting, in a way that prevents either distinction from getting a grip. The qualities of the doer in the case must coincide with the qualities of the thing done, in a way that leaves no room for talk of blameless wrongdoing or blameworthy rightdoing. The relevant qualities of the action, conceived as an object of *moral* assessment, are the same as those of the agent in doing it (where there is no error or ignorance, of course).

It is important to notice the similarities between this result and that of Kant. The first chapter of Kant's *Groundwork* might be thought to contain reasons for saying that moral assessment is focused on the agent rather than on the act. Consequentialism focuses on the act and its effects, deontology on the agent and her intentions or motives. But this would be a mistake, in my view, on both sides. First, as I have argued in the present chapter, consequentialism can adopt a non-causal criterion for acts which effectively allows consideration of motive to re-enter evaluation of act. Second, Kant should not be seen as accepting the relevance of the act/agent distinction for ethics and arguing that we should focus on the agent side of it. Rather he is rejecting the distinction altogether, in so far as it is supposed to be of moral relevance.[16]

8 CONCLUSION

With this the story is now complete. This book has been about moral reasons. I have argued that they are cognitive and holistic, that the action which one ought to do is the one that meets the demands of the situation, and these are to be identified with the shape in which the relevant features present themselves there. I have suggested that generalist conceptions of moral rationality are incoherent, and offered an account which stresses very much the role of judgement in the particular case. I have offered a relevant conception of objectivity which renders neutral moral reasons objective, and argued that agent-relative reasons are no less objective than the neutral ones. Finally, I have suggested that consequentialism cannot accept the existence of the agent-relative.

To what extent is this story presented as a package deal? I definitely wanted to suggest that a particularist form of cognitivism is the one best fitted to survive a common objection, and the notion of the moral shape of a situation gives us a moral metaphysics that is especially well suited to particularist conceptions of moral reasoning and to the associated attempt to dismantle the distinction between argument and description. The support for my favoured conception of objectivity is independent, however; to that extent there is a new start at chapter 9. And from there on the main structural considerations are in place, and the question is whether the picture offered is one which makes room for the agent-relative.

So the story is intended to have the virtues of coherence, but one could hardly hope to deduce any one part from any other part. Which elements in it are the least secure? I had trouble in establishing that particularism can accept the existence of constraints. If I had to choose, I would abandon the constraints. Beyond that, especially insecure elements seem to be:

1 The account given of the claim that all and only moral imperatives are categorical.
2 The commitment to the existence of tragic dilemmas, and the idea that a situation can have two shapes at once.
3 The underlying metaphysical picture of the relation between value and reasons.

Of these, the first and the third are related. I suggested in 2.2 that moral reasons are requirements (or at least that they demand or call for a certain response from us). This claim came obviously unstuck with the recognition of non-insistent reasons (7.2). These are in some sense moral reasons, but not ones which generate even a weak sort of demand; for one can discount them, though not ignore them. These reasons, then, are reasons recognized by morality. Is this enough for a consideration to count as a moral reason? The suggestion has been, throughout this book, that moral reasons are ordinary considerations such as the pain I will cause her if I don't tell her soon. This is a moral reason because it is a salient feature of a situation which generates a demand – the demand that I tell her soon, perhaps. (It is not *itself* moral in any sense.) Not all moral reasons are quite like this, however. Non-insistent reasons are not, for a start, for when they are counted it may be that no demand is generated. They stand as moral reasons because they are relevant to the question whether any demand is generated. In this sense they are reasons recognized by morality. Non-insistent reasons are grounded in the cost to the agent. Again, this cost is a morally relevant consideration, but it is not itself moral in any sense. Viewed in this light, the notion of a moral reason is not very exclusive.

Similar remarks can be made about values. Values are not in themselves moral or non-moral. A value is a moral value here if it is morally relevant.

Reasons stem from values. The cost to the agent is a disvalue, as is the pain I will cause her if I do not tell her soon. These considerations function as reasons (except when silenced) because of the values which they are. Not everything that functions as a reason is in this sort of way a value. For instance, a reason for doing it today (and a moral reason, in the sense above) might be that I have some time to spare today, or this is my last opportunity, or that I promised to do it today. There are values in the offing here, of course, in the light of which these reasons are moral reasons, but these reasons are not themselves values.

NOTES

1 This problem seems to bedevil David Gauthier's attempt to take us from self-interested to moral motivation. See Gauthier (1986).
2 This material is presented in chapter 1 of Parfit (1984). (Unattributed references to Parfit's work in the present chapter will be to this book.) In this chapter he offers an extended comparison between a theory of rationality (the self-interest theory) and a moral theory (consequentialism). In Dancy (1993b) I argue first against his defence of the self-interest theory, as well as trying to show, as I do here, that his defence of consequentialism will not work in its own terms.
3 Parfit (1984), p. 24.
4 This definition is on *ibid.*, p. 5. There is a more damaging sort of self-defeatingness: a theory is 'directly self-defeating' when it is certain that, if someone successfully follows it, he will thereby cause the aims it gives him to be worse achieved than they would have been if he had not successfully followed it (p. 55).

5   Ibid., p. 24.
6   Ibid., p. 24.
7   Notice that this notion offers an evaluation of the agent in doing a particular act; it purports to be atomistic.
8   Parfit (1984), p. 5.
9   Ibid., p. 27.
10 Ibid., pp. 27–8.
11 Ibid., pp. 32–3.
12 He doesn't suggest that it is strong, to be fair. He is more interested in the consequences of C's being self-defeating than in whether it is self-defeating or not. (The second example he uses to show that C is self-defeating turns on the objective/subjective distinction, which is officially not the point he is meaning to address.)
13 Parfit, pp. 27–8.
14 For more on this theme, see Dancy (1992b).
15 See Joseph (1931) for the main elements of this story.
16 The Kantian distinction between acting out of duty and acting in accordance with duty does not need to be interpreted in such a way as to reintroduce the act/agent distinction.

Appendix I Internal and external reasons

For Williams, an internal reason expressed by the statement 'There is a reason for A to F' is one which is comprehensibly related to A's subjective motivational set. A reason is comprehensibly related to A's subjective motivational set if it is possible to take A from that set to a new set which contains that reason by a rational process – standardly a process of reasoning or argument (this includes the correction of false belief). Williams then raises the question whether there are any other reasons than these.[1]

This question is distinct from the question whether we should be internalists or externalists in the theory of motivation. A Nagelian internalist is not committed either to accepting or to denying the existence of external reasons in Williams' sense; an internalist may allow that there are external reasons (in Williams' sense), so long as when those reasons come to motivate they require no additional psychological sanction to motivate our compliance. Equally, a Nagelian externalist can happily hold that there are no external reasons. An externalist only holds that where a moral truth or judgement is a reason, it still requires some additional psychological sanction to motivate our compliance. And in general it should be no surprise that the two distinctions, that between internalism and externalism and that between internal and external reasons, fail to coincide. We should not forget that the first distinction applies not to the theory of reasons as a whole, but only in certain areas. I have been taking it as restricted to moral reasons, though there could of course be parallel distinctions elsewhere – in the theory of prudence, say. The second distinction applies across the board, and is really in a different ball-park. However, this does not mean that there are *no* interconnections between the two at all. I suggest below that those who accept the existence of external reasons had better be Nagelian internalists.

Here is the crucial part of Williams' reasoning. All reason statements are potentially explanatory of action. If there are reasons, agents could act on them, and these reasons could then contribute to the explanation of their acting. When we say 'There is a reason for him to do A', we normally mean that *he has* that reason, in the sense that either he already recognizes it or he would recognize it if he lost some false belief (or something like that). But sometimes we mean (or think we mean) that *there is* a reason which means nothing to him. Williams' example is of Owen Musgrave, whose father takes it that the family military tradition is a reason for him to join the army but who himself despises all things military. Williams writes:

> Even if it were true (whatever that might turn out to mean) that there was a reason for Owen to join the army, that fact by itself would never explain anything that Owen did, even his joining the army. For if it was true at all, it was true when Owen was not motivated to join the army ... So something else is needed besides the truth of the external reason statement to explain action, some psychological link; and that psychological link would seem to be belief.[2]

The idea here is that when Owen comes to believe an external reason statement about himself (that there is a reason for him to join the army), this would help to explain his action. And Williams goes on: 'this agent, with this belief, appears to be one about whom, now, an *internal* reason statement could truly be made.' But what is the point here? We knew all along that external reasons become internal when recognized by the agent as reasons. Williams suggests that:

> it does not follow from this that there is nothing in external reasons. What does follow is that their content is not going to be revealed by considering merely the state of someone who believes such a statement, for that state is merely the state with regard to which an internal reason statement could truly be made. Rather, the content of the external type of statement will have to be revealed by considering what it is to *come to believe* such a statement.[3]

And when we consider this, what do we find?

> Owen might be so persuaded by his father's moving rhetoric that he acquired both the motivation and the belief. But this excludes an element which the external reasons theorist essentially wants, that the agent should acquire the motivation *because* he comes to believe the reason statement, and that he should do the latter, moreover, because, in some way, he is considering the matter aright. If the agent is to hold on to these conditions,

he will, I think, have to make the condition under which the agent appropriately comes to have the motivation something like this, that he should deliberate correctly; and the external reasons statement itself will have to be taken as roughly equivalent to, or at least entailing, the claim that if the agent rationally deliberated, then, whatever motivations he originally had, he would come to be motivated to φ.[4]

This is the argument Williams actually gives. As such, it is defective in various ways.

Let us allow for argument's sake that if the fact that p is a reason for S, this entails that if S were to believe that p, this would motivate him. This could be in either of two types of situation. The first is where the new belief would fit in with existing motivational structures in some way, so that its ability to motivate depends on keeping the main block of previous motivation intact; reasons of this sort would be internal reasons. The second is where the new belief is able to motivate in its own right, and so does not depend for its efficacy on being brought into some suitable relation with the agent's original motivational set; in this case the reason would still be an external one.[5]

When we say that a moral fact is a reason for one, whether one recognizes it or not, we allow that if one were to recognize it, one would be motivated by it. We do not require for this, however, that one could be brought by rational means from a non-moral motivational set to a moral one. (This requirement is the one that collapses external reasons into internal ones.) Why does Williams think that this is required? His reason for this is that the external reasons theorist believes that those reasons are there to be seen, and hence, if one is 'considering the matter aright', one will see them. But this notion of considering the matter aright is ambiguous. It might either mean that if one makes only rationally permitted or endorsed moves, one will emerge with the relevant belief, or that if one comes somehow to see things as they are, one will see this. It is the latter that the external reasons theorist wants to insist on, and the former is no part of the programme. Moral facts are such that if we see them for what they are, we will be motivated by them.

Note again that there is no suggestion that in what we have said so far we have committed ourselves either to an externalist or to an internalist picture of moral motivation. However, it now appears that if we want to be external reasons theorists, we do better to be internalists. For suppose (with the externalists) that moral facts are essentially inert, but we have a standing desire to do whatever may be right. If I discover that this action is right, I am motivated to do it. But this is just the sort of situation described by the internal reasons theorist in his discussion of replacing true beliefs for false ones. This moral fact is a reason for me now, because I have a standing disposition to pursue the right. So externalists should deny the existence of external reasons.

This gives Williams a further argument against the external reasons theorist. There can only be external reasons if externalism is false and internalism true. But internalism is false.

Williams would argue, I think, that a mere fact cannot motivate, and hence there is no real sense in talking of facts as reasons unless we take this to be a roundabout sort of way of talking about how we would act if we believed these facts. (This is a broadly Humean position.) Only beliefs (and desires) can motivate, and so since reasons are essentially capable of motivating no mere fact can be a reason.

Why should we believe this? I can see several possible reasons in the offing, suggested by things that Williams says. The first is a version of the argument from illusion. The idea here, as Willams puts it, is that 'the false/true distinction cannot affect the form of the appropriate explanation.' Suppose that a fact is offered in explanation of an action. We know that the agent would have acted whether that *fact* obtained or not, so long as she retained the relevant *belief*. So what explains her action is not so much the fact believed as the belief. Belief-based explanation will be always of the same form, whether the belief is true or not. I do not accept this argument; it is a switching argument, as are all versions of the argument from illusion, and as such suspect.

The second is that no mere fact can motivate; a fact motivates when believed, and then it is the belief that is motivating, not the fact. (One might hold this not for the reason that the false/true distinction cannot affect the form of the appropriate action-explanation, but because facts cannot cause and action-explanation is causal.) But this is far from cast-iron. One obvious point is that a belief is often explained by appeal to the fact believed. (Consider the causal theory of perception.) If so, where fact causes belief and belief causes action, why not suppose that the underlying explanation of the action is the fact? Second, we could argue that though the fact is never a reason unless believed, the belief is a necessary or enabling condition for motivation, not part of what motivates and not exactly a cause.

A third may be closer to Williams' text. He seems to suggest that if the fact is there already, as it were, without generating the action, then when the action does eventually take place the fact cannot be the sole (or main?) explanation of it. This reminds one of Hume's views:

> Tis an established maxim both in natural and moral philosophy, that an object, which exists for any time in its full perfection without producing

another, is not its sole cause; but is assisted by some other principle, which pushes it from its state of inactivity, and makes it exert that energy, of which it was secretly possest.[6]

However, that the fact is not the sole cause is no point against the external reasons theorist, even if we allow that an enabling condition such as a belief is a causal contributor as well.

NOTES

1 See Williams (1980). Page references are to the version reprinted in Williams (1981).
2 Ibid., pp. 106–7.
3 Ibid., pp. 107–8.
4 Ibid., pp. 108–9.
5 I have been helped here by McDowell (forthcoming).
6 Hume (1739–40), 1.3.2; ed. Nidditch, p. 76.

Appendix II
Hare's later views

In this appendix I relate what I said in chapter 5 about Hare's earlier work to the position outlined in his later *Moral Thinking* (1981). In this book Hare uses the term 'universalizability' to mean what most people mean by 'supervenience'. In fact, he abandons entirely the use of what I have been calling universalizability in his account of moral rationality. I make no apologies for the examination of that earlier use in chapter 5, for the question whether any such system can be got to work is not answered by noticing that Hare has abandoned it. It is right, however, to ask whether his later views are subject to criticism on similar grounds.

According to Hare, there are two levels of moral thinking, the intuitive and the critical. The intuitive level is that at which we operate with a set of comparatively unspecific universally quantified prima facie principles. These principles are the ones which all of us use some of the time, and most of us use all of the time. But there must be another level of moral thinking, for two reasons. First, without further resource we would be completely unable to resolve the common occurrence of a conflict between our principles. Second, without further resource we would have to take our intuitive principles as simply given by intuition, in a way about which Hare is quite rude. He argues that appeals to substantial moral intuition should be altogether excluded from any self-respecting moral theory, and that the only permissible intuitions are linguistic ones. So there must be another level, the critical one. At this level we construct moral principles out of the judgements we are willing to make about individual cases, by asking what we would say about an *exactly similar* case in which we play a different role – we are the slave rather than the master, for example. Since we are only concerned with exact similarity, our critical moral thought uses the supervenience of moral judgement as its main tool. There is no place at either level for thoughts about universalizability.

In criticism of this story I offer two comments. First, Hare calls his intuitive principles prima facie principles, and in this way adopts for his own purposes the theory which I discussed in chapter 6. If my complaints about that theory are sound, then, this would cause problems for Hare unless any defects at the intuitive level can be compensated by the existence of the critical level. And since my criticisms concern the *coherence* of the notion of the prima facie, I take it that this would subvert Hare's use of the notion as much as anyone else's.

Second, it is just not clear how much of Ross's theory Hare wants to buy into. He refers to Ross as if it were obvious what is implied.[1] But when properly worked out, Ross's theory seems to offer at least the chance that the intuitive level needs no supplement. One of Hare's criticisms of a system which tried to make do merely with the intuitive level, namely that conflict of principles cannot be resolved at that level, could be directly answered by Ross. Hare, I think, conceives of his 'prima facie' principles as 'first blush' principles; for him, each is universally quantified in a very simple way. Thus the principle 'Do not lie' is of the form 'All lying is wrong', the principle 'Save life' is of the form 'All saving life is right'; and so when we have to lie to save a life we are told by our intuitive principles that our action is both somehow overall right and overall wrong, in a way that is impossible to sort out without radically different resources. This is, as we have seen, not at all the way in which Ross conceives the matter. For him, conflict of principles is quite a different sort of affair, in which the moral worth of life-saving is mitigated by the moral evil of lying; conflict is just a matter of the coexistence of negative and positive moral contributions of this sort. Judgement resolves these conflicts by determining where the balance lies; essentially this is a matter of adding and subtracting. No *principle* determines one's overall judgement, which comes into play when all the principles have made whatever contribution they are capable of. But the principles themselves do not contradict each other, even in the particular case, so that what they do say about the case is much more easily reconciled.

Hare's second criticism, that the intuitive principles are *merely* intuitive and stand in need of external support, is a different matter. Whether his own theory eventually does better in this respect is too large and particular a question for me to enter into here, even if I wished to. We should notice, however, that Ross would claim that his prima facie principles are not supported by intuition but by *experience*. This is then another respect in which Hare wants to borrow from Ross very selectively. In fact, to be plain, I don't think it right for Hare to describe his intuitive principles as prima facie principles at all.

The final question, at least from the point of view of a particularist, is whether critical thinking will ever come up with substantial universal moral principles. Let us for the sake of argument admit the use of supervenience to give us a judgement about the particular case before us in which we have abstracted the identity of the participants, so that we would say the same thing even if it were ourselves on the receiving end. This judgement, of course, tells us nothing about any other type of case whatsoever. There is no possibility that we can rely on supervenience to take us from this case to one which differs in even the slightest particular. And we cannot hope to restrict the supervenience base to those properties which we take to be morally relevant. Hare explicitly rules this move out on the grounds that only previously accepted principles could establish which properties are morally relevant.[2] So there is no chance that we could use what we already have to help us decide what to do in a new case, if we remain entirely at the critical level. We have to return to the intuitive. How might results gained at the critical level serve to ground intuitive principles? One possibility would be that we see the full range of intuitive principles as some sort of theory intended to make the best sense of our critical principles (a sort of inference to the best explanation), but Hare does not take this line. He holds instead that at the critical level we ask ourselves which intuitive principles should be inculcated – which it would be best, by and large, for people to use. But, quite apart from the question whether we can consider matters in sufficient generality at the critical level to pronounce on such a topic, this manoeuvre simply returns us to the problem whether Hare has a working account of the intuitive principles which he calls 'prima facie', on which I have already expressed a rather negative opinion.

NOTES

1 Hare (1981), p. 38.
2 Ibid., pp. 62ff.

Appendix III Nagel on incommensurability

Nagel starts by suggesting that there are five different sorts of moral reasons, deriving from obligations, rights, utility, perfectionist ends and private commitments.[1] He then asks what we are to do when a conflict occurs between reasons of different types. His general view is that if the conflict were between reasons of the same type, those reasons can be ordered in degree of strength and so either one or the other side will win, or there will be a tie. (We will see reasons to worry about all of this later.) However there is no possibility of ranking reasons of different types. Such reasons are incommensurable. Nagel goes on:

> When faced with conflicting and incommensurable claims we still have to do something – even if it is only to do nothing. And the fact that action must be unitary seems to imply that unless justification is also unitary, nothing can be either right or wrong and all decisions under conflict are arbitrary.[2]

So Nagel has presented himself with a problem. His solution is this:

> I contend that there can be good judgement without total justification, either implicit or explicit. The fact that one cannot say why a certain decision is the correct one, given a particular balance of conflicting reasons, does not mean that the claim to correctness is meaningless. Provided one has taken the process of practical justification as far as it will go in the course of arriving at the conflict, one may be able to proceed without further justification, but without irrationality either. What makes this possible is *judgement* – essentially the faculty Aristotle described as practical wisdom, which reveals itself over time in individual decisions rather than in the enunciation of general principles. It will not always yield a solution: there are true practical dilemmas that have no solution,

and there are practical conflicts so complex that judgement cannot operate confidently. But in many cases it can be relied upon to take up the
slack that remains beyond the limits of explicit rational argument.

The general idea here is that no reason of one type is equal to, stronger
than or weaker than any reason of another type. (This is an extreme
form of incommensurability.) What is more, there are no overarching
reasons to which we can appeal in case of conflict. So conflict between
types of reasons cannot be rationally resolved. All resolution is achieved
by *judgement*, which operates at the level of choice but not at the level
of reasons.

It seems to me that the problem here is one that Nagel has created
for himself, and it arises because of the extreme form of generalism he
adopts, which I discussed in chapter 6. Nothing else can explain the
ease with which Nagel moves from the idea that there can be no ordering
of types of reason to the much more damaging claim that there can be
no ordering of reasons of those types. We might well admit that reasons
deriving from rights are not in themselves either stronger than or weaker
than reasons deriving from utility. But this leaves us well short of holding
that no reason deriving from rights can be stronger or weaker than a
reason deriving from utility, which seems to be Nagel's position. This
extreme form of incommensurability claim is not forced upon us.

Nagel's position is both too strong and too weak. It is too strong
because, with five incommensurables, *any* conflict between them calls
for the sort of judgement which comes into play when principles are
exhausted. This makes interesting incommensurability far more prevalent
than it really is. It is too weak because it does not address the question
how there can be practical dilemmas without solution *within* one of his
five types; for Nagel, these only arise *between* types. But this renders
them too unusual. Consider the nice example of the choice of a violin
teacher for one's child. One teacher is known for his musicality, another
for her ability to work with children, another for her knowledge and
understanding of bow technique, another for the success of his pupils
in local competitions. This looks like the sort of case where practical
judgement is called for, since we have surely already outrun the scope
of any musical principles, and yet Nagel can only suppose that there is
interesting incommensurability here if he can see the conflict as lying
between reasons of different types, in his sense.

Nagel's demand is for 'total justification'. He supposes that without
this there is a problem about how a choice of action can be rational.
But he conceives of total justification as the sort of justification achieved
by an appeal to a set of suitably ordered general principles. He hopes

that 'our capacity to resolve conflicts in particular cases may extend beyond our capacity to enunciate general principles that explain those resolutions'. Where this latter capacity runs out there can be no justification, but there can be rationality because there is still 'good judgement' to take up the slack. Nagel appeals to Aristotle here, but his appeal seems to me to be a misconception. Aristotle's conception of judgement is one of a faculty based on reasons, not one which comes into operation when the reasons have been exhausted. Nagel has left no space for judgement of Aristotle's sort to operate in, and the idea that such a faculty can 'take up the slack' once reasons are all used up seems to me to be an empty answer to a fictitious question.

I conclude that the problem which Nagel gets himself into here derives from the combination of two questionable assumptions: first, his extreme generalism and, second, the related view that justification can only proceed by subsumption under general principles.

NOTES

1 This is in his 'The Fragmentation of Value', pp. 128–41 of Nagel (1979) and reprinted in Gowans (1987).
2 Ibid., p. 134.

Bibliography

Anscombe, G. E. M. (1957) *Intention* (Oxford: Blackwell).

Baier, K. (1958) *The Moral Point of View* (Ithaca: Cornell University Press).

Berkeley, G. (1710) *A Treatise Concerning the Principles of Human Knowledge*; reprinted in *Berkeley: Philosophical Works* ed. M. R. Ayers (London: Everyman, 1985).

Blackburn, S. (1981) 'Rule-following and Moral Realism', in Holtzman and Leich (1981), pp. 163–87.

Blackburn, S. (1984) *Spreading the Word* (Oxford: Oxford University Press).

Blackburn, S. (1985) 'Errors and the Phenomenology of Value', in Honderich (1985), pp. 1–22.

Bond, E. J. (1983) *Reason and Value* (Cambridge: Cambridge University Press).

Brink, D. O. (1986) 'Externalist Moral Realism', *Southern Journal of Philosophy* 24 (suppl.), pp. 23–41.

Brink, D. O. (1989) *Moral Realism and the Foundations of Ethics* (Cambridge: Cambridge University Press).

Broome, J. (1991) *Weighing Goods* (Oxford: Blackwell).

Brown, C. (forthcoming) 'Moral Truths and Moral Principles', *American Philosophical Quarterly*.

Cornford, F. M. (1908) *MicroCosmographia Academica: Being a Guide for the Young Academic Politician* (Cambridge: Bowes and Bowes).

Dancy, J. (1981) 'On Moral Properties', *Mind* 90, pp. 367–85.

Dancy, J. (1983) 'Ethical Particularism and Morally Relevant Properties', *Mind* 92, pp. 530–47.

Dancy, J. (1985) 'The Role of Imaginary Cases in Ethics', *Pacific Philosophical Quarterly* 66, pp. 141–53.

Dancy, J. (1986) 'Two Conceptions of Moral Realism', *Proceedings of the Aristotelian Society* 60 (suppl.), pp. 167–87.

Dancy, J. (1988a) 'Contemplating One's Nagel' *Philosophical Books* 29, pp. 1–16.

Dancy, J. (1988b) 'Supererogation and Moral Realism', in Dancy, Moravcsik and Taylor (1988), pp. 170–88.

Dancy, J. (1991a) 'Intuitionism', in Singer (1991), pp. 411–20.

Dancy, J. (1991b) 'An Ethic of Prima Facie Duties', in Singer (1991), pp. 219–29.

Dancy, J. (1992a) 'Agent-relativity: the Very Idea', in R. Frey and C. Morris (eds) *Value, Welfare and Morality* (Cambridge: Cambridge University Press), pp. 00–00.

Dancy, J. (1992b) 'Externalism for Internalists' in E. Villanueva (ed.) *Rationality in Epistemology (Philosophical Issues* vol. 2).

Dancy, J. (1993a) (ed.) *Reading Parfit* (Oxford: Blackwell).

Dancy, J. (1993b) 'Parfit and Indirectly Self-defeating Theories', forthcoming in Dancy (1993a).

Dancy, J., Moravcsik, J. and Taylor, C. C. W. (1988) (eds) *Human Agency: Language, Duty, Value* (Stanford: Stanford University Press).

Darwall, S. (1983) *Impartial Reason* (Ithaca: Cornell University Press).

Darwall, S. (1986) 'Agent-centred Restrictions from the Inside Out', *Philosophical Studies* 50, pp. 291–319.

Davidson, D. (1980) *Essays on Actions and Events* (Oxford: Oxford University Press).

Davis, L. (1979) *Theory of Action* (Englewood Cliffs: Prentice-Hall).

Falk, W. D. (1948) '"Ought" and Motivation', *Proceedings of the Aristotelian Society* 48, pp. 492–510. Reprinted in Falk (1986), pp. 21–41.

Falk, W. D. (1986) *Ought, Reasons, and Morality* (Ithaca: Cornell University Press).

Foot, P. (1978) *Virtues and Vices* (Oxford: Blackwell).

Foot, P. (1983) 'Moral Realism and Moral Dilemma', *Journal of Philosophy* 80, pp. 379–98. Reprinted in Gowans (1987).

Foot, P. (1985a) 'Morality, Action and Outcome', in Honderich (1985), pp. 23–38.

Foot, P. (1985b) 'Utilitarianism and the Virtues', *Mind* 94, pp. 196–209. Reprinted with some changes in Scheffler (1988a), pp. 224–42; page references are to the latter version.

Frankena, W. K. (1958) 'Obligation and Motivation', in Melden (1958), pp. 40–81.

Gauthier, D. (1986) *Morals by Agreement* (Oxford: Oxford University Press).

Gay, R. (1985) 'Ethical Pluralism: a Reply to Dancy', *Mind* 94, pp. 250–62.

Goldman, A. (1970) *A Theory of Human Action* (Princeton: Princeton University Press).

Goldstein, I. (1989) 'Pleasure and Pain: Unconditional, Intrinsic Value', *Philosophy and Phenomenological Research* 50, pp. 255–76.

Gowans, C. W. (1987) (ed.) *Moral Dilemmas* (Oxford: Oxford University Press).

Guttenplan, S. (1979/80) 'Moral Realism and Moral Dilemmas', *Proceedings of the Aristotelian Society* 80, pp. 61–80.

Hare, R. M. (1963) *Freedom and Reason* (Oxford: Oxford University Press).

Hare, R. M. (1981) *Moral Thinking* (Oxford: Oxford University Press).

Holtzman, S. and Leich, C. (1981) (eds) *Wittgenstein: To Follow a Rule* (London: Routledge and Kegan Paul).

Honderich, T. (1985) (ed.) *Morality and Objectivity: A Tribute to J. L. Mackie* (London: Routledge and Kegan Paul).

Hookway, C. J. (1986) 'Two Conceptions of Moral Realism', *Proceedings of the Aristotelian Society* 60 (suppl.), pp. 188–205.

Humberstone, L. (1992) 'Direction of Fit', *Mind*, 101, pp. 59–83.

Hume, D. (1739/40) *A Treatise of Human Nature*, ed. P. Nidditch (Oxford: Oxford University Press, 1978).

Hume, D. (1751) *Enquiry Concerning the Principles of Morals*, ed. P. Nidditch (Oxford: Oxford University Press, 1975).

Hurley, S. (1985) 'Objectivity and Disagreement', in Honderich (1985), pp. 54–97.

Johnson, W. E. (1921) *Logic* (Cambridge: Cambridge University Press).

Johnston, M. (1989) 'Dispositional Theories of Value', *Proceedings of the Aristotelian Society* 63 (suppl.), pp. 139–74.

Jonsen, A. R. and Toulmin, S. (1988) *The Abuse of Casuistry: a History of Moral Reasoning* (Berkeley: University of California Press).

Joseph, H. W. B. (1931) *Some Problems in Ethics* (Oxford: Clarendon Press).

Kagan, S. (1984) 'Does Consequentialism Demand Too Much?', *Philosophy and Public Affairs* 13, pp. 239–54.

Kagan, S. (1988) 'The Additive Fallacy', *Ethics* 99, pp. 5–31.

Kagan, S. (1989) *The Limits of Morality* (Oxford: Clarendon Press).

Kant, I. (1785) *Groundwork of the Metaphysic of Morals*; translated by J. Paton as *The Moral Law* (London: Hutchinson, 1972).

Korsgard, C. M. (1986) 'Scepticism about Practical Reason', *Journal of Philosophy* 83, pp. 5–25.

Lewis, D. (1989) 'Dispositional Theories of Value', *Proceedings of the Aristotelian Society* 63 (suppl.), pp. 113–37.

Mackie, J. L. (1973) *Truth, Probability and Paradox* (Oxford: Oxford University Press).

Mackie, J. L. (1976) *Problems from Locke* (Oxford: Oxford University Press).

Mackie, J. L. (1977) *Ethics: Inventing Right and Wrong* (Harmondsworth: Penguin Books).

McDowell, J. (1978) 'Are Moral Requirements Hypothetical Imperatives?', *Proceedings of the Aristotelian Society* 52 (suppl.), pp. 13–29.

McDowell, J. (1979) 'Virtue and Reason', *The Monist* 62, pp. 331–50.

McDowell, J. (1981) 'Non-cognitivism and Rule-following', in Holtzman and Leich (1981), pp. 141–62.

McDowell, J. (1985) 'Values and Secondary Qualities', in Honderich (1985), pp. 110–29.

McDowell, J. (forthcoming) 'Are there External Reasons?', in J. Altham and R. Harrison (eds) *World, Mind and Ethics: Essays on the Moral Philosophy of Bernard Williams* (Cambridge: Cambridge University Press).

McGinn, C. (1982) *The Character of Mind* (Oxford: Oxford University Press).

McNaughton, D. (1988) *Moral Vision* (Oxford: Blackwell).

McNaughton, D. and Rawling, P. (1991) 'Agent-relativity and the Doing/Happening Distinction' *Philosophical Studies* 63, pp. 167–85.

Mandelbaum, M. (1955) *The Phenomenology of Moral Experience* (Glencoe: Free Press).

Melden, A. I. (1958) (ed.) *Essays in Moral Philosophy* (Seattle: University of Washington Press).

Mill, J. S. (1863) *Utilitarianism*, edited by A. Ryan (London: Penguin Books, 1987).

Nagel, T. (1970) *The Possibility of Altruism* (Princeton: Princeton University Press).

Nagel, T. (1979) *Mortal Questions* (Cambridge: Cambridge University Press).

Nagel, T. (1986) *The View from Nowhere* (Oxford: Oxford University Press).

Parfit, D. (1984) *Reasons and Persons* (Oxford: Oxford University Press).

Pettit, P. and Smith, M. (1990) 'Backgrounding Desire', *Philosophical Review* 99, pp. 564–92.

Philips, M. (1987) 'Weighing Moral Reasons', *Mind* 96, pp. 367–75.

Phillips, D. Z. (1977) 'In Search of the Moral "Must"', *Philosophical Quarterly* 27, pp. 140–57.

Platts, M. de. B. (1992) *Moral Realities* (London: Routledge).

Prichard, H. A. (1912) 'Does Moral Philosophy Rest on a Mistake?', *Mind* 21, pp. 21–37. Reprinted in Prichard (1968), pp. 1–17.

Prichard, H. A. (1968) *Moral Obligation*, ed. J. O. Urmson (Oxford: Clarendon Press).

Rachels, J. (1975) 'Active and Passive Euthanasia', *New England Journal of Medicine* 292, pp. 78–80. Reprinted in Sher (1987), pp. 646–51.

Railton, P. (1984) 'Alienation, Consequentialism, and the Demands of Morality', *Philosophy and Public Affairs* 13, pp. 134–71. Reprinted in Scheffler (1988), pp. 93–133; page references are to the latter version.

Raz, J. (1975) 'Permissions and Supererogation', *American Philosophical Quarterly* 12, pp. 161–8.

Raz, J. (1986) *The Morality of Freedom* (Oxford: Clarendon Press).

Ross, W. D. (1930) *The Right and the Good* (Oxford: Clarendon Press).

Ross, W. D. (1939) *Foundations of Ethics* (Oxford: Clarendon Press).

Ross, W. D. (1949) (ed.) *Aristotle's Prior and Posterior Analytics* (Oxford: Clarendon Press).

Scheffler, S. (1982) *The Rejection of Consequentialism: A Philosophical Investigation of the Considerations Underlying Rival Moral Conceptions* (Oxford: Clarendon Press).

Scheffler, S. (1988a) (ed.) *Consequentialism and its Critics* (Oxford: Oxford University Press).

Scheffler, S. (1988b) 'Agent-centred Restrictions, Rationality, and the Virtues', *Mind* 94, pp. 409–419. Reprinted in Scheffler (1988a), pp. 243–60; page references are to the reprinted version.

Searle, J. (1983) *Intentionality* (Cambridge: Cambridge University Press).

Sen, A. (1982) 'Rights and Agency', *Philosophy and Public Affairs* 11, no. 1, pp. 3–39. Reprinted in Scheffler (1988a), pp. 187–223; page references are to the reprinted version.

Sher, G. (1987) (ed.) *Moral Philosophy: Selected Readings* (Orlando: Harcourt Brace Jovanovich).

Shope, R. (1978) 'The Conditional Fallacy in Contemporary Philosophy', *Journal of Philosophy* 75, pp. 397–413.

Sidgwick, H. (1874) *The Methods of Ethics* (London: Macmillan).

Singer, P. (1991) (ed.) *A Companion to Ethics* (Oxford: Blackwell).

Slote, M. (1985) *Common-sense Morality and Consequentialism* (London: Routledge and Kegan Paul).

Smart, J. J. C. and Williams, B. A. O. (1973) *Utilitarianism, For and Against* (Cambridge: Cambridge University Press).

Smith, M. (1987) 'The Humean Theory of Motivation', *Mind* 96, pp. 36–61.

Smith, M. (1989) 'Dispositional Theories of Value', *Proceedings of the Aristotelian Society* 63 (suppl.), pp. 89–111.

Stocker, M. (1976) 'The Schizophrenia of Modern Ethical Theories', *Journal of Philosophy* 73, pp. 453–66.

Stocker, M. (1990) *Plural and Conflicting Values* (Oxford: Oxford University Press).

Stalnaker, R. (1984) *Inquiry* (Cambridge, Mass.: MIT Press).

Urmson, J. O. (1958) 'Saints and Heroes', in Melden (1958), pp. 198–216.

Urmson, J. O. (1975) 'A Defence of Intuitionism', *Proceedings of the Aristotelian Society* 75, pp. 144–52.

Wallace, R. J. (1990) 'How to Argue about Practical Reason', *Mind* 99, pp. 355–85.

Warnock, G. J. (1967) *Contemporary Moral Philosophy* (London: Macmillan).

Wiggins, D. (1976a) 'Deliberation and Practical Reason', *Proceedings of the Aristotelian Society* 76, pp. 29–51. Reprinted in Wiggins (1987), pp. 215–37.

Wiggins, D. (1976b) 'Truth, Invention and the Meaning of Life', *Proceedings of the British Academy* 62, pp. 331–78. Reprinted in Wiggins (1987), pp. 87–137.

Wiggins, D. (1979) 'Weakness of Will, Commensurability, and the Objects of Desire', *Proceedings of the Aristotelian Society* 79, pp. 251–77. Reprinted in Wiggins (1987), pp. 239–67.

Wiggins, D. (1987) *Needs, Values, Truth: Essays in the Philosophy of Value* (Oxford: Blackwell).

Wiggins, D. (1991) 'Categorical Requirements: Hume and Kant on the Idea of Duty', Inaugural Lecture, Birkbeck College, London.

Williams, B. A. O. (1973) *Problems of the Self* (Cambridge: Cambridge University Press).

Williams, B. A. O. (1976a) 'Persons, Character and Morality', in A. O. Rorty (ed.) *The Identities of Persons* (Berkeley: University of California Press). Reprinted in Williams (1981), pp. 1–19.

Williams, B. A. O. (1976b) Utilitarianism and Moral Self-indulgence', in H. D. Lewis (ed.) *Contemporary British Philosophy* fourth series (London: Allen and Unwin). Reprinted in Williams (1981), pp. 40–53.

Williams, B. A. O. (1978) *Descartes: The Project of Pure Enquiry* (Harmonds-
   worth: Penguin Books).
Williams, B. A. O. (1980) 'Internal and External Reasons', in R. Harrison (ed.)
   Rational Action (Cambridge: Cambridge University Press, 1980). Reprinted
   in Williams (1981), pp. 101–13.
Williams, B. A. O. (1981) *Moral Luck* (Cambridge: Cambridge University Press).
Williams, B. A. O. (1985) *Ethics and the Limits of Philosophy* (London: Fontana
   Press).
Williams, B. A. O. (1988) 'What Does Intuitionism Imply?', in Dancy, Moravcsik
   and Taylor (1988), pp. 189–98.
Winch, P. (1972) *Ethics and Action* (Oxford: Blackwell).
Wolf, S. (1982) 'Moral Saints', *Journal of Philosophy* 79, pp. 419–39.
Wright, C. J. G. (1988) 'Moral Values, Projection and Secondary Qualities',
   Proceedings of the Aristotelian Society 62 (suppl.), pp. 1–26.

Index